The Great Executive Dream

THE GREAT EXECUTIVE DREAM

The First Myth of Management Is That It Exists

Robert Heller

DELACORTE PRESS
NEW YORK

*Originally published in Great Britain by George Weidenfeld
& Nicolson Ltd. under the title* The Naked Manager.
*Copyright © 1972 by Robert Heller
Illustrations Copyright © 1972 by Robert Osborn
All rights reserved. No part of this book may be
reproduced in any form or by any means without the prior
written permission of the Publisher, excepting brief
quotes used in connection with reviews written specifically
for inclusion in a magazine or newspaper.*

Designed by Joel Schick

*Library of Congress Catalog Card Number: 77-38894
Manufactured in the United States of America
First American printing*

*Library of Congress Cataloging in Publication Data
Heller, Robert, 1932–*
    The great executive dream.
    *1. Management. 2. Executives. 3. Conglomerate corporations.
I. Title.*
HD38.H43   658.4   77-38894

*This book is dedicated to all those executives
who did the right thing for the wrong reason,
and were acclaimed as geniuses and heroes;
and to all those who did the wrong thing
for the right, the wrong, or no reason at all
and still hold their overpaid jobs.*

CONTENTS

ACKNOWLEDGMENTS

THIS BOOK could not have been started without the help, direct and inadvertent, of the many managers I have met since becoming a journalist in 1955. Nor could it have been written without the education received from Sir Gordon Newton, my first editor. I am permanently in his debt, not least for sending me as a correspondent to the United States, where I learned plenty. His chairman at the *Financial Times*, Lord Drogheda, among many kindnesses, encouraged me to start *Management Today*. At that magazine I have been taught as much about business as journalism—thanks largely to colleagues such as the late Jim Hunter, Michael Heseltine, Lindsay Masters and Geoffrey Foster, and to the support of John Marsh and the British Institute of Management, and of Roland Bird and the *Economist*. The genesis of the book lies in the fortnightly column "Management in Action," published in the *Observer*. Some of the material and most of the ideas in these pages have appeared in the *Observer*. I am everlastingly grateful to David Astor, the *Observer*'s editor, and to Anthony Bambridge, the business editor. Leopold Ullstein, the managing director of Barrie & Jenkins, thought of the book almost before I did; and so did my agent, Hilary Rubinstein. Ross Claiborne and Manon Tingue at Delacorte have buoyed me up at moments when buoys were badly needed. The help of Felicity Krish in getting the typescript fit to print, and in many other ways, was indispensable. I owe many other debts I can never fully repay. Among others: to Sheila Black of the *Financial Times*; to John Davis of the *Observer*; to Hugh Parker of McKinsey & Company; to Wally Olins of Wolff Olins; to Sir Arnold Weinstock of the General Electric Company; to Tommy Wilson of the London Business School; to John Diebold; to Peter Drucker, who has set the standard of perfection in writing about management: and to John Thackray, whose articles on U.S. business in *Management Today* were as invaluable as they are brilliant. Finally, like everything I write, this book should really be dedicated to the late David Roberts, senior history master at Christ's Hospital.

I _Myths_

1
Why the Executive Has No Clothes

THE NAKED emperor in Hans Christian Andersen's story was magnificently dressed, not only in the public's mind, but in his own. The business executive, ruler of economic empires richer than many nations, has gone one better. The public believes in him: he believes in himself: but his clothing is not simply that of personal prestige and power (though both can be great): the manager is wrapped in a rich and seamless garment, which, going by the name of management, has become a pervasive religion of our time. But management, like the emperor's clothes, does not exist: the prime myth of management is that it does.

Management's nonexistence explains why there are so many confused and conflicting attempts to define a pastime that all but monopolizes the waking hours of earnest men, many of them able, creative, and industrious; many of them none of

3

these things. Any definition of management must be right, because almost any definition must fit something so amorphous and shifting. "Achieving results through other people" is one of the more popular definitions. It applies to the president of General Motors, but it also fits the madam of a brothel. And she is an executive facing real problems of personnel selection, marketing, and accountancy—not to mention her tax and legal arrangements.

The president of GM may not fancy the idea that a madam is in the same business, but she is—the business of business. All executives are in this racket—organizing something or somebody in such a way that somebody else, somehow or other, will pay for it. The job of a big business executive is basically the same as that of a small shopkeeper—turning a (more or less) honest penny. And the executive forgets this (as he usually does) at his peril.

Efficient businesses and brilliant executives are those who turn the most pennies, make the most money. The public never bothers about the methods. It accepts the results as evidence of their excellence. And this seems perfectly right and proper. So the good executive is the effective one, and the effective executive is the good one—or is he?

Effectiveness means more than goodness, but not much more. This little difficulty explains how a professor of management can write: "Effectiveness is best seen as something an executive produces from a situation by managing it appropriately." Substitute "effectively" for the last word in that mishmash, and you have a sentence that means exactly the same, i.e., nothing. There is no absolute criterion of managerial achievement. A manager is good and a company efficient only because others consider the results of their work good: their so-called goodness endures only as long as this good opinion holds.

Ivar Kreuger, the European match king, and Samuel Insull, the American utilities magnate, are early figures in a line that stretches to the crack of corporate doom. President after president, honest and less honest, has been turned into a hero-figure, sometimes without benefit of assiduous publicity.

Cornfeld, Ling, King, Bluhdorn, in the U.S.; Maxwell, Bloom, King, Lord, in Britain. These feet-of-clay names are paralleled by those of fallen idol companies: some, like Litton or Rolls-Royce, are too conspicuous ever to forget: others have slid so far from grace that nobody remembers either their names or the exact astronomical height of their former price/earnings ratios.

In management, wonders nearly always cease. One day, events will surely expose any executive, in all his nakedness, for what he is: a fallible human being trying with the help of others, who are equally fallible, to cope with circumstances that are constantly changing. In the kingdom of the uncertain, the one-eyed man makes mistakes. And that is why corporate goodness, even measured on the standard scales, is infrequent.

A study of Britain's leading companies showed that over the 1960s only 16 percent could claim to be good—if you defined goodness as doubling profits in real terms in the decade, maintaining return on stockholders' equity over the ten years, and having only one off-year. The average performance of big companies is just that—average. In the United States, half of the five hundred largest companies had annual earnings per share growth of less than 5 percent in the period from 1960 to 1970; and any company that couldn't double its earnings in an inflationary era, in which all manner of juggles for the painless boosting of earnings per share were invented, has no claims to any managerial skills, even low cunning.

Executives are not always to blame for mediocrity. Running large corporations, or middling or small is never easy: To run them effectively is always tough, and is sometimes impossible. This explains the management that is excellent in everything except its results—as in aluminum. You won't find a nicer, harder-working, keener, better-educated, cleverer, better-developed bunch of men anywhere than in companies such as Alcoa and Alcan (Heaven knows why, since aluminum is the world's second most boring industry, after cement). Yet the result of all their effort and massed brainpower is an insignificant return on capital, profitless growth, and a terrible

5

proneness to accident. Alcan, possibly the most expert of the groups erecting aluminum smelters in Britain, naturally had the project that went most grievously awry; and the whole industry has an uncontrollable urge to plunge into excess capacity.

John D. Harper of Alcoa once made the immortal remark, "There is no overcapacity, only underselling"—another of those management sayings that read the same backward or forward. Executives are bad judges of their own actions, their own talents, their own stock prices. Every member of the board thinks his company's shares are too cheap, although few are foolish enough to buy them (they don't mind having them free). Whenever a company boasts of its managerial excellence, sell the shares; and if you own the firm, fire the boss.

Bids bring out the worst in executives. They can't judge their own ability fairly, which is understandable. But they can also be awful judges of other managers. When you hear a chief executive say, "You should not forget that in buying a company we are buying management as a primary asset" (to quote one merger fanatic), run for the hills. Management does not exist, and here's this colossus paying good money for the invisible and evanescent. You can't buy management, but you can very easily buy trouble. Better executives can, and often do, walk out; and sometimes after the reality emerges from the image, the worse ones have to be fired. An American group bought a red-hot British growth company for a tycoon's ransom and discovered subsequently: "(a) it does not have good reporting and control data; (b) the production output per person employed is very poor; (c) it has too many people for the job they are doing; (d) it has never really set good targets; (e) it is much too diversified." Otherwise, the buy was in pretty good shape.

The optical illusion of goodness arises from the one-idea phenomenon. Sigmund Freud called *The Interpretation of Dreams* his greatest work, noting that inspiration of this order only came to a man once in his lifetime. Companies and chief executives are subject to the same law. A company such as

Control Data Corporation has a large notion about large computers and a couple of brilliant men who can make it work. In the process, the company—and their fortunes—swell from $600,000 of value in the summer of 1957 to $3.9 million in 1968. All this proves is not that the CDC crew are super-managers, but merely that their one super-idea was good, wonderfully good. The managers will look good as long as the big idea does; but so will all their other ideas, including the foolish ones, until—as happened to CDC when the large computer market dematerialized—the profits turn to loss.

Skepticism in the face of success is an impudent posture. But corporate history must foster the skeptical approach. The eye-opener lies in the way that respectable, established, conservative corporations and their no less clean and decent executives start off in one direction and end up facing the other way, with equal ardor for both postures. Sad examples, here are the copper companies, who threw fortunes into the laps of other people in a doomed and silly effort to keep prices down: and then discovered the virtues of the free market they had sought to destroy.)

In corporation land, you learn rapidly that there are some villains, but no heroes. I once had to write the profile of an oilman reputed to be the hero-genius behind one of the world's greatest companies. Research showed that, after an incomparable early career battling against the arch-enemy, he had long since sat on the sidelines. In despair, I asked the real boss to say what the hero did. "Well," he said, after deep thought, "he has the office next to mine." The profile, inevitably, perpetuated the legend. Nobody would have believed the reality—any more than most people would believe that a young family scion, famed (falsely) for internationalizing an introverted Midwest business, was once so claustrophobic that he held conferences in an open bus. Cured by his shrink, he then became so agoraphobic that he could work only in a windowless room.

Men like him, or the Cunard chairman who never took a ship to America, are the human factors, the real stuff of management—eccentric to the point of lunacy in a few cases, and

7

generally odd enough in multitudinous smaller ways. Time and again, what happens in corporations cannot be explained by economics. It can only be understood by realizing that, naturally enough, men express in their work the same motive forces that drive them in their ordinary lives. Management is an arena for human behavior at its most naked—under stress, but freed from many restraints of civilization. You can yell and scream at a subordinate in a way that would not be tolerated even by a wife. You can force a man to lose all his assets, though you wouldn't trespass on his lawn. You can tell lies, but if the lies are good enough, they will be applauded as universal truth.

This is the background against which one Harry Figgie can be seen as a real management hero of our times. Figgie, a manager of brilliant reputation, had won high academic respect and an avid stock market following for his "nucleus theory of growth," which he applied to Automatic Sprinkler. The nucleus theory proved to be an empty sham. The reality was that in rapid succession Figgie bought a fire-hose nozzle company whose profits promptly fell from $939,000 to $76,636; a vacuum cleaner firm whose sales methods were outlawed just before acquisition; and a metalbending defense contractor that managed to lose $8 million on a $6.3 million Pentagon contract. There are no theories of growth, nuclear or nonnuclear. There are only actions—intelligent, not so bright, and stupid. And the only thread binding the intelligent actions is that they work.

Theories of management can work in individual companies —but only because they suit the way in which individual men like to act. The methods that Robert Townsend, of *Up the Organization*, used to run Avis were a marvelous way for Robert Townsend to run Avis. But they might paralyze a different company with different men—even Hertz. Yet executives, beset by corporate ailments, reach for a theory formed in a different context as if it were a broad spectrum antibiotic, a wonder drug. They see their businesses as suffering patients requiring medical treatment: though there is seldom anything wrong with a company that better, or better-directed, executives won't cure. Executives, however, will undergo almost any treatment rather than amputation of themselves.

But self-amputation is far more effective for the stockholders. I know of two companies, one large, one gargantuan, which found themselves with cuckoos in the nest—two tough, aggressive, ruthless entrepreneurs whose drive, hunger for profits, and magical rapport with figures couldn't live with the passive, profitless vagueness on the existing board. Laying their own heads on the block, the older directors voluntarily handed the ax to the new men. In the next few years, both companies grew by such prodigious bounds that some of the superannuated oldies became very wealthy—and they deserved every penny. They followed the golden rule: if you can't do something yourself, find somebody who can—and then let him do it in his own sweet way.

In contrast, many cures that less self-effacing boards purchase are subject to the same objection as psychoanalysis: they are expensive, they take a lot of time, the patient does all the work, and there's no way of telling that he wouldn't have got better, anyway, with the mere passage of the years. If it takes two years (to take one example) to draw up a new shop floor management structure in a car company, the problem won't be the same at the end as it was at the beginning.

Any improvement, moreover, can always be looked at two ways. You can thump yourself on the back (as most executives do) for your brilliant advance, or you can kick yourself for the imbecility that made improvement necessary. If the executive doesn't like one view through the telescope, he can turn it around and look through the other end—precisely because management is not a scientific and objective activity, but a subjective historical process, full of ifs and buts. Thus Roy Ash, president of Litton, forced to explain how the management wasn't to blame for errors that wiped out billions in stock market value, had no trouble at all: "Operationally, we could have made sure of never facing the problem by never undertaking the venture." Nothing ventured, nothing lost, in fact. That's like the guilty party in a midair collision offering as excuse that if he had never learned to fly the accident would never have happened.

The literature of Litton bears careful reading by anybody who believes that the emperor-manager is wearing clothes. In this book, although there are no heroes, there are Goodies and Baddies, and Litton is among the Baddies, along with Rolls-Royce, Lockheed, the International Publishing Corporation, Ling-Temco-Vought, and a strong supporting cast, mainly of conglomerates, whose badness lies in the damage done by arrogant managers to innocent stockholders. There are also the Heavies—such as du Pont, General Electric, ICI, and General Motors—companies, which are neither very good nor at all poor, whose enormous potential for goodness is constantly frustrated by their own bad habits. And there are also Goodies: men such as Sir Arnold Weinstock of General Electric, Forrest Mars of Mars, Leslie Lazell of Beecham, and the gang at Marks and Spencer—men who (unless and until I am proven wrong) can be trusted with the stockholders' money to the last line on the balance sheet.

Think before you act; the money isn't yours—the First Truth of Management—is a home truth. But management is a far more homely business than its would-be scientists suggest, more closely allied to cookery than any other human activity. Like cooking, it rests on a degree of organization and on adequate resources. But just as no two chefs run their kitchens the same way, so no two managements are the same, even if they all went to the same business (or cookery) school. You can teach the rudiments of cooking, as of management, but you cannot make a great cook or a great manager.

In both activities, you ignore fundamentals at grave risk—but sometimes succeed. In both, science can be extremely useful, but is no substitute for the art itself. In both, inspired amateurs can outdo professionals. In both, perfection is rarely achieved, and failure is more common than the customers realize. In both, practitioners don't need recipes that detail timing down to the last second, ingredients to the last fraction of an ounce, and procedures down to the last flick of the wrist; they need reliable maxims, instructive anecdotes, and no dogmatism. This is a cookbook for managers who want to get their clothes back.

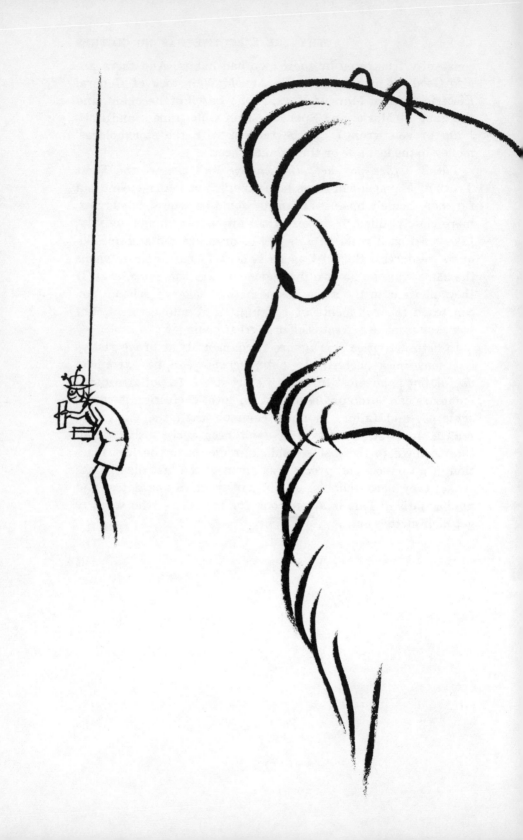

2 God Save the Stockholder

To HEAR THEM tell it, big company directors on both sides of the Atlantic are quite dedicated to the stockholder. Strangely, devotion turns to irritation, almost a sense of betrayal, if the love object asks offensive questions about the company's performance at the annual general meeting. The stockholder whom the directors love is better than a good Victorian child or a chairman's yes-man, neither seen nor heard: one who merely collects his dividend (if any) and dutifully returns his proxy form if, by some mischance, one of the directors' projects needs a democratic rubber stamp.

Most top executives are sincere men. When they say they hold the stockholder dear, they really and truly mean it— because they truly can't imagine any conflict between the stockholder's interests, as seen by the directors, and the directors' own desires. What's good for the board of General Motors

13

is good for the stockholders, and vice versa, more or less sums up the philosophy. Suppose that the stockholders would be better off with a whole new management: the existing managers won't share the horrible idea, and they won't protect stockholders by lopping off their own heads. The stockholder is not expected to criticize. It's enough to know that managements, in deciding what they want, will have general objectives that directly promote the stockholder's everlasting comfort—or will they?

Rich targets for growth in earnings per share were once standard corporate objectives. (That was before President Nixon, in the routine of the right-wing, political friend of business, manufactured a recession that gave business hell.) In happier days the hotter giants, the Honeywells and so on, dreamed of a 15 percent annual compound increase in earnings per share. The number was plucked out of the air—10 percent looked too small, and 20 percent (doubling every three and one-half years) absurdly large for a swollen corporation. A steady 15 percent clip, doubling monotonously every five years, would surely guarantee a high price/earnings ratio for all eternity.

But this corporate target has a secret advantage for the men in charge of companies. Earnings per share are engineered by dividing profits attributable to ordinary stockholders (that is, after tax and minority interest) by the number of shares in issue—which is a beautifully elastic sum on both sides. For instance, if Wonder Company A buys Wonder Company B with stocks, kindly valuing B at the same noble price/earnings ratio as its own, the earnings per share of A (now A plus B) stay exactly the same. But if A uses money borrowed at fixed interest, any margin between B's profits and the interest paid comes through as a straight, juicy increment in earnings per share.

As the conglomerates noted, many tricks can be worked around this basic dodge—simply buy earnings without diluting the equity, and by a stroke of the computer, management seems to achieve the results of years of honest toil. This cult of earnings per share has never been worshipped so widely in

14

Britain as in the U.S., where management has elaborated much the same concept into something called "return on invested capital" or "on stockholders' equity." But the British beginnings were visible long before 1970. (Another of Britain's typically late imports of American technology: in this case, opening the British stable door after the American horse had bolted.)

The notion behind invested capital is that only the money that belongs to the stockholder counts. So you conveniently forget about loans, however overpowering, and take the often much tinier sum of stockholders' capital. This in turn relates to asset values that have been shrunk by so-called depreciation over the years. To this much skinnier residue, you apply the net profit figure—and the result is a much zestier index of performance than could be got in any other way. For example, General Electric puffed out 12.3 percent on invested capital in 1970; its yield on total assets was only 5.2 percent.

Few managements consciously fix their figures in the most flattering light—but that's what happens when they define their objectives by stockholders' finances alone: it is dangerous —it sustains the myth that high debt is good for the company, and it also misrepresents the motivation of the board. Though the director chatters about the stockholder as the owner of the company's assets, he doesn't really see the investor as a proprietor—and still less as a member of the company. The members, in the director's inner mind, are those sitting on the payroll, above all the upper management itself.

The stockholders are remote licensers. They get a cut of any profits, and in return they license the managers to do as they please with the assets. More, they let managers do what they like (apart from outright theft) with the value of the shares. If the management longs to dilute those famous earnings per share by some overpriced acquisition, the stockholder can seldom kill the deal. And if the management wants to change the entire business of the company, the stockholder is expected to sit tight and watch, clapping loudly.

The tobacco companies, faced with evidence that they were merchants of death, could have taken their profits, remitted the maximum loot to the stockholders for as long as the going was good, and then folded into graceful liquidation. No law ordains that American Brands (née Tobacco) or Imperial Tobacco must be preserved in perpetuity. Yet the company's executive officers (who would otherwise have liquidated themselves out of good jobs) proceeded to act as if in slavish obedience to such a law.

At all costs, the corporate entity must be perpetuated. So the Imperial stockholders, like it or not, were swiftly switched from owning a lucrative cigarette manufacturer, with minor diversified interests, to possessing a notably unprofitable food group with major tobacco interests. Disgruntled giants all over the world have found it hard to resist the sight of food. Along the way the giants' stockholders have been forced by corporation officers to pay prices for independent provision merchants that made the latter positively drool.

Management's liberties are guaranteed by the weakness, apathy, and ignorance of stockholders, by the stockholders' lack of time to harass bad management, and by the stockholders' perpetual freedom, if disenchanted, to sell out. However, not all stockholders are weak, apathetic, and ignorant; at least, they shouldn't be. The directors' real masters are institutions —the mutual funds, insurance companies, pension funds, and unit trusts that control the dominating chunks of the equity; the banks that hand over short-term finance; the investment banks and merchant banks that are pipelines to the long-suffering investing public. These solid institutional citizens are not always stockholders—the banks in Britain and the U.S. do not, as on the Continent of Europe, own industry. But in several respects, the banks' interests are no different from the stockholders', individual or institutional: since they want their booty back, the banks—like the stockholders— need to ensure that inefficient management doesn't drain or dribble the money away.

Yet the institutions, on both sides of the Atlantic, are almost as supine as the little old lady in Toledo, Ohio, or Melton Mowbray, Leicestershire. When they do zero in on a lagging management, the move is ponderous and far too late. Take

Vickers, once famous in British weaponry. In 1970 the chief stockholders, led by the mighty Prudential Assurance and a merchant bank, promoted a slight earth tremor on the board. The sleeping dog of capitalism had barked—but only after twelve years of inept performance. When the watchdog awoke, profits at Vickers were two-thirds of the 1958 level (and that was after a spunky recovery), while return on capital was just 7 percent. Annual profits had slipped in five of the eight years after 1958.

In this company, traditional management at its least magnificent escaped a worse fate only by the Labour government's providential nationalization of its steel (even then Vickers collected £16.3 million for a plant on which it had sagely and very recently spent £20 million). Why did the dog take so long to bark? The executives who lead financial institutions are, if anything, more conservative, more deeply dyed in tradition, happier to rest on seniority and security, and more thoroughly inbred than industrial directors. They have a vested interest in stability at the top, especially a top manned by personal friends or men of higher rank in the arcane lists of business snobbery. Those who run mammoth banks and insurance companies (let alone those who merely handle multimillion-pound investment portfolios) seldom reach the exalted heights or salaries of captains of industry; and they feel the difference.

Nor are financial men especially knowing about business and business management, in their own trade, or in other people's. Financial institutions are better at burying their million-pound mistakes in multimillion aggregates than at displaying commercial drive, managerial acumen, and marketing enterprise. The expertise needed on Wall Street or in the City of London is not that of the industrial executive suite—and the financier's judgment of directors is therefore fallible. That is why banks lend gigantic sums to managements of bewildering incompetence. The unsureness of investment managers and their bosses about how to judge management in industry partly explains their profound reluctance to tackle nonperforming boards—and of those there is never any shortage.

Even if you use their own soft criterion of growth in earnings per share, the top fifty U.S. companies made a feeble showing from 1960 to 1970: in fourteen cases, earnings per share fell over the decade; in twenty-four further cases, they rose by less than 7 percent compounded annually; the magic 15 percent mark was hit in only four cases. The next fifty were no more inspiring. A dozen showed declines; another sixteen grew by less than 7 percent; and only two managed 15 percent. The Nixon recession of 1970 can't be blamed, either. In 1969, a marvel for growth in sales, there were nine companies in the top fifty whose earnings per share were lower than in 1959, a further fifteen managing less than 7 percent growth over the decade, and just three in the 15 percent wonder-bracket.

The British picture warms no more hearts. In twenty-seven cases out of the two hundred biggest companies, the share prices were lower in early 1970 than a decade before; in sixty-seven companies, stockholders had not obtained a 7 percent annual return on investment. Yet few knives have leaped out, Vickers-style; nothing has disturbed the slumber in the executive suite of such as U.S. Steel (with a negative 1960–70 growth rate of 6.22 percent for its earnings per share). Unless companies are on bankruptcy's brink (in which case the directors have other anxieties), managements have little cause to fret about their mighty, weak stockholders. They only need watch out for the rare rich-and-determined individual investor.

Thus, coal tycoon George H. Love injected new management into Chrysler (he jacked it up high enough to plunge it right back into distress). Thus Chicago financier Colonel Henry Crown twice intervened to arrest General Dynamics' slide into bankruptcy. Thus Donald Forrester, another loaded and independent businessman, harassed the Cunard management; without him, that once-great Atlantic name might have missed its lucrative, short-lived revival. When Forrester left later, the good ship Cunard was visibly listing once again and heading straight for the take-over rocks. In all three cases, trouble remained endemic. Maybe even effective gingering up by rich stockholders has its limits: it usually comes too late, when too much vitality and cash have already been sucked away by years of travail.

Can only God save the stockholder? Investors could save themselves by trying to avoid companies that on past performance can't outdo the returns from an American savings and loan company or a British building society. But most individual investment in shares goes via the insurance companies and investment companies anyway, and the sheer weight of the money that they must invest presses them to buy into big companies, and with little discrimination. Only the heavyweights have enough shares on the market for heavy buying, and only large-scale purchases are any use to a large fund. Big companies and big investors are locked into each other by nature, which is one good reason why the investment record of the great funds is generally so insipid: they are stuck with insipid investments.

The myth that men who run investment funds or manage companies can always do more with the stockholder's money than he could for himself still stands—despite its destruction by all manner of evidence. A recent theory of stock markets has, almost irrefutably, shown that stock prices follow a haphazard statistical pattern known to mathematicians as the "random walk." If so, all the beavering "fundamental" analysis designed to prove that a company's stock price must soar is beside the point. In reality, security analysts, however closely they nuzzle up to an industry, judge the favored managements too kindly: being articulate men themselves, the analysts especially fall for executives who can actually talk.

It also follows that the expert is no more likely than the inexpert to pick a growth stock that grows. In 1970, top American investment professionals picked Viatron, an electronics outfit, and a company called National Student Marketing, as the two hottest growth prospects of the year. Both slid down a slippery slope. This follows the equal success of earlier U.S. analysts in selecting Edwards High Vacuum, a high technology outfit, and London Grocers, a supermarket chain, as the two hottest British growth stocks. Both bumped down a trail of declining profits into the mouths of larger firms.

Another enchanting story is of a data processing company that had a rousing reception on Wall Street—until its sponsors saw the prospectus. Unlike other similar gee-whiz ventures, which were all losing money handsomely, this one was making profits. The sight of its price/earnings ratio, up over the 100 mark, so terrified the sponsors that they sold out of the stock: had it reported losses, they would happily have held on for some later deluge.

The fallback argument is that all equity investment, taking the lean years with the fat, will wax rich. First, the money purchases productive assets that (however inept their management) become worth more year after year through the simple magic of inflation: second, the company can do massively what the individual can seldom do—get "leverage" by borrowing at fixed interest, achieving double the financial horsepower from the same engine.

Both arguments rest on one unsafe assumption: that management will, year in, year out, boost earnings by a statistically significant amount. If, like most companies, it doesn't, the market value of the stocks, which is all that matters, may slump below the book value of the assets—let alone their supposed inflation-proof real value. And all that leverage is mathematically bound to accelerate the profit declines nastily when, as happens more often than not, the company steps firmly on a banana skin.

Maybe there is a haphazard statistical pattern, a "random walk," in profits. Since in most human affairs there is only a fifty-fifty chance of being right, half the actions of any company are likely to be wrong. Certainly the records of many corporations (after extracting the impact of acquisitions) look more random than planned: and in such circumstances the highly geared company is a menace to one and all.

Surveys by *Fortune* in the U.S. and *Management Today* in Britain show conclusively that the most profitable companies have the least debt and that the most indebted are the most likely to be unprofitable. *Fortune* found that the fifty highest-debt corporations among the five hundred biggest companies in the U.S. included fifteen in the lowest bunch for profitability and not one in the top fifty; the fifty lowest-debt companies included twenty-three, nearly half, in the top lot for profitability and not one in the bottom. In Britain *Management Today* noted that the twenty lowest-debt companies had an average profitability that was 70 percent higher than that for the twenty highest-debt firms.

Like many earthshaking management finds, this one enshrines childish logic. If a company generates great profits, it rarely needs to borrow; if it needs to panhandle heavily, the overwhelming odds (as with an individual) are that it is earning too little. In most cases, it never will earn enough either—the borrowing becomes a permanent burden on the sore backs of management and unwitting or witting stockholders.

Financial institutions don't pause to wonder why they lend most generously to managements that show themselves least capable of making the money grow. Without its friendly neighborhood bankers, for instance, Lockheed would have gone to the wailing wall long ago. Yet the banks, on all external evidence, went on showing nothing but confidence in Lockheed's Daniel Haughton and his merry men as nine-figure sum after nine-figure sum was literally sunk into the company.

Lockheed's partner in calamity, Rolls-Royce, soaked the City of London for money time and again on the strength of a balance sheet that would have worried Mr. Micawber. And yet the big business executive, who finds it relatively easy to get around the allegedly sharp-eyed men with the big money, says that he is genuinely concerned about the little stockholder up-country. He can safely leave the stockholder to look after himself: nobody else will.

3 *The Inefficient Americans*

GREAT IDEAS commonly turn false when they are most widely promulgated, applauded, and received. For a decade Europeans groaned under what J.J. Servan-Schreiber nicknamed "The American Challenge." Superefficient Americans were supposed to deploy the bottomless riches of magnificently organized corporations to trample, take over, and mesmerize European competition. But the thesis was untrue even then— and it has been getting further from reality with every passing trans-atlantic flight.

In reality, American executives are no abler than Frenchmen, Japanese, Germans, or even Englishmen. U.S. corporations, including the most highly praised, suffer from all the same inefficiencies as their competitors. American technology, in most fields, is not some magical, insuperable advantage, and (so much for Servan-Schreiber) many European firms—

even in Britain—have outgrown the Americans by a mighty margin. The beauty of the invader lies only in the eyes of the invaded.

For a start, the awesome figures of American invasion overstate the challenge. Take away oil and cars, and U.S. investment dwindles severely; and almost all the original investment in these capital-hungry industries dates back well before World War II. There are only a few exceptions, such as Continental Oil's unprofitable efforts to off-load Libyan oil or Chrysler's stakes in Simca and Rootes (to which it is welcome).

In computers, the most typical, most publicized, and most glamorous postwar industry, American dominance is based largely, not on the miracles of Pentagon-financed technology, but on IBM's prewar lead in punch card machines; the Watson family business had 80 to 90 percent of this market back in 1935, more than it has ever managed in computers. In the new industries in which transatlantic hostilities have begun since the peace—chemicals, say, or convenience foods—Europeans have often had little trouble defending themselves, and Americans even less difficulty in losing glorious sums. Much of the superior quality of American management in Europe in fact consists of this endearing ability to suffer losses that would send most Europeans to the poorhouse.

While admirable, in its way, the attribute is not on the curriculum of the Harvard Business School. But that seminary, and its like, were launching pads for the most truly challenging American invasion. More pervasive, and more profitable, than the computers of IBM are the acolytes of American management technology. They came from all sides—highly motivated professors of motivation, consultants commanding the world's highest fees, expatriate managers whose salaries (and tax positions) would embarrass an Italian boardroom, visiting lecturers of every posture, sellers of packaged management development aids—witch doctors whose spells, if they won't cure all corporate ailments, will definitely provide hours of harmless, profitless diversion.

The arrival and acceptance of this flood seemed logical

enough. When a powerful commission under Lord Franks, a former British ambassador to Washington, compared the defects of British management with American virtues, it saw one prime difference. The Americans had myriad business schools, Britain none. Ergo, build British business schools, native imitations of Harvard, and British management would improve. Nobody unkindly observed that the Germans, whose managers have also handily outstripped the British, had no business schools either.

The Franks theory rested on two improbable or at least unprovable notions: that American business management actually is more efficient and that the business schools have been critical in creating this lead. The grains of truth are only that management, as a body of theoretical knowledge, is almost entirely an American creation, and that business management, as a professional racket, attracts far more highly educated U.S. citizens than Britons or Frenchmen.

It is also true that American business, chasing the economies of scale in the richest market in creation, and in a society that is indulgent toward high profits, has spawned corporations of immense success and, for all practical and some highly impractical purposes, unlimited resources. Some of these resources have been invested in some grave, sometimes despairing, attempts to combat the disadvantages of scale by constructing new corporate systems. And these are truly built with a thoroughness and theoretical justification worthy of that great free enterpriser, Karl Marx.

But a system, or a management theory, or a posse of business school graduates are only as good as their achievements. Forget the long string of American disasters in Europe—the Betty Crocker cakes, the Dial soap, the Gerber baby foods, the Frigidaire refrigerators, the Campbell's soups (those lost $6.1 million in a single year as the obstinate British refused to change their tastes), and so on and so on. Consider instead events back home in corporations that, by common consent, are among America's finest.

Nobody can wander through the thickets of management lore for long without bumping into General Electric and

25

American Telephone & Telegraph. GE is virtually a free business school: its investment in management theory, organization, and development is legendary. AT&T's fame spreads from the invention of the transistor in its Bell Labs via experiments in human relations and job organization to the courteous efficiency of the phone service. At least, that was the story until the New York telephone system had its coronary in 1969.

GE's record would shame a British electrical giant. Between 1963 and 1969, while its sales doubled, its profits budged scarcely an inch. Over the decade from 1960, GE's rise in earnings per share was a pitiful 4.8 percent annually. The malfunctions of these two giants are in no way extraordinary: running a business with 396,583 employees (GE) or 772,980 (AT&T) is a crucifying task. The oddity is only that no gleaming theory that the two have tried to implement will ever be soiled by their self-evident lack of success.

The records had little to do with the damage inflicted on U.S. growth by Nixonian economics. Right through the Kennedy-Johnson boom, the performance of GE was inferior: its management of its computer business, stuck out on a limb in Arizona, was a dream of decentralized failure that only ended with a humiliating sellout. AT&T in New York was brought low, not by a shortfall in demand, but by inability to cope with the expansion that it stimulated through its own homey, costly advertising.

Neither GE nor AT&T lacked management talent. Very few American leviathans do. They all claim otherwise, but many consultants outside the U.S. agree that the American corporation multiplies executives like mice. Just as paperwork breeds paperwork (every memo demands at least one answer), so one executive breeds more executives (every executive vice-president needs at least two vice-presidents reporting to him).

This overbreeding and interbreeding of executives, mostly hot from the business schools, is the root of the fashion that reached its apotheosis at the end of the 1960s—the corporation decentralized on product lines, with management responsibility devolved to profit centers within profit centers, bound together by tight financial controls and meticulous forward planning, activated by regular reviews of plans and progress.

The system, imitated slavishly by one European corporation after another, seems a sensible answer to diversity and to problems of maintaining individual responsibility and initiative inside the whale. With the rose-colored spectacles off, the system can be seen as a monumental bureaucracy, with veins made of paper, subject to blood clots at any point. To work at all, the system demands more layers of management, a great burgeoning of staff work, and heavy expenditure of line managers' time, simply to cover the control, planning, and review. Much of this managerial time is frittered away on meetings for "coordination," "consultation," and "approval"—in other words, in committees.

Take AT&T's macabre New York fiasco, as detailed by the *Wall Street Journal*. Under pressure for good figures, the New York profit center pushed up earnings by 16 percent in 1966 and 10 percent in 1967—and cut capital spending significantly in both years. Down the line, each subsidiary profit center was under strict budgetary control. This meant that in one area, grossly overworked men were transferred from repairs to installations (a separate profit center on a separate budget) "to get them off the maintenance account." The installers, in turn, were the bottom of a line of command that ran through foremen, service superintendent, divisional superintendent, assistant vice-president, and operating vice-president to the president.

This was the long, long trail up which the bad news about New York's overload wound its way. AT&T executives, being human, were reluctant to face the facts—and the consequences for their budgets. A former sales manager from the main disaster area, Wall Street, told the *Wall Street Journal*, "We were well aware that these problems were coming, and we kept passing it up the line. But nothing much seemed to happen." The story has been repeated, and will go on being repeated, in many U.S. corporations with similar dire results. In this case, fifteen hundred expensive technicians were imported six months too late and an additional $200 million was pumped in as capital spending—also belated.

Since Americans have (or had) a wondrous talent for regeneration, the big company will probably swing to some other fashion before long, casting into outer darkness the kind of decentralization that isolated AT&T's top management so effectively from what it was supposed to be managing. Already the brightest business school graduates are said to prefer the individualism of hot shops of various kinds to climbing the mountainsides of corporate bureaucracy. Suppose the future does sharpen the reflexes of the American executive, shake off his bonds, and flex his managerial muscles. Before the renewed might of management and money, will America's wizard technology, financed by the taxpayer through defense contracts, and no longer hampared by an over-valued currency, win again as it always has?

This too is an American daydream. Some bitter U.S. disappointments of the late 1960s (GE, General Dynamics, Litton Industries, Lockheed, Ling-Temco-Vought, etc.) have been leading recipients of federal largess. True, the U.S. spends some $16.8 million on research and development, supplies $13 million of defense plant and equipment free with $10 million of working capital thrown in, and gives two-thirds of all its bounty to just one hundred lucky companies.

But this lavishly financed technology has often not worked. Very little has been directly useful in civilian markets; the real gee-whiz stories, such as Xerox or Polaroid, were private ventures; and even in industries that U.S. firms do lead worldwide, such as chemicals or cars, the few technological advances have mostly been made outside America. American defense contractors, like government-financed firms everywhere, have stumbled over the myth of their own efficiency, forgetting that the marketplace is no respecter of legends.

Lockheed was so fabled a defense performer that its executives never conceived that they could flop over military projects or even make civil bloomers—even though their earlier Electra turbo-prop airliner, several years too late and accident-prone, was an awesome augury. The Cheyenne helicopter, SRAM missile, and Galaxy supertransport military disasters were promptly compounded by overstretching what was left of Lockheed's resources on the Tristar jet airbus. Almost from take-off, the Tristar flew far in the vapor trail of its Douglas rival. Yet in beautiful downtown Burbank in the autumn of 1969, Lockheed's directors seemed oblivious of onrushing financial doom. They could neither see nor admit that any management error lent a hand to the $2 billion (or 60 percent) excess on the Galaxy.

"We've asked ourself what we did wrong," said one executive, "and we concluded that there really wasn't anything." However rich Lockheed is in usable technology, blind conceit made it as vulnerable in management terms as any European corporation stuck in the fog of its between-the-wars mentality. Look down the list of prime American defense contractors—very few have made any significant new impact in postwar European markets. Where their technology was relevant, their cost structure was often too high. Until the 1960s, the Americans could trust greater productivity to offset higher costs, but that possibility was eroded long before the decade's end.

Companies operating in highly unionized Megalopolis, U.S.A., have horrendous problems even in maintaining productivity, let alone accelerating its rise. Gigantic plowback of funds into new capital equipment was supposed to offset declining productivity of labor, but a heavy price has been paid in plant that lies idle because it can produce too much or because (like all new, complicated machinery) it has broken down. Despite blatantly protective devices, such as oil import quotas, the U.S. began the 1970s with no insulation against the dollar's overvaluation; and the inevitable devaluation duly followed, humiliatingly, before the end of 1971.

Countries with happier currencies had no real disadvantage against the armies of U.S. management—armies which send ten men to do one executive's job. In 1969 and 1970 *Fortune*'s roster of sales by the two hundred largest non-American companies lifted sales by 16.2 and 16.7 percent. Those listed by *Fortune* as the five hundred biggest U.S. groups grew by only 9.7 percent in 1969 and 4.3 percent in 1970, the first statistical proof that the American challengers are actually on the defensive, and that no managerial alchemy, taught at business school or anywhere else, can overcome basic facts of economic life.

American executives share all the normal human qualities, including incompetence. Where their own myth has made them overconfident, they are more vulnerable than Europeans wrestling with their managerial inferiority complexes. Europeans will find this hang-up hard to shift. Whatever the growth figures, isn't American business still more profitable than European? And don't American subsidiaries in countries such as Britain tend to earn more than the local bumpkins?

On the first point, accountants' ideas on profits vary across the Atlantic, which makes comparison tricky. Moreover, for a long time, U.S. levels of return depended on the cheapest money rates in the world (no longer, though, which was another reason for the fading of the American challenge). Even the margin between the U.S. invaders and the locals seems to be narrowing, too, as American satellites become more mature and less able to live easily off the technology and output exported cheap or free by their ever-loving parents.

These Americans, by definition, are offshoots of the more aggressive, better-heeled, and better-equipped U.S. corporations. It would be shameful if they couldn't outperform the mass, or gloomy average, of local industry. Yet some U.S. subsidiaries don't even manage that. Ideal Standard, proud offshoot of American-Standard had a three-year profit record from 1968 of $1.21 million (half its 1963 peak). Even that is much less grim than Dow Chemicals' $43.3 million write-off on the Phrix joint venture in textile fibers with Germany's BASF. Dow, in its despair, even asked an American competitor what production standards should apply to the Phrix operation. "We don't know," came the answer. "We've never seen a plant that small."

The final evidence lies in the blowing up of the conglomerate. The conglomerate was an American invention, founded on the supposed supremacy of modern management, nurtured on business school graduates, fueled by theories such as "the free-form corporation" or the effective use of high debt. Non-Americans watched in awe as the conglomerate star rose, but didn't draw the obvious moral as it sputtered and exploded. That passage through the corporate heavens is symbolic of the American challenge. It was founded, not on real managerial, technological, and financial supremacy, but on passing circumstances, myth, and the infinite capacity of people for self-delusion.

4 _The Myopic Marketing Myth_

THE 1960s as a management decade were vastly influenced by one question: What business are we in? The question was put by Theodore C. Levitt in a _Harvard Business Review_ article, "Marketing Myopia." He cited the U.S. railroads, which chugged off into penury under the delusion that their business was railways, not transportation. And there was a myopic buggy whip company that went bust because it too had defined its business by the product, not by the market.

Levitt's thesis sounded plausible, although it did raise certain questions. Would dumbheaded railroad proprietors have been any brighter at managing truck companies or airlines? And what if the buggy whip firm had decided that, instead of being in transport accessories or guidance systems, it was in flagellation?

But executives love a new panacea; so companies all over

the world chugged off, as the American railroads didn't, into the business of defining their businesses. The bigger the company, the greater their pain—because large firms, like rocks acquiring barnacles, build up an encrusted deposit of unrelated activities over time. In the U.S., for instance, the biggest conglomerate in the sense of operating in the most different markets, was not Charlie Bluhdorn's Gulf and Western or Hal Geneen's International Telephone and Telegraph or even Jimmy Ling's Ling-Temco-Vought. It was good old General Tire.

The search for definitions led off in strange verbal directions. Of all odd results, Britain's Tube Investments had the most alliterative and meaningless—metal manipulation. This fine phrase can cover everything from the tubes that provide most of TI's profits to hairpins, which it doesn't make; but the company's products include some that use no metal, and others, such as gas heaters, in which manipulating metal is about the least important factor.

Dunlop, deeply influenced by the McKinsey consultants, who are in turn high on the marketing concept, came up with an equal beauty to explain its confusion of activities. "What do rubber and its successors do?" asked chairman Sir Reay Geddes rhetorically. "They absorb shock. They cushion. They grip. They bounce. What binds us together is the extension of these kind of things."

A binding that grips mattresses, tennis rackets, antiskid devices, and slippers is not tight. Any diversified giant's business is seldom logical. It is nearly always founded on one basic well-defined market—such as tires, which make up roughly two-thirds of Dunlop. The logic of Levitt, if strictly applied, would lead here to one of two conclusions. Either everything unrelated to the cushioning and care of transport equipment should be dropped as time-wasting diversion: or Dunlop should be treated, not as homogenous, but as a bunch of different and unrelated businesses.

Neither course is attractive. Company directors never (or hardly ever) voluntarily reduce their imperial sway; failed conglomerates have been slow to reduce their mass, or deconglomerate, even under acute financial pressure. If a big company does dump a major interest (as GE and RCA did with their computers), there are only two explanations: either the disposed fragment was losing money in floods, or the trustbusters (as with ITT and Avis) have forced the issue.

Most executives are no happier accepting the fact that they have a ragbag, which cannot be managed as one company in one way by one group of top men. They have mostly risen through the one homogenous business that makes sense for the company. They used to manage that business positively, by day-to-day involvement. They will not admit that their skills are of little help to the companies clustering round the mother planet. So they interfere and produce some concept of the company that lends rhyme and reason to their fiddling.

The marketing myopia question thus inadvertently nourished a policy of widening spread, which is the antithesis of the marketing concept—although that is by no means unforgivable. Marketing has attracted piles of unenlightened prose. Its definitions wander into long, echoing sentences littered with the ugly word "orientation." Marketing seems to mean finding out what the customer wants, putting on the market something that meets his need at a price the sucker is ready to pay, producing whatever it is for a cost that yields a fat profit at the price it is sold for, and knitting in the distribution and advertising with the marketing idea. All very sound and satisfying—until you ask what a nonmarketing company is up to.

Reversing the definition, that kind of company makes things whether anybody wants them or not, prices them any old how (except at the right price for the market), manufactures without any thought of the market, and distributes and promotes the result at random. Many companies are guilty of all these sins, but it isn't their marketing that is at fault. They need a new management.

Marketing's definitions end up describing every activity of top management, including even mergers, and stopping short only at personnel relations (on which top management spends no time, anyway, except when there are strikes). If marketing equals management, and bad marketing equals mismanagement, why all the fuss? And why, if marketing is a nonexistent mystery, do companies hire graduates wholesale from firms such as Procter & Gamble that are supposed to have the knack? (What P&G knows best is how to sell soap, and that not always: Camay was a fair flop in the U.K., and soap selling is rarely the secret P&G's management poachers are after).

Good books or articles on marketing are suspiciously thin. Except for recondite areas, such as the impenetrable equations of market research, there isn't much to write about—merely general management. One executive turned marketing professor, now retired, believes that marketing as a subject will eventually wither away, as executives finally master, for good and all, the outlandish notion that they have customers.

Marketing (not successful marketing, but marketing as the provision of bright ideas) is the easiest function in business management—which is why smooth-talking confidence artists have created such havoc. An ex-soap man, whose impeccable credentials included creating near-chaos in his first nonlather post, proceeded to tie up nearly all his next employer's working capital in the unsold stocks of just one division. The employer learned too late that any fool can produce a plan to capture 20 percent of the market. The excruciating job is making products that work at a cost that brings profits within earthly possibility. You can (the Germans did) successfully flog a well-made product for decades without having a marketing man or marketing notion on the premises.

But nobody, for more than the shortest period, can market mangled goods—no matter if every marketing consultant ever to wing the Atlantic is massed on his side. In a way, the old, despised production orientation had more logic. Any business has to be adept at its basic physical operations: without that, nothing is possible. This truth was partly obscured in British industry of the 1960s by the marketing myth, which even shrouded the bizarre events at the British Motor Corporation in its mist.

BMC's plagues were universally laid at the door of production orientation of bad, absent, or absent-minded marketing. It did indeed have many marketing problems, possibly every one there is. Its real problems, however, began with production—and ended there, at the time of its merger with Leyland, with serried stocks of unordered, even uncompleted, cars. Yet BMC's critics looked across at Ford, where everybody is supposed to talk marketing, and concluded that, since BMC had apparently little use for the word, that was the crunch.

In fact, BMC designer Sir Alec Issigonis had met marketing's first requirement—divining what the market wants—by unassisted genius. His Mini concept was a wholly original, highly acceptable consumer package. Enlarged into the 1100 to 1300 range, it gave BMC the best sellers that were its only life belts. The questions which BMC consistently got wrong were those of engineering design, cost of production, purchasing policy, balance of productive capacity, manpower deployment, and compatibility of components between models.

In a period when British industry was being lashed for marketing lapses, its sins of production were far more heinous. Americans are (or were) more deeply indoctrinated in the arts of marrying engineering and manufacture to meet product and profit requirements. But lately there have been signs that the old black magic has fled, possibly because of all U.S. specializations, production is the least likely to lead to the top and therefore, presumably, the last functional area into which bright young things from Harvard will direct their pattering feet.

As the marketing thinkers and their disciples have taken over, so Americans have imitated British disasters—for instance, in the aircraft industry. Their problem was not designing an aircraft that the market wants. The trouble has come mostly from failing to get enough working planes or engines flying at economic cost, and at the scheduled time.

Even the best-versed American companies can come to grief these days. Ford Motor has long prided itself on understanding the interrelation between car manufacture and marketing, which isn't too difficult. You invest heavily to keep down manufacturing costs and to introduce new models; you engineer desirable qualities into the cars and so push up the price;

you seek maximum interchangeability of parts between different lines; and you never launch a car until volume production is running smoothly and the dealers are stocked with the shiny new toys.

So what happened in Britain when Ford introduced, in late 1970, the replacement for its biggest profit earner, the Cortina? Well after the launch and before Ford's crippling strike, the dealers had no cars, and the few thousands made had all been recalled because of a production defect. The recalls of U.S. cars seem to have reached epidemic proportions—and it is no coincidence that, while you can call VW's beetle ugly, noisy, uncomfortable, slow, and inconvenient (and, if you're Ralph Nader, unsafe); you cannot say, by the industry's standards, that the machine is badly made. The marketing man, of course, won't let that escape. Reliability, he will say, is VW's gimmick—in other words, whatever a company does right is good marketing, and whatever it does wrong is because its marketing is bad.

The marketeers have not only pushed production men into the cold, but have also ousted the salesman. The standard sneer against "nonmarketing-oriented" companies is that they have merely called the sales manager a marketing manager. This is more sensible than importing a costly and expensively educated marketing manager and downgrading the little matter of selling. Just as you cannot market anything you cannot make, so you cannot market a product you cannot sell.

Selling, like production, is one of the grubbier aspects of management. Instead of hitting machines that break down, you come up against people who say no, or maybe. The great marketing companies were all founded on nothing more elaborate than the hard sell—3M, National Cash Register, Procter & Gamble, Coca-Cola, Shell, and IBM. IBM's acolytes would sing, of Thomas Watson, Sr., "He is the fairest, squarest man we know. Sincere and true, he has shown us how to play the game. And how to make the dough." The further they drift (like the men in head office aeries) from the hard base of making dough by selling, the more ineffective the companies become in the marketplace.

What business are we in? may help in brooding about the future and about the delicious directions that the company could or should take. But even that is dubious. Every single large company that diversified into computers had excellent reasons, based on realistic definitions of its business, for adding computer capacity. Yet every single one suffered untold grief as a result. They failed not by misunderstanding what business they were in, but by not seeing what business computers were in—and that, overwhelmingly, was the replacement of punch card machines.

The first real marketing question is this: How do we truly make our money? The answer, even in the largest conglomerates, usually comes down to that one basic area, established since its time began, in which the company is the lord of the market. Defending and extending this position must have the overwhelming priority. The next two marketing questions are How can we improve the key products and their manufacture? and How can we improve our selling?

The major asset of any business is the expertise acquired over time in its fundamental activities, and that is defined not by broad markets but by specific products. The U.S. railroaders would have made a mess of road or air transport because, lacking equipment and experience, they would have failed to understand unfamiliar technologies of selling or operation. The moral is not "Look after your production and selling, and your marketing will look after itself," but simply that stuffing the company into a bag marked Marketing Concept makes not a whit of difference to its myopia, arthritis, constipation—or any other of the diseases to which corporate flesh is heir.

5 *Bigness Is Best*

EVERYBODY KNOWS that the bigger the company, the sloppier its management, but everybody is wrong. The big company has the best managers, the best management, and generally the best technology, the best products, and the best production equipment—because the big company has the big money, and all these pleasures cost plenty. True, the large corporation is constipated, tongue-tied, muscle-bound, spendthrift, and overweight and does all it can, via these disadvantages, to outweigh its assets. But the mammoth's strengths give it an invaluable asset—staying power.

Large corporations are as durable as Old Man River. The whiz-kid companies come and go, rise and fall, but even a rudderless vessel such as U.S. Steel goes rolling along forever. It takes prodigies of mismanagement—usually in thorny industrial forests such as aerospace, into which many a man

41

has disappeared without trace—to break a large company. Short of mislaying its trains (which it did, too) the Penn Central had to commit every folly in the book to sink into bankruptcy.

The received view, which looks at the failures and fiascos of the leviathan rather than its strengths, requires correcting by what an American writer nicknamed the "Lestoil syndrome," after a once obscure New Jersey detergent firm. Expounding the Second Truth of Management, that *all good management is merely an expression of one great idea,* Lestoil broke out of obscurity by bottling the heavy-duty detergent which it sold to industry, and offering the heavenly liquid to housewives as well.

TV advertising, cautious at first, bolder as sales soared, quickly shifted Lestoil out of New Jersey and into the New York big time. The highly salaried managers at Lestoil's massively larger competitors, Procter & Gamble and Lever Brothers, had (as is their wont) totally missed this opportunity, despite their massed brainpower. In the end, however, the mammoths reacted with multimillion dollar force, swamping Lestoil in a sea of green bubbles. Hence the Lestoil syndrome —and it happens all the time.

In Britain a tiny concern, Alexander Duckham, was the first to produce a multi-grade lubricating oil for cars. It doubled its turnover in four years, enormously enlarging its market share until it had about one quarter of sales nationwide, and all under the very noses of the skilled big company managers at Shell, British Petroleum, Esso, Mobil, Castrol, and the like.

The leviathans had every motive to defend themselves; lubes are the most profitable end of their racket. Yet tiny Duckham (with assets one four-hundredth of BP's) produced a better product first and marketed it best. Enter the Lestoil syndrome. Duckham incurred the penalty of success. The giants retaliated, the competition intensified, the growth leveled off, the profits fell, and Duckham stock fell by half. Finally BP swallowed up little Duckham in its capacious gullet, obeying an ancient management maxim; If you can't beat 'em, buy 'em.

This has its tragic aspects: little David hurls his stone against Goliath, who takes his bruises and then, with ridiculous ease, plucks up his adversary. But the tragedy is inherent in two facts. First, the Davids are worse managed than the giants, and this is hidden behind the smokescreen of their success. Second, an essential ingredient of the little guy's success is the somnolence of Goliath. Outside every big, fat company there are sectors of the market waiting for a lean competitor to thrust his way in. No corporation, no matter how rich and superbly staffed, can preempt every possibility in the market or in technology; and the wealthier the company is, and the more massively entrenched in its chosen sectors, the harder it may be for its directors to react—for reasons of economics as well as pure inertia.

Gillette's initial failure in the stainless steel razor blade war was not simply its refusal to accept the fact that a little British sword company called Wilkinson's could provide serious competition. Gillette could compete technically—it made stainless blades for the Swiss and Swedish markets before the word "stainless" ever dropped into Wilkinson's consciousness, and Gillette even owned the patent for the critical PTFE coating of Wilkinson's wonder blades.

But Gillette had a huge worldwide production apparatus geared only to make carbon steel blades, which, because they became blunt quicker, were bound to sell in larger quantities and at lovelier profits than stainless blades. No wonder Gillette didn't want to know about the horrible things. But in management you can't (though executives do it constantly) shut your eyes and hope the competition will go away. Eventually Gillette was forced to compete, after losing significant slices of a seemingly impregnable market in country after country.

The oil companies learned a similar hard lesson in the British petrol market. Prices were fixed on a cozy formula linked to the free market quote in (of all places) the Gulf of

Mexico: the logic was only slightly stronger than fixing the price of beef in Chicago by that of yak's meat in Siberia. Under this umbrella of artificially high prices crawled the first cut-price independents; these tiny folk made handsome profits while charging much less. The big companies faced a horrid dilemma. Did they cut prices to cut out the independents, and sacrifice profits? Or did they maintain their profit margins and forget about the new competition? In the end, the issue was settled for them: the independents made such fast inroads that, thus getting the worst of both worlds, the majors lost market share and still had to cut prices. In the end, after much painful loss of profits, the Lestoil syndrome came into play and the independents were bought up—at the traditional premium prices.

The harder a leviathan is hit by small fry competition, the more likely it is to undergo the whalelike upheaval from which its progress mostly springs. The leviathan can bask for decades at a time before some terrible shock (like the great lumps that Wilkinson carved out of Gillette) makes it shoot out of the water on a sudden, usually brief career of high-speed performance. And it is easier for giant companies, despite their inertia, to react to challenge than it is for the little challenger to meet the awakened giant's attack. For the challenger's deficiencies are the mirror of the champion's strengths.

The sudden growth star normally has one or two thrusting and forceful personalities at the top—entrepreneurial types who lack interest in the routines of administration and organization. Below these leaders are few, if any, middle executives able to plug the gaps. First, the needs of the company rapidly outgrow the capacities of the men on board at the start of the upward trajectory, when the company was much smaller. This calamity hit even the Italian domestic appliance makers, long after they had become incredibly rich by flooding Europe with their refrigerators and washing machines so efficiently that even the mighty Philips was forced to surrender.

Second, people with high management talent tend to go where it is most recognized and best rewarded—and that generally means not the up-and-coming growth company (which usually underpays) but the heavyweight corporation. Any investor, or any take-over bidder, who buys a second-rank growth company for its management is flying blind. The management only looks good through the distorting glass of the boom-type profit record.

Some challengers do make it to the top—more in America where risk capital is relatively abundant than in Europe where the established companies have a hammerlock on the available financing. Xerox and Polaroid are the two stimulating examples of challengers turned champions, riding new technology that the giants wouldn't touch. Without detracting from either achievement, however, their two biggest competitors—3M and Eastman Kodak—have prospered mightily, all the same. Both achieved relatively good annual growth in earnings per share during the Polaroid-Xerox era. (3M's annual rate was 9.27 percent from 1960 to 1970, Kodak's 12.21 percent).

In fact, the Polaroid apparition galvanized Kodak into producing, in the Instamatic camera, its first great marketing innovation since a couple of concert pianists turned up with Kodachrome—just as Gillette was stung by Wilkinson into marketing the Techmatic razor, its first improvement in basic wet shaving technology since the royal days of King C. Gillette.

A benevolent circle produces these wonders. Because they are relatively well managed and exceedingly rich, the leviathans attract most of the new talent, which helps to soup up their management horsepower and to make them richer still. But the managerial talent of larger companies differs from that of growth stars. Its quality is shown in the effectiveness of formal systems, in the recognizable ability of individuals deep down inside the organization, in consistent performance over the years, and in this very power to regenerate.

Royal Dutch—Shell is the biggest example that Europe can offer of this, as of everything else. Its managerial reputation was so potent as the 1960s began that *Time* magazine fulsomely lauded Shell's superiority over the American oil majors. It often happens that the summit of pride for a corporation precedes a fall. When the profits stuck fast shortly thereafter and the McKinsey consultants were called in, Shell was revealed as another constipated, overweight bureaucracy that could only be cured by painful slimming at the managerial health farm. Recognition of its own defects is an excellent

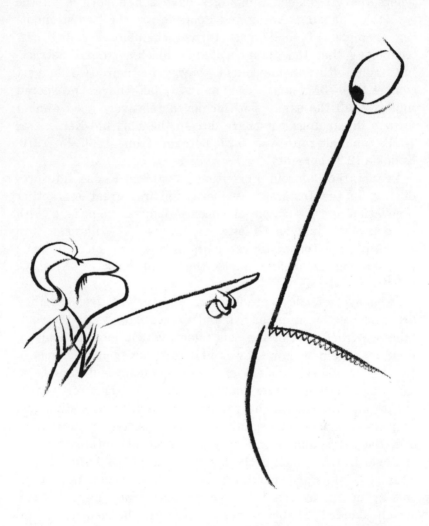

therapy for management. Shell led the oil majors into the giant tanker era and prospered accordingly; its pretax margins went up by no less than one-fifth, which on a turnover in the billions has a perfectly marvelous effect.

Because it builds up so much blubber over the years, a large corporation is relatively easy to pare down: great lumps of fat can be sliced away without any visible effect on corporate efficiency. This is the lesson of Sir Arnold Weinstock's calculated surgery on the General Electric Company. Its net capital employed rose from 1962 to 1965 by only £4.5 million, while sales galloped up by £23.6 million and profits by £10.6 million. As Weinstock wielded the knife, critics argued that the cutting would go too far, until the very heart of the old electrical giant would be chopped out. In fact, the amputation of superfluous offices, factories, and staffs left GEC so formidable that its two bigger rivals, English Electric and AEI, couldn't stay in the game: both succumbed to GEC bids.

Cutting is not the same thing as creating—even though eliminating £1 million of running sores is just as effective financially as creating a new business earning £1 million. Loss elimination, moreover, requires no capital, and may actually free it, if the culprit can be sold off; new businesses always involve investing new money, a job at which large firms are worse than they know. The weakness of the big corporation lies, not only in the sluggishness and inefficiencies bred by long chains of command and entrenched bureaucracies, but in inability to behave like small company entrepreneurs, no matter how it tries.

Big company managers are far better at running an ongoing, soundly based business: the money that Honeywell, for instance, has milked out of thermostats over the years would buy up every small gee-whiz company along Boston's Route 128 and still leave change. On this argument, big companies should give up the seldom successful effort to launch new businesses. If they discover bright aggressive entrepreneurs in their midst, managements should encourage these rarities to go into business for themselves—and keep a slice of the equity for the good old company. Most of the offshoots, however, will fail. (Fear of failure within the big company is a prime cause of its entrepreneurial inertia; the key to making a personal fortune in business is to lose inhibitions about going bankrupt).

Those breakaways who succeed can always be acquired in the big company's own good time. Cynical, perhaps; but it's the only way. Xerox provided clinching evidence of its own passage from entrepreneurial creation to established corporation in its first major diversification. It bought up Scientific Data Systems, a little computer breakaway turned sometime bonanza; and Xerox (behaving like an established giant all the way) paid far too much for a company that promptly lost much fine gold.

Few corporation men have the wit or psychological insight to concentrate on and refine what they can do—running large commercial bureaucracies—and to avoid the activities at which they fail. No chief executive will ever say, even to his inner soul, We're no good at doing new things; we'll let somebody else do it, then buy them up. The corporate mythology dictates, to quote a vice-president from du Pont, that the entrepreneurial man who bucks the system is the man who makes it. Asked to give an example, the du Pont vice-president came up with a hero who started the company's antifreeze business—back in the 1930s.

In more modern times, plagued by a lack of entrepreneurs, du Pont pioneered a device designed to break any logjams. Called by the fancy name of venture management, this sets up businesses within the business. One manager gets total responsibility for a new project. It is all his, to nurse to profitable fruition; all his, that is, subject to the normal limitations of corporate budgeting and policy restraints.

There's the rub. The corporation's checks, changes, habitual slow, grudging reactions, and heavy overheads are exactly the forces that stifle entrepreneurial initiative. A new business may need new forms for its success; the old norms of a corporation may be deadly. For all du Pont's depth of resources, hefty research spending, and sophisticated techniques such as venture analysis (computerized assessment of projects, renamed "venture annihilation" by aggrieved managers), its flow of new riches has disappointed deeply. Its trumpeted Corfam synthetic leather had to be folded for a pretax loss of $100 million, after a series of marketing and manufacturing errors. There may be lush things in du Pont's cupboard—although one item on its list of unmarketed new ventures is discouraging. This is an office copier that uses ordinary paper. As a du Pont man told *Time* magazine, "We may just be too late. Perhaps we should have moved faster."

The tragedy of the new venture manager in the large corporation is what seems to be his strength—the fact that all the corporation's resources are behind him. The small men, like the two Gross brothers, who foolishly tackled National Cash Register head-on in the British market, can't take four years to launch a product; they don't have the time, so they take four months. They can't install expensive engineering, because they haven't got the money—so they find a cheaper way to manufacture, which produces a cheaper price and so automatically builds in a marketing advantage.

The brothers pinched half the U.K. cash register market, quadrupling their sales in five years. If the Grosses of this world save money, it's money they badly need. But if a corporation man is given a budget to invest, he spends it—for there is no personal gain in economizing. The small man runs hard because the bet is all or nothing. The corporation man is on double or quits. If the project comes off, he is a hero. If he is a Corfam-coated failure, he probably stays put. In the rare cases of dismissal, there is always some other job somewhere. Curiously, the man dismissed for disaster seems to have less trouble in finding a new home than the manager who loses out under some impersonal economy drive, perhaps because the former has active, aggressive qualities that interview better than the latter's passive misery. Like some of Bernie Cornfeld's lieutenants in IOS, the dismissed aggressor, too, can always claim that his past was perfection—it was just Bernie or his sidekick, Ed Cowett, who loused up the deal.

The big corporation that is really serious about innovating will have to loosen the whole structure of checks and balances, reports and committees in which decisions are arduously taken and painfully executed. At the same time, the routine operations that go on for eternity are always a happy hunting ground for improvement. A great deal of work inside an organization serves only the organization; it has no direct relevance outside, which is the only place where the money is. All this work can be dumped without loss.

Large companies further compound the perennial problem of effective management of large numbers by overhiring. Far too many able executives sleep peacefully within those ample bosoms. As a former ICI executive once wrote, "If everyone in giant corporations of this nature who is earning over £2,000 a year were lined up, and the even numbers dismissed, not only would those left behind cope more easily with their tasks, but those dismissed would have a major impact on industry."

The paradox of too many competent executives when (according to the complaints of most chief executives) there are not enough to go around, is easily resolved. The extant executives are used for the wrong jobs or pointed toward the wrong objectives by the kind of big company top management that (to quote a case) maintains a separate sales force to sell its own commodity to its own subsidiaries, who (naturally) are not allowed to buy from any other source. This management had imported bright, aggressive market-minded newcomers to run the businesses closest to the marketplace; but it offset the contribution from any of its ventures that survived pregnancy by losing all the money it could in older parts of the company.

Great companies would crash into these barriers less often if they saw themselves as they really are—not as thrusting, entrepreneurial commercial go-getters, but as bureaucracies with a tendency to domination by *apparatchiks*—people who have grown old in a company's service and traditions. The delightful chairman of one of Britain's international jewels once said, "You can't turn a group like this upside down every eighteen months." That is the authentic voice of the apparatchik: if a corporation urgently needs turning upside down, even eighteen months after the last upheaval, inversion it must have. It is the apparatchik who stops the big corporation, time and again, from cashing in on its innate superiority.

6 *Your Least Important Asset*

REBELLION BY THE workers alarmed managements all over Europe and North America as the 1970s began. The upsurge of unrest followed oddly on a decade in which, thanks to the blessings of behavioral science, the workingman's well-being had ostensibly received more nurture than ever before. Inventions in employee relations ran from the joys of job enrichment to the rewards of productivity bargaining. Yet the unions wanted still more—mysterious gains such as employee participation and co-ownership, as well as that simple, age-old need, more money.

Putting cash aside, labor feels hard done by—which is strange, given that the leaders of big business cast themselves as leading humanists. Most annual reports contain ritual tributes to the labor force ("Again the staff distinguished itself by its team effort, its enthusiasm, and its loyalty . . ."). Corporate heads are also fond of phrases such as "Its able and dedicated employees continue to be the company's most valuable resource" or "People are our most important product" or "our most important asset." How strange that those assets (or products) are increasingly prone to strike.

Actually, people are often less important than physical assets—companies sometimes move whole operations to new towns, leaving their labor forces in the lurch. Almost the entire New England textile industry shifted to the more pliable South: but its executives took care not to forget the up-to-date machines. Even if people can't be replaced collectively, they are always disposable individually. Against this background, few managements—and this is a far greater cause of unrest than Communist agitation—pay a labor force much attention until trouble actually breaks out.

Applied to machines, the same procedure causes instant chaos. But the labor force is not regularly maintained. It is treated as an asset, possibly, but as a fixed asset that only requires attention when the wages plumbing goes wrong, or the pay boiler blows up in a strike. The failure is patched up (usually with money) by use of whatever conventional negotiating system is at hand; and most managements let their reactions to the emergency be dictated by external forces— the unions, the Government, the law.

Boards seem to regard the care and maintenance of the labor force as an inferior function—witness the low number of personnel directors in British companies, and the still smaller squadron of personnel experts who actually sit on British boards and executive committees. Even in America, the personnel chief is rarely a director of the company; he is almost always a specialist (often hired principally to conduct the biennial wage negotiations, or strike). He has as much chance of becoming president of the U.S. as president of the company. His status matters less if the chief executive makes labor relations his responsibility and knows how to manage them. Few do, and most wouldn't want to. The deterrent is that human beings in the mass are hard to handle; they are unpredictable, obstinate, demanding, intractable, and the wretches answer back.

Boards prefer to mull over multimillion dollar investment projects, negotiate large and comforting mergers, and compose optimistic five-year plans, rather than getting involved with the messy events on the factory floor. This is a fatal error, precisely because manpower is not in reality an asset. It is more like a supply of raw material, changing but essential —the most important supply that a corporation consumes. Because this is so, the unions are a company's most important suppliers, which makes it all the sillier that boards of directors have so little contact with union leaders, either at national or factory levels.

In large tracts of America, the necessity for unwholesome contact can be avoided by keeping the plants free of union contamination. This usually involves either locating factories in the equivalent of the Australian outback—far from civilization—or continually keeping a jump ahead of whatever the unions might demand. The same gymnastic trick has been tried by American subsidiaries in Britain, and it works; moreover, it works for the right reasons, even if done for the wrong ones. It demands that management think how to bribe the worker. It means switching from passive management of labor to active concern with its desires, treatment, and satisfaction.

Even at the simplest level of forestalling strikes, no managerial effort can produce a better return on investment. After all, if the men don't turn up, no other resource, except the stocks, has any current value. Yet managements are constantly surprised, even hurt, when their own folly makes the men march out. At one British engineering works, where the loyalty of the men and the company's prestige were both taken for granted, the management was so shattered by a walkout that it called in consultants. They found that a complex pay claim had been submitted two years before—so complex that the management, unable to understand it, had never replied.

The late, great A. J. Liebling tried in vain to persuade the American public that there are always two sides to any strike, that a deadlock requires an obdurate management as well as an obstinate union. The public, however, starts from the idea that the union is the protagonist, presumably because the men have to take the first active step by leaving the premises and posting pickets. Very few strikes are ever studied to discover who really is to blame; and the cause is often some abject management failure.

In one British car incident (typical of countless unofficial disputes), the men had been laid off during the week, were recalled at the weekend to make up a shortage of parts, and were to be laid off again the next Monday. They struck, of course. In another car crisis, two men accidentally got each other's pay slips—and the more skilled worker found he was getting less than a relatively unskilled man. Strike two.

British managements have longed for long-term contracts, American style, with strikes kept down to one every three years, but few have taken any such initiative: perhaps they couldn't face the cost in fringe benefits. For decades, British managements have soldiered on with archaic pay systems that opened up yawning gulfs between take-home pay and basic pay, produced wildly irregular earnings, and worst of all, placed control of output rates in the hands of union shop stewards. Hardly any managements did anything to correct a situation that was neither in their interests nor that of the workers—they let the sleeping dogs lie.

In labor management, a dog left lying too long can bite the hand that thinks it feeds him. The strikes at Leyland Motors and the great Pilkington Brothers glassworks, both without stoppages of any kind since the general strike of 1926, shocked both managements. Both supposed smugly that all quietness on the Western front indicated worker satisfaction, not seething discontent.

Alas, however, you do have to ask the men if you really want to know their feeling; and you get some funny answers. In one fast-growing small company the men turned out to hanker after a long-lost mythical past: "We used to sing at the machines, and the buzzer at the end of the day was just an annoying interruption." In Leyland and Pilkington, it was the managements that lived in the past, and the managements paid the price.

This isn't the same as a failure of communication, the usual scapegoat. Again, communicating (i.e., putting out costly house journals, or some similar waste of cash) is easier than tackling real, tough problems. You can find out some of these by buying an employee attitude survey, an expensive goodie dreamed up by the sociologists. The risk of bringing the entire place to a standstill while unlettered workers wrestle with the questionnaire may be worthwhile if the results rub management's nose in the usual sorry truths; for instance, that the workers have taken amiss some pet managerial scheme for the advancement of mankind. The reason is not bad communication, but bad blood: workers distrust executives even more than executives distrust workers.

The ideal worker, from management's point of view, does what he is told without argument; never makes mistakes; is punctual, clean, and tidy; produces maximum effort on a consistently rising scale; accepts any working arrangements his superiors ordain; and never demands more pay than the firm can afford (i.e., the minimum that the management thinks it can get away with). The blue-collar paragon is expected to live a working life far more virtuous than that of the average executive—for that individual argues, makes mistakes, sometimes slacks, always expects big annual increments (larger than a blue-collar man usually even demands), and though mostly clean and tidy, is often unpunctual.

Yet the executive, cosseted with fringe benefits to the limit of the law, looks forward to substantial advances in real wealth year after year on the long road to a heavily pensioned retirement. This gap—the true difference between Us and Them—yawns wider in Britain than in the U.S. The British worker, apart from a factory canteen, has hardly any fringe benefits. An inadequate welfare state has to provide for all needs—sickness, death, retirement—even if a man has given a lifetime's service to a wealthy corporation.

In Britain neither side of the bargaining table gets what it wants. Company directors need stable and predictable labor costs and effective control over organizing and allocating work. The men want the security of stable and predictable earnings, with a rising standard of living over the years, but they don't want any part of management's job. "Industrial democracy" and "worker's participation" sound well on a militant unionist's lips or on the brochure for an expensive management seminar. But it's hard enough to achieve democracy in any group of executives (or executive participation) in most companies; letting the employees into the act is impossible. It has been tried: Britain's Glacier Metal has such elaborate consultation machinery that somebody once gibed, "Why doesn't Glacier give up making bearings, and concentrate entirely on its joint consultation?" The effort doesn't seem to affect the way the Glacier management manages, and nobody else has flattered the approach by imitation.

The executive at the middle level puts up with being frozen out of the big decisions because he feels that he belongs. Only in rare circumstances, and in carefully paternal companies, does the British or American worker share the same faith. In West Germany and Japan, the world's most strike-free industrialized economies, belonging is built into the social system, and paternalism cements the structure. Although the recipe is difficult to follow without the same social ingredients, that is the only way of making "the most important asset" *feel* important.

But paternalism is no panacea. Real paternalism doesn't mean that father knows best. Like everybody else, father is wrong half the time. The real need is to find managers who can look at the treatment of labor from labor's angle as well as their own. But this is not only hard work; it offends against the Third Truth of Management—*no manager ever devotes effort to proving himself wrong.*

Instead, companies prefer to try the newest device for satisfying the unsatisfied worker. Take "job enrichment," a marvelous piece of word coining, because who can resist being "enriched"? It means asking the worker about his work and finding ways to make the worker's job more interesting and his performance more effective—the enrichers are peddling goods that sensible managements have always kept in stock.

The annals of enrichment are full of ripe successes. There was huge improvement in performance at one U.S. factory that completely altered procedures to give more initiative to the workers: one old sweat promptly recalled that "this was how the job used to be years ago." The old method had been abandoned to improve productivity, and now engines were being reversed for exactly the same reason and with exactly the same result. All changes that grab the interest of workers raise their performance—installing piped music or (preferably) taking it out; painting the walls red, white, and mauve; returning them to plain green; enriching jobs or taking out the skill element by mechanization; making the lighting brighter or changing its color.

Typically, the improvement in performance lasts for a limited period and then trails off; the workers regress toward their norm. They respond to the stimulus of somebody taking an interest, and backslide as the stimulus wears off. Executives lose interest too. Detroit Edison in the mid-1950s reorganized one thousand employees in the accounting office, proving that job enrichment worked—but the office has been reorganized several times since and everybody has forgotten about it. Similarly, workers whose operations are studied in an unchanged operation habitually raise their performance (unless the study is designed to cut their pay per job in a piecework system, in which case they naturally *lower* their speeds). But managers operate on the assumption that labor forces respond only to the one stimulus of money: hence the invention and brief flowering of so-called productivity bargaining.

This seed was first planted in Britain by American consultants working for an American oil company, Esso, at its Fawley refinery. U.S. firms find the refusal of British workingmen to behave like Americans peculiarly irritating; and the Fawley experiment could do little harm, since the plant, like all oil refineries, employed few men. The Fawley deal in effect bribed the men to accept new working conditions, the theory being that improved productivity would pay for the bribes and leave plenty of jam to spare for the company.

Another U.S. oil company, Mobil, followed. Later on, manufacturers using labor forces of significant size climbed on the bandwagon—and sometimes fell off with a crash. Some paid bribes that greatly exceeded the initial productivity benefits, and then discovered (as did Esso after the original Fawley deal) that the process is subject to diminishing returns as new restrictions grow up like weeds, to be bought off in their turn. In one plant, the workers were shrewder than the managers. "They want more productivity," said one. "But all they will get is more fiddles."

So the urging in 1970 of American corporations to start productivity bargaining as an anti-inflation device was hilariously inapt. The deals are often uneconomic and hideously complex (cabalistic documents that only a union official, a management consultant, a labor lawyer, or a linguistic philosopher could understand) ; they also enshrine a hopelessly wrong principle—that you should pay people more to work sensibly, which means, of course, that up to now you have been paying them to work stupidly.

Unless all pay is reward for cooperative and intelligent working, total absurdity must result. For instance, at Dunlop's main U.K. tire plant, the new automated machines making radial tires were capable of outputs so high that the tire workers, all on piecework, stood to outearn the managing director. Only long and unbelievably tedious negotiations— altogether eleven and one-half months of talks with the unions were needed to evaluate 1,180 jobs—kept some of the productivity gains for the company. Management paid the price, in misspent time as well as higher wage rates, for perpetuating a system that made no managerial sense.

If you have a long-standing incentive pay system, like Dunlop's, the instinctive course should be to drop it for a day wage. If you have a day-wage system, however, maybe you had better try incentives. At least, in Britain in 1970 and 1971 incentive schemes were going out of one factory while going into the one next door. On the whole, however, it is simpler and more dignified to pay a man a fair wage than to tie his pay to his output—an oversubtle task that is bedeviled by horrors such as the learning curve (labor costs reduce by one fifth with every doubling of output and without one liquid ounce of extra employee sweat). As Steve Keating, president of Honeywell, observed, "It takes a very good factory management to make incentives work well. It takes outstanding supervision and if you have that, you don't need incentives."

Like fighting wars, managing labor relations is full of disappointments—logical policies may not have logical results when you are dealing with human psychology. But illogic doesn't have to reign. Management must give its labor force a guaranteed acceptable level of earnings; give labor full consultation, but with management retaining the right to change equipment and methods; create a long-range manpower plan designed to provide steady employment; plan opportunities for promotion and good raises even for the unpromoted; and equalize fringe benefits between all grades of employee.

The dockers of Rotterdam were superbly treated in more or less this manner. For many years they were held up as paragons of virtue and cooperation and as standing rebukes to their London equivalents—tough, obstinate cookies, who, whipped on by the odd Communist, fought a running guerrilla war, breaking out in pitched battles, against some of Britain's most purblind employers. The London war culminated in a mammoth productivity bargain that notoriously achieved minimum productivity at maximum cost.

They don't manage likewise in Rotterdam. But for all their good treatment, the nice, undemanding Dutch dockers struck viciously over a pay claim in late 1970, demanding gigantic raises, blocking the traffic, and using violence in a way unknown even to a London dockside militant. The moral is not that the Rotterdam employers were wrongheaded to treat their dockers well. The lesson is that the good employer does not practice truly good labor policies because he expects manna to fall from heaven as a result. It won't. He manages men humanely, generously, and thoughtfully because it is right.

II Money

7 *The Case of the Crumbling Profits*

IF MANAGEMENT had a god, it would be Mammon—symbolized by a column of profits. Even in the deepest British backwaters, the most stagnant Midwest hinterland, the darkest Ruhr iron foundry, possibly even the most paternalistic sweatshop in Osaka, every executive knows that profit is the name of the game, the objective and the measure of managerial performance. But what is a profit?

In common or garden life, the answer sounds easy: profit is the difference between what something costs and what you sell it for. Common or garden ideas, however, become complex and slippery in the higher (or lower) reaches of business management. Sure, profit is the difference between costs and revenues, but what are costs and what are revenues?

In Britain, Associated Electrical Industries—a crumbling monument to a previous era of capitalism—fought a vain fight against take-over by the General Electric Company. It forecast, notoriously, a £10 million profit for a financial year that was almost over. GEC's sharp-penned accountants looked at the same books after victory. They worked the math out to a £4.5 million loss; and £14.5 million seems a hard sum to mislay.

The essential point—that conventional accounting does not produce the one accurate figure by which managers are supposed to live—was obscured by the violent GEC–AEI struggle itself. After all, strange things happen in the heat and dust of battle. But odd things also occur in time of peace. The first spots of sickness at Lockheed broke out in 1968, when it added 50 percent to alleged profits by a switch in accounting for overhead on the government contracts that provided all but a tenth of its takings.

Even then, Lockheed's performance was distinctly earthbound, which added fiercer point to the vital question, Had Lockheed actually made that extra 50 percent or hadn't it? Even if the previous method understated "true" profits, could the Lockheed management take credit, in reputation or in pocketing bonuses and salary increases, for extra profits that had been "earned" by its accountants? Lockheed's example is made more glaring by the nemesis that lay in wait; but other managers all over the world constantly recook the books by which they are judged.

In one typical week not long ago, two British worthies, Fison's (fertilizers-cum-drugs) and Plessey (electronics), added a combined, effortless £2.3 million to profits. Fison's managers stumbled across an extra £1 million (or 19 percent) of pretax profits by, in effect, charging less depreciation—the process that assumes that a part of all assets withers away each year—and valuing stocks on a more cheerful basis. Plessey's £1 million plus arrived through liberalizing its depreciation policy (yes, that again) and reshuffling other accounting odds and ends. Neither business had improved or even influenced its efficiency by this fancy footwork. Yet their return on capital employed—the most hallowed barometer of corporate competence—seemed to have surged smartly upward.

The breasts of these two managements were no doubt clear, their motives pure. But either before revision or after, they must have portrayed an untrue picture of their lovely corporate finances. Strangely, or not so strangely, all three—Lockheed, Plessey, and Fison's—ran into financial setbacks shortly after these fine exhibitions of dynamic accounting. Perhaps the plucking of profits out of thick air is a sign, registered in the conscious or subconscious of executives, that real profits are drying up. For there is a real profit, just as there is reality behind the notion of capital employed. However, conventional profit is outstretched for elasticity only by conventional capital employed; and expressing one of these prize uncertainties as a ratio of the other mystery—dividing the profit by the capital to get a pretty percentage—cannot measure anything at all. (The British government even judges the efficiency of its mammoth nationalized industries by return on capital, mindless of the fact that, in a snug monopoly, the figure only measures the size of the latest large price increases.)

Businesses and heads of corporations don't earn profits: they earn money. Profit is an abstraction from the true, underlying movement of cash in and cash out. Any small businessman who has had trouble meeting the payroll knows the painful principle: without enough cash, you drown. Larger businessmen have learned the same lesson in the same brutal way; the mighty Penn Central in the U.S. ran out of hard currency; so did Rolls-Royce; so did a one-time British textile star, Klinger. A later Klinger chairman recalled to stockholders, "We were unable to pay the interest on the loan stock, or the wages on the Friday night, and already several checks had bounced." A big company's checks can rebound just as high as those of a little shopkeeper. But many top executives, even in suave and sophisticated organizations, have never mastered the truth that what counts at the end of the day is the cash in the kitty—not the abstractions in the books.

The object of the honest manager is to fit the abstraction

to the reality as neatly as he may. Any managers who toy with procedures to invent a higher profit must search their souls long and harshly. Will the change paint a truer likeness, or will it obscure the truth? For high technology companies, the dilemma is acute. They need, and badly, lofty stock market ratings to attract the capital for which they slaver, so they have high incentive to report high profits. Yet their spending on research and development has an unpleasant way of devouring any cash left over from financing equally voracious long-term manufacturing projects.

How such stars treat research and development, and how they value stocks and work in progress, determines their "profits" far more than what they actually manage to sell. Back in 1961, the managers of Rolls-Royce, as one later put it, "were having trouble showing a profit." So the directors adopted a new magic formula. They assessed "the value of R and D recoverable from sales resulting from existing aero-engine orders." This lusty sum was not charged against the income for the year in the accounts (though it was paid out of that income). The money spent was instead counted as an asset, and Rolls (hey, presto) duly showed a profit.

This handy device has been employed by utterly respectable companies with the noblest intentions. But the money to be made from *future* engine sales was not the question that should have bugged the engineers of Rolls. The real issue was whether they could earn enough bread from *existing* business. The answer was crystal clear several years before the Rolls-Royce calamity. The company couldn't, and didn't, earn nearly enough.

In 1967, the accounts showed a £17.5 million trading profit after interest: Rolls lavished £9.6 million on research and development (charging only £5.7 million against income) and set aside £4.2 million for tax. Trading profit, minus research and development, minus tax left £3.7 million in a year when the company paid out £6.1 million (every pound of it real) in dividends. The kitty tells the same caustic story. The poor benighted stockholders handed over another £17.4 million during the year as the company raised more money by selling them new shares—yet the 1966 net overdraft of £25 million shot up to £41.3 million. In effect, stockholders paid for their own dividends, which was kind of them. Much the same tale was repeated in 1968, and thereafter Rolls went on having "trouble showing a profit" because there was little or none to show.

It was bad books, as much as the RB 211 engine for the Lockheed Tristar, that ran Rolls out of cash, unhorsed chairman Sir Denning Pearson (an apprentice turned chief executive of the old school), and unraveled the company. If published accounts, with a little easy disentangling, can reveal hard reality to outsiders, there is no excuse for insiders missing the point. The harsher the truth, however, the happier executives are to hide it from everybody—especially themselves. The lives and ambitions of the Rolls-Royce men were bound up with building "the best aero-engines in the world." As Pearson put it, "We don't care whether you propel 'em with squibs or with elastic bands. We'll be up in front whatever the method." To admit that they could not be up in front at a profit would have negated their whole existence.

A misinformed executive is a doomed one. Witness the brave boss of a small British company. He went after export business on the heroic scale at prices that covered only component costs and direct labor—and failed to take any account of increased overhead and indirect expenses. "Why didn't somebody tell me this before?" demanded the poor fellow, as they led him away to liquidation.

The first fact of life that any manager needs to know is the likely cash effect of his decisions: what he must pay out, how that spending will be financed—including what income the firm will receive—and when. Cash flow accounting excludes notional expenditures (items such as depreciation that don't represent physical cash leaving the premises) and also deletes notional income (such as the money that will be earned when, please God, somebody buys the inventory). It includes all real spending (such as research and development) and is only interested in real receipts (the safe arrival of somebody else's cash).

True, if company accounts were written only in this hard-headed way, a different distortion would follow. For instance, if the inventory is about to be snapped up by a screaming public, just counting its cost, without taking in any added value, must understate the lucky company's profitability. There is a British building contractor who only takes in profits when his bills are settled—and accountants think him dangerously eccentric. But is the distortion as severe, or as dangerous, as the folderols of conventional profit or loss accounting? That is a subject on which Saul Steinberg, the whiz-kid of Leasco Data Processing, should have interesting views after his costly tangle with the ex-wizard of British publishing, Robert Maxwell of Pergamon Press.

The boy genius who invented Leasco by dazzling financial maneuvers (not least by switching into insurance and out of leasing computers before the latter business died on him) should have a good and twitching nose for a balance sheet. Yet he accepted Pergamon's declared 1968 profits and 1969 forecast and compounded his folly by buying shares in the open market—an escapade that eventually cost Leasco the write-off of some ten million sorely needed pounds.

The 1968 balance sheet showed, to a casual, but curious glance that in the year of a reported £2 million profit, Pergamon's cash ran downhill by £2 million. That £4 million slalom should have led Steinberg to ask some tough prior questions. As it was, tough later researches—much too late for Leasco—turned that £2 million profit into only £495,000: and that was before taking account of stupendous losses on Maxwell's fatal effort to imitate the *Encyclopaedia Britannica*.

Books illustrate beautifully why a profit need not be a profit. The highest point at which the publisher can value a book is his own selling price. This assumes that the books will all be sold. If they are not, the publisher has taken credit for an unearned profit, and future losses lie literally in store. Books can be valued at cost (which assumes, less hazardously, that sales will at least reach the break-even point) and then written down yearly. Or they can be valued as pulp (virtually nil), which accurately mirrors the cash position, at the expense of favorably distorting profits in future years. Of the two extreme positions—stating current year's profits at the highest or lowest possible level—the latter must be more desirable, less misleading to the honest publisher, less tempting to the dishonest.

Always select the most conservative accounting portrayal that is consistent with previous years and with the inexorable reality of cash flow in and out of the business—and that puts off paying tax as long as possible. Precisely when the cash reality shows up is less important than the knowledge that, one day, show up it will. One small company reported large monthly losses although its bank balance was mounting sky-high. The explanation lay in ultraconservative accounts (subscription revenue was coming in but being phased over a whole year): and the prognosis was rudely healthy. The reverse situation—a business combining high, wide, and handsome profits, with a rapidly rotting cash position—more often than not leads but to the grave.

With financial half-truths (or downright untruths) the outcome is the same as with boxers: the bigger they are, the harder they fall. Yet sometimes the "truth" produces absurdities on the capital side of return on capital employed. The return (or the profit) is what executives choose to make it within a latitude wide enough to cover most sins. But the similar Yo-Yo characteristics of capital employed operate differently. For instance, should you value property at cost or present-day worth? Because of the endless inflation of property values, revaluation of a store chain could easily double the capital employed. This is a more "realistic" and conservative figure—yet, if you do revalue, the return on capital will halve.

Assuming (extravagantly) that profits are truly calculated, which is the more accurate return? The conservative one may be more misleading; it puts forward, as a realistic alternative (it seldom is), the proposition that the properties could be sold off en bloc at market value. You could argue that whenever the property worth of a business rises above its value as a going concern, the business should be folded and the property leased. What's the point of sweating to make a profit if you can earn the same in easy rent? Alas, on this criterion, half the businesses in the world would be forced to close.

There are sometimes potent reasons for revaluing your assets, and rapidly. When the British government announced that it would switch to a return-on-capital basis in working out its price for milk, the dairy chains reached for higher valuations as one man. Upvaluing can also help to guard against take-over marauders, or provide bigger security against borrowings. But none of these aims, though they may be quite sanitary, has anything to do with efficiency as such.

By an unhappy coincidence, every disappearing or appearing trick that can be worked with profits must, under the laws of double-entry bookkeeping, have a reflection on the capital side. Revaluing (assiduously avoided in the U.S.) is only one way of bumping up capital employed. You can charge a low depreciation rate, which elevates both profits and capital. If you boost the depreciation, you cut the capital, and then in some later year, when you decide on lower depreciation again, up and up goes your return. You can buy a business for much more than its asset value and keep the excess in your balance sheet as "goodwill" (whatever that means), or you can manfully wipe out the goodwill there and then. Since you don't expunge any of the acquired profits, your return on capital will again shoot up.

A favored wheeze for companies losing money on favorite ventures, borrowing a leaf from the aerospace accountants, is to call it "development spending" and capitalize it (i.e., overstate profits by that amount). Lord Thomson, busy dissipating some of the profits of North American monopoly newspapers and broadcasting, in the doomed effort to turn *The Times* into a goldmine, called his staggering losses "development" and created them as such. But the accounting treatment made the drain no less. Financial gimmickry has nothing to do with managing a business; the company director is only playing with numbers. The trouble is that not only investors and financial writers get mesmerized by the number game: so do the directors themselves. And when the profits in the case finally crumble away, it is too late for the mesmerized director to wake up.

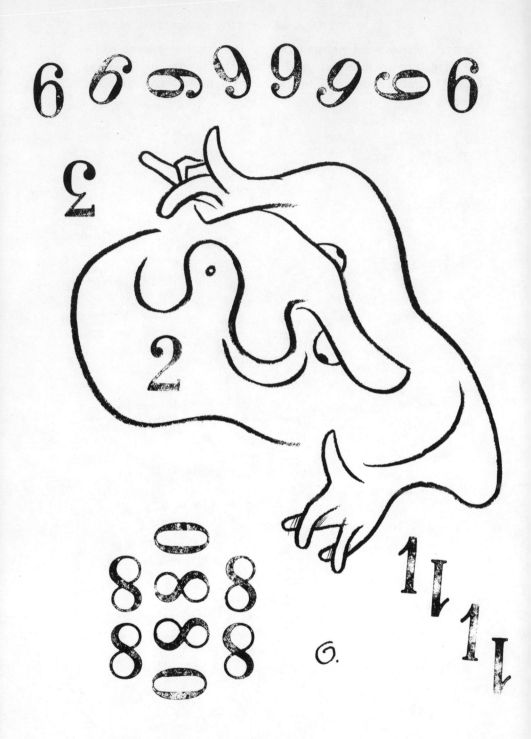

8 *The Accountancy Dodge*

WHENEVER A company fails, or a management wakes up covered in financial mud, one relevant question seldom gets asked: What were the accountants up to? Every failed management was advised, hectored, and helped by its own accountants, its auditors' accountants, possibly those of its favorite moneylender. Accountants are highly trained professionals in the management and recording of financial transactions. Yet crash and calamity reveal them blithely or blindly accepting figures (such as the Rolls-Royce forecasts for the RB 211 engine) that would set alarm bells ringing in a half-trained mind. The Penn Central's crash in the U.S. too raised doubts about the efficiency of audits—given the lack of resemblance between reality and that befuddled railroad's published reports.

Such a sequence of disasters questions the accountant's

usefulness as a source of management information, as auditor of the accounts, and even as a reliable keeper of the financial score. But that should be no surprise. The accountant is playing an elaborate game, whose purpose is not to tell the truth (for truth is a chimera), but to obey the rules. The rules in turn are not designed to make managers more efficient, or to inconvenience crooks, or even to keep companies solvent. They are there simply to allow the game itself to proceed. That explains how accountants can usually wash their hands of blame or dirt when disaster strikes. They can nearly always prove that they played their game according to their rules. Unfortunately, management is a different game entirely—that of producing more resources than the ones you started out with.

It's not the accountant's fault, moreover, if the executives they work for suffer from the widespread malaise of good old financial ignorance. Most executives, like most people, but more oddly, do not truly understand money in a personal sense (they handle their own financial affairs unintelligently) or in their business capacity, certainly in Europe, very possibly in the U.S. It was in America that big business managers (even unto the sharp-eyed hawks employed by moneylender Walter E. Heller and the cautious corporate owls of American Express) tripped over in their eagerness to become the victims of Billie Sol Estes, filler of phantom harvest silos, and Tino de Angelis, filler of phantom salad oil tanks.

The problem is not even that managers lack the accountants' technical education in money—although that, too, can produce strange effects. One respected chairman of a family company complained bitterly when told that he couldn't finance a pet project. "What," he grumbled, stabbing at the left-hand side of the balance sheet, "about all those reserves?" Nobody had told him that reserves in accounting terms merely exist to make the left-hand side of the balance sheet equal the right-hand side. More often than not, however, guilty executives (assuming that they are also honest) are more innocent than unlettered.

A grim story about one crashed company reveals the distinction. One of its too-late rescuers put the corporate figures in a new presentation. The recast showed, sadly but convincingly, that the outfit could never make a profit, no matter what. He duly presented his findings to his fellow directors. "Your figures are wrong," answered one. "But they are *your* figures," said the outsider. "Well," remarked the inside man, "that's an interesting way of looking at it." Financial genius, fortunately, is not required of the business manager. But managers, the uncrashed as well as the crashed, often possess the reverse of genius—blind refusal to see inconvenient financial facts or, if confronted with the revolting truth, to admit its significance. The results of their innocence (which in the case of artists in the company promotion racket may not be so innocent) are written all over their overdrafts.

The essence of money in management is, first, that *cash in must exceed cash out.* This Fourth Truth of Management is the Law of the Barrow—known to every sweatshop on Seventh Avenue or barrow boy in Petticoat Lane. A cash deficiency is not solved by borrowing money from stockholders, from equally innocent financiers, or from far too friendly neighborhood bankers. Debt merely postpones the day of reckoning: sooner or later (and the sooner the better) there must be a cash surplus, and the more you borrow, the bigger that eventual surplus has to be. But like any small businessman sprinting for trouble, a great many top executives incur immense expense, and allow subordinates to pile up still more extravagance, without more than a misty idea of the monetary consequences.

One management consultant learned the law of the barrow by starting four businesses of his own. He saw two flourish, while two shriveled up. With a bookkeeper as chastity belt, he had watched over the cash of the two ripe successes like a jealous husband. In the two sour failures, the cash was left to look after itself. Yet in Britain a company director is under no legal necessity to know either the amount of his existing cash or its future availability (to make sure that he doesn't run out of the stuff). His accountants and auditors too are under no legal obligation to make sure that their client does discover these two indispensable facts. Accountants, since they are often called in as undertakers, know more than anybody about the life-or-death importance of cash. But as auditors they habitually certify accounts, referring to events long past, though they don't know (and are in no way expected to know) whether or not at the moment of approval cash is pouring out in great lukewarm gouts.

The bigger the company, the more academic an audit becomes. The auditors (all three of them) for Royal Dutch—Shell presumably earn every pound, guilder, and dollar of their magnificent fees. But they can't do much more, in a company that gets through £4 billion of business each year, than approve the performance of Shell's own internal accountants, advise the directors on knotty points of tax law, do the odd spot-check to see that nobody has run away with the company—and collect their fees.

The notion that auditors are at arm's length from directors is, in any case, a blatant fairy tale of accountancy and management. The stockholders in theory appoint the auditors—but in annual general meetings that are under the thumb of the directors and their captive proxies. Finance directors and auditors are in close and cosy contact. Even suppose an auditor does smell an accounting rat: he won't dream (except in nightmares) of making a public row. He will try to persuade the director to change his malodorous figures, or, more commonly, the director will persuade the auditor that the stocks in Nicaragua really have doubled in value overnight. In the end the auditor almost always has to accept the business judgment of the director.

Remember, accountants aren't businessmen. (As one accountancy firm proved by going into a wine company, noting correctly that it was wildly overstocked with 1953 Red Bordeaux, and instructing its customer to sell off those marvelous wines—now worth much fine gold—at cost price.) In the end, the accountant adjusts his fiction to the executive's version of the facts. Dishonesty need not enter his head. Accountants know perfectly well that firms that gain a reputation for being uncooperative don't get audit work—and

audit work is their main source of money, to which accountants are not wholly indifferent. The key is that they are free
within the rules of their game to choose whichever version of
the same truth they like.

This tale of two truths is an intrinsic part of "turnaround
jobs"—of the company revival game. New management moves
into a deadbeat, loss-laden company and turns it around—as
Lynn Townsend did with Chrysler or Don Burnham with
Westinghouse, and as a host of British turnaround men have
done with local industrial relics. But the key is more easily
turned than appearances suggest. If the past conduct of the
company has been paralytic, doing better is no terrifying test
of the new men. The accountant, moreover, can help to make
the turnaround man look more beautiful than he is.

The technique is to examine the corporate patient coldly
from top to bottom. Every loss that could or should be taken
is written back into the accounts, thus flatly contradicting the
previous accountants' version of events. If the sick business
has only rudimentary financial controls, every cupboard will
be full of old bones; simply installing a sensible system
ensures that no more skeletons will accumulate in the subsequent year. That year, the first of the new management,
inevitably shows an inspiring improvement because of the
absence of the previous year's bumper write-offs. This only
heightens the optical illusion effect that arises in all turnarounds, even if the accountants lean over backward not to
gild the new man's lily.

The British Printing Corporation, self-titled "the biggest
printer in Europe," was left in hazardous condition by one
Wilfred Harvey, a septuagenarian dictator who after his
departure was faced by charges to do with transactions between himself and the company. The new broom appeared
to sweep scrupulously clean—and after profits rose 150 percent in three years, the shares responded warmly, and the
new management won golden respect. Innocents (the turnaround executives, as well as investors) often look at the
before-and-after figures and beam broadly: but what about
the absolute figures? The best profits swept up by BPC's new

brooms were lower, before interest and tax, than the best
under Harvey's care. The most that the new brooms managed
by way of return on capital was a pathetic 6.2 percent; the
worst (later on) was a £4 million loss.

Turnarounds should always be compared, not with the bad
old days, but with present standards of good performance.
Even a phrase like "present standards of good performance,"
however, leaves an executive in the helping hands of accounting conventions. The profit that an executive shows is "after
depreciation." Many British executives believe that the wither-
ing away of depreciating assets is real. You can, of course, go
too far the other way. Back in 1926 (which shows that the

more things change the more they are the same), Armstrongs, the famous British defense contractor showed a profit "conjured out of optimistic depreciation figures" when on its way to the slaughterers.

The distinction is between profit and cash flow. If you buy a machine for £1 million and it has to be scrapped after ten years, it makes evident sense to knock off 10 percent each year; but in the process a fiction is created—that the company has made £100,000 less money in the first year, £90,000 less the next, and so on. In fact, the directors get their hands on the "depreciation" money, to do with what they will, and the company pays less tax. The real depreciation, and its real financial impact, only takes place when the thing is scrapped.

The reverse analogy is that of a man who buys a house, reckons it will be worth twice as much in ten years' time (7 percent per annum compounded) and credits his income with the 7 percent appreciation each year. Clearly ridiculous. But the stockholder has no way of knowing whether the directors have allowed too much for depreciation or too little. Some accountants argue that in the U.S. the amounts written off in depreciation over the years have been excessive. In other words, higher profits should have been reported to stockholders—and higher dividends could have been handed out.

But tax laws encourage the stockholder to shun dividends anyway. The net result, as Peter Drucker pointed out, is to put more and more easy money into the hands of fat, old, established corporations and their executives—who, by every test, are least adept at using the stuff. The inferior use of capital by big companies is self-evident even from the accountants' figures. Over the 1960s a before-tax return on capital employed of 15 percent or so was required to cover the replacement of assets at inflating costs and to reward the British stockholder at going rates of interest. Yet the median return averaged over the whole decade by 185 large U.K. companies was 14½ percent—half these companies had less than nothing left over to create new resources for expansion. In 1969, the median return on invested capital of the 500 largest U.S. companies was 11.3 percent (in horrible 1970 it fell to 9.5 percent) after tax, and that too can't have left much nourishment for the future.

The case of Imperial Chemical Industries is especially moving. This giant failed to earn enough in the 1960s to cover the 11 percent interest charges on its first big long-term borrowing of the 1970s. An ICI director explained that a business of its colossal size, doubling every seven years, can't hope to generate all its capital internally. But if the cost of capital exceeds the rate of return, a manager can't hope to generate any income at all from investing the new money.

Directors don't deal in concepts like the marginal cost of capital. So they gladly borrow long-term money at 11 percent when they have existing businesses earning below that mark —unless they have the fortune to find and listen to an accountant who spots their folly. Far better to close or sell the corporate drags to finance the new and hopefully more rewarding ideas. Yet most executives, because of their fond attachment to what they manage rather than to its results, insist on retaining interests or products that run the gamut from poor profitability to aching loss, without understanding that even a low-profit business is a tax on the company's good apples. (In cases of real misfortune, such as Dunlop's merger with Pirelli, which promptly ran into horrendous Italian losses, the accountants may kindly arrange to have the losses put outside the company's accounts altogether.)

Financial figures are not, however, the be-all and end-all of a business. Far from it—accurate money statistics are valuable only as a universal way of portraying physical reality. Profit is the *result*, not the objective of efficient management: it is the outcome of selling, pricing, producing, distributing, and organizing effectively. If the figures are terrible, it is always because the directors have failed in more tangible areas than the books. The latter, as an index of performance, serve as weapons to control, as guides to make physical efficiency less inefficient—provided you have the will. One tasty little financial graph produced inside a big company showed a line plunging down right off the graph paper: it was a chart of the downward *variance* from budgeted losses. In situations like this, accounting has ceased to have any relevance to management. Control means taking action when the instruments give their warning. It's no good sitting helplessly in mission control, like many accountants and their bosses, while the company spins off forever into financial outer space.

9 *Inflation Is A Board's Best Friend*

NOBODY TAKES A tougher line against inflation than the big business executive. Nobody deplores high wage claims with greater fervor—or greater self-interest—since nobody else faces those monstrous demands. Nobody applauds right-wing, anti-inflation politicians louder or backs their parties, Republican in the U.S., Conservative in Britain, more willingly or with more cash. And nobody is more baffled when, as the right tries to damp down inflation, sales fall, profits crumple, orders melt away, stock prices slide, and money gets hard to find and ruinous to borrow. Corporate man never pauses to note that, of all beneficiaries of inflation, nobody out-benefits the corporate boss.

Every executive knows that the ultimate proof of corporate success is growth (a few suspect that profitable growth, while tougher, is far more meaningful). The blue chip that doubles sales in seven years, assuming that some profit cream goes with the jelly, can reckon to earn the thanks of stockholders, the warmth of stockbrokers, and hot options for the brains in the boardroom. For the leviathans, more dazzling progress looks pure pie-in-the-sky: to double every five years, a $2 billion monster must find $300 million of extra sales in the first year alone.

Short of acquisition, there is little hope of reaching this nirvana, and acquisition is not true growth. Of itself, a $2,000 million company's ability to pay $300 million for somebody else's sales says nothing about the purchaser's managerial quality. Even a self-generated (or "organic") growth target of only 10 percent a year must be a definite stretch: at least, most corporations can't seem to reach that mark without the benefit of inorganic acquisitions.

Taking capital employed as the measure, 47 of the 200 biggest British commercial and industrial companies failed to double in size (a 7 percent growth rate) in the 1960s. Of the 10 largest by turnover, only four managed to grow by 10 percent annually, and giant mergers were partly responsible in three of the cases. In the U.S., in an era of rampant pursuit of growth, only 38 percent of the 500 largest companies doubled earnings per share, measured in inflated dollars. On the record, organic growth of 10 percent should dangle in front of stockholders' eyes like a vision of earthly paradise.

However, the 1960s saw intense and accelerating inflation. In the U.K. the average rise in prices (or average fall in the internal value of the pound) was 3½ percent a year. A company that merely moved its profits in step with general inflation, with no increase in physical sales at all, would have expanded by 36 percent in the decade, and one tenth of the 200 Britons grew only at this rate or more laboriously still. Despite avoidable and unavoidable accidents that forced down prices in some sectors, the overall level responded quite generously to treatment—in Britain the manufacturers' price index in 1970 stood 35.5 percent higher than in 1960; in America the figure was 16.3 percent.

In many companies, real growth—of the physical variety—

has been all but invisible. Physical output as an indicator means nothing in a large diversified company, and that definition fits almost every significant firm. But unit sales of vehicles in the big car companies have grown by significantly less than their cash results. GM sold 53 percent more vehicles in 1969 than in 1960, while cash turnover rose by a thumping 91 percent. Company directors only fail to see that general inflation makes their money growth much easier because they share a common delusion of people throughout the world.

Next to depression (which today nobody believes in, except John Kenneth Galbraith and Eliot Janeway) inflation is the dirtiest word in economic jargon—and that was true long before the price explosion of 1969/70. Enormous ingenuity went into discussions of cost push and wage pull, of spirals and equilibrium levels. However, economic expansion is a good thing for nations, companies, and individuals alike—right? Now, the faster a market or an economy expands, the more demand will press against supply and the more prices are likely to rise. The only big exception is when (as in the U.S. after Eisenhower) a yawning reservoir of spare capacity is waiting to be filled. Once that has been done (as under Johnson), prices gallop away; politicians reach itchily for the economic reins; and the complaining voice of the housewife is heard in the land.

Consumers, like executives, have been brainwashed. They think of money as a constant measure when (as they constantly complain) the measure constantly changes its length. If the value of money is falling, it means little to say that prices (or sales or profits) are rising by that same sinking criterion. The man whose $25,000 house sells for $50,000 seven years later claims that he has doubled his money— though he should know that, because of the inflation that pushed up the price of the house, his $50,000 is worth nothing like twice the $25,000 of seven years back. Managements know just as surely that a $50 million profit is not worth twice the $25 million of 1964; but that won't stop executives from boasting that profits have doubled, or from being applauded for their splendor.

87

The executive has also personally exploited the hidden truth about inflation. It isn't what you can buy with your pounds or dollars that counts, but what you can buy with your time. Expressed in these terms, most prices have fallen substantially —and more so for the executive than for lesser hired hands. A decade or so back it took an ordinary British worker a year's pay to buy the cheapest car on the market. It was less comfortable and less sporty than he drives today for six months' pay. Average British weekly earnings rose by 90.7 percent in that decade, and the American worker's pay by 49 percent. How much the average executive salary has risen is a matter for debate, but it has probably risen at least as rapidly; and that doesn't count increased fringe benefits, capital appreciation on his house, a share in inflationary stock markets, and all the other goodnesses of the good executive life.

That's not the end of the executive's blessings. If inflation reflects rising demand, sales must be rising, and rising sales (other things being equal) mean rising profits. New plant put in at today's lower capital costs, too, will earn profits at tomorrow's higher prices. Typically, however, executives do not rejoice over this fact: instead, they fret because the plant will have to be replaced at higher prices. But this may also work to the executive's joy. It implies that depreciation rates are too low, in which case current profits (on which the stock price and management bonuses depend) are being exaggerated to the benefit of the board. Even if depreciation rates are raised to the right level to compensate for inflation (and nobody knows what that is), the higher depreciation (if the Revenue Service can be conned into accepting it) will result in lower taxes.

Most corporations, and most executives in their private capacity, are heavy borrowers, often over long terms at fixed interest. This too has a lovely result—or would have, if executives could curb their weird insistence on investing borrowed money at rates of return below the interest cost. The real cost of the interest payments declines as inflation rolls onward; and the final repayment is worth much less in real terms than the original loan. So the opportunities for exploiting inflation are always there. If executives fail to cope with its problems, the reason may lie in their own weakness.

The executive is pulled in opposite directions by self-interest and by conditioning, which includes the belief that corporate actions should be in the public interest. Self-interest dictates that directors should charge the highest price that the traffic will bear. The public interest dictates (or is thought to) that prices should never rise at all; but since rise they must, should do so by the merest smidgen. So administered pricing creeps onward and upward like lichen.

Prices are not treated as they should be, as the most decisive element in the marketing and economic mix. They become a fixed base to which inflationary increments are added from time to time. The cost-plus mentality takes over: firms fix their prices by costs plus a percentage, and accept increases in costs as some God-given plague to be passed on to the consumer if at all possible; if not, the costs get handed over to the stockholder in massacred profits, slashed dividends, and tumbled stock prices.

In 1970 and 1971, company after company blamed miserable profits on unprecedented rises in wages and other costs. The rises really were unprecedented; but exceptional cost pressures were not so unreservedly to blame as companies liked to maintain. One poor performance was that of Cunard. Its £3.2 million profit, hard won by comeback from years of financial anemia, turned into a £1.9 million loss. The one-time queen of the North Atlantic, though it blamed its cost burdens, had another disappointing year purely as a trader: turnover fell by 3.3 percent against a 3.4 percent rise the year before. In ten years its turnover hadn't risen by as much as one pound; new ventures (such as the container consortia) took over the debilitating role of old, axed ships (the dead Queens Mary and Elizabeth).

Cunard's prices, of course, were under pressure at a time when costs (meaning other people's prices) were rising. One key to this conundrum was overcapacity on the container routes—itself a result of bad decisions by several shipping managements, including Cunard's. The worst embarrassment that a company can contrive is to get caught in its own private deflationary spiral in an inflationary era; and it happens, more often than not, because managers put expansion first and profits well behind. This folly severely stained the pure growth records of the chemical companies of West Germany in 1970. They too blamed wage pressures, though labor costs matter much less in chemical plants than in car factories. Price weakness was a far more serious cause; and much of it resulted from their own errors of capacity planning and pricing policy.

An American chemical executive, coming into Europe from the lush green home pastures where companies know a pretty price when they see it, complained, "There is awful and unjustified price weakness in Europe." The Europeans have cut prices to keep the Americans at bay; a self-defeating gesture, since the Americans, being richer, can better afford to give away their goods. Not that the Americans are blameless. Early in the 1960s, every executive in synthetic fibers knew that the amount of nylon-making plant being planned would eventually flood every nook and cranny of the market. But knowledge never stops a determined expansionist. American executives went on buying their way into Europe at prices that became still more ruinous, as the backwash of the world surplus hit their cosseted home market.

The airlines showed with equal thoroughness how to create your own private deflation by overordering Jumbo jets, just as they had overordered 707s a few years before. If capacity had only been balanced with demand, prices could have been slashed and yet profits would still have risen. A glut absolutely guarantees that prices will slump at the same time as operating costs soar, because of the heart-breakingly low use of capacity. At this point, executives customarily institute sweeping cost-reduction programs, laying off employees on all sides, without reflecting that the costs being cut must have been inexcusably fat before.

Inefficient use of labor is endemic in industry. Whether the men down tools for tea-breaks, as in Britain, or stand guard around the Coke machine, as in the U.S., or get sick with suspicious regularity, as in Germany, or are kept in full employment when they can't lift a finger, as in Japan, the results are the same. Their companies don't reap the full harvest of their new equipment; and they don't get maximum protection against the impact of inflation on their wage bill.

Companies waste more than men; they also throw away expensive material. On one estimate, only half of the materials bought in by the U.K. engineering companies is gainfully employed; the rest is scrap. But executives look through the wrong end of the telescope. Budgeting first in terms of sales, and setting targets in terms of profits, they pay too little attention to costs. Even when stringency and crisis force them to carve away at everything in sight, they choose the soft targets, such as advertising budgets, first, rather than the hard target, which is the corporate incompetence.

Excessive costs arise, not only from maladministration, but from bad equilibrium. The deliberate creation of excess capacity is only one example. Another is making too many products and offering the excessive lines at tempting prices that are bound to yield amazing losses. If their cost accounting is weak enough, the executives may not even know that the losses exist (in disaster after disaster, the mortician's diagnosis is the same: "inaccurate costing and lack of financial information"). But higher prices will weed out losing lines that can be dropped forever, preserving only those for which the customers are prepared to pay; and the results can be delectable. One new British management, anxious to escape from big unprofitable contracts in an underdeveloped country, but also anxious to keep face, elevated its tender (twice) to a level that looked certain to lose. It got the job (and might even make a profit).

In mythology, the executive is a rapacious creature who charges as much as he can as soon as he can. But the robber baron spirit of John D. Rockefeller seldom rides in the great corporation. Its executives charge prices that are too low (i.e., unprofitable, and less than the traffic will bear) for too long— and then make bad worse by offering discounts on the listed price. The sales side, in particular, has to be heaved away from a natural lust for low prices: no commission-crazy sales-man ever willingly accepts any change that might, by any stretch of his imagination, make his selling task harder.

But price increases and discounts often have only marginal effects on demand; and the price increases, or saved discounts, then flow through as pure, pretty, and undiluted profit. The former boss of Mars in Britain agonized for months over whether to raise the Mars bar price from a handy 6d to an awkward 7d—the hardest decision he ever faced. He never regretted the plunge for one sweet minute.

Those who argue that inflation is a destructive economic force are bound to oppose maximizing returns by maximizing prices; and many managers likewise miss the management logic. "You can't charge that much," was one sales manager's anguished cry. "It cost so little to produce." Anti-inflationists ignore the economic damage of underpricing. For years Jaguar managers labored under the delusion that their spiffy cars had to be cheap, starting at under £2,000 in the U.K. home market. This outlandish value for money produced a vociferous pileup of unsatisfied, waiting customers—many of them Americans, who wait for nothing. The lost income robbed the company of the resources needed to raise its production capacity to something near the level of demand. As a result of Jaguar's self-denial, BMW, whose prices have never been restrained by scruples, stole the market. It was making more cars in a day than Jaguar did in a week.

Executives find it just as hard as governments to leave the correction of prices to the forces of the market. The pressure of governments anxious about inflation has greatly reinforced the businessman's own fear of public reaction, his own instinctive sympathy with the irrational feeling that there is a "fair" price that results in a "reasonable" return on capital. Words like "fair" and "reasonable" are purely emotive. For instance, General Motors in a nonstrike year earns twice as much on its assets as Ford. Does this mean that Ford's prices are fairer? Or that its products are better value than GM's? Or does it mean that GM is managed more effectively?

In British mass retailing, the great Marks & Spencer chain earns profit margins of over 12 percent: its pretax return on stockholders' capital is nearly twice that of the Woolworth outfit, which (though American controlled) has long shown legendary clumsiness. Yet Marks, which has offered progressively higher quality at relatively low prices, is considered a leading fire-fighter against inflation. In point of fact, its price levels have risen steeply over the years: the moral is that, even at higher price tags, M&S goods are well within the customer's vital willingness to pay.

The company that gets inflation on its side will rush past those who are content to be its victims. After all, when all prices are rising, it's easier to put up your own without anybody noticing. So long as inflation is publicly execrated more than deflation (a process that is much nastier), wise directors may have to hide the fact that they charge the maximum price —not simply the price that covers the movements of costs and the competition. But even if a management manages badly in pricing and everything else, inflation, with luck, will partially conceal its failure, upgrading executives who would otherwise be done down professionally—and (far more painful) in their own pockets.

10 Mergers Make Strange Bedfellows

BUSINESS HISTORY IS festooned with amalgamations. The mightiest manufacturers in the U.S. and Britain, General Motors and Imperial Chemical Industries, were created by merger artists. The colossus of Europe, Royal Dutch-Shell, arose from another bout of corporate love fever. But in the 1960s merger as a fine art got elevated to the upper reaches of the management stratosphere, stamped with the seductive, scientific-sounding word "synergy." Ostensibly, this meant a magic process in which two and two made more than four. More properly translated, synergy means that the deal makes no financial sense, but (please, God) something will come out of it in the end.

Most mergers are created in pious hope; their guiding drive is not financial or industrial logic, but, in various forms, the urge to aggrandize. Yet a merger is nothing but a straight financial investment. One company pays cash, or stocks (i.e., the right to participate in future cash earnings), or some hybrid security for another company's cash potential. The maneuver is no more sophisticated fundamentally than an investor's phone call to his broker—except that only a consummate sucker would pay a broker twenty times earnings for stocks selling in the market at a multiple of ten.

Industrial companies, however, play the sucker all the time (in 1971, Britain's ICI did precisely this in buying Atlas Powder of Wilmington, Delaware, to draw up to the local champion, du Pont, in the global chemical stakes). The more cunning conglomerates, in their happy heyday, at least avoided this trap. Their key deals were schemed to elevate earnings per share, never mind whether the morsel was worth eating for any other reason. (As time wore on, the conglomerate executives grew careless; contrary to their own myths, they picked up the bad habit of buying companies for ransoms that diluted their earnings.)

Conglomerators, in their prime, pursued only the financial goals of mergers, because money was their obsession, lifeblood, and governing lust. Others merge regardless of cost because, for all their pretensions, financial maximization—or getting truly richer—is not their object. Maximization is the name of their corporate game, true; but maximizing the corporation, not its effectiveness or its share price, is the mainspring.

In Europe, especially in Britain, this urge for bigness has been reinforced by politicians who believe that economies of scale (i.e., the unreliable idea that bigger equals cheaper) are required weapons for fighting the good fight against U.S. economic imperialists. Many ill-starred British mergers were put together under this strange banner—including Rolls-Royce (which married Bristol Siddeley in the years leading to its demise). The conventional wisdom has consequently reversed. Europeans have begun to learn, as did the conglomerates, that the opposite of synergy is dissipation: that two and two can make less than four, and that sometimes they don't add up at all.

These awakenings have still left most boardrooms dreaming of glory. Bids and deals preempt more top management time than any other pastime—and to minimal effect. Every study has shown that polygamous companies grow no faster, in terms of earnings per share, than firms that stay resolutely single. In the 1960s, the average earnings growth rate of thirty intensively merged British companies was under 5 percent per share per annum. Marvelous benefits are desperately hard to buy, and grotesque losses too easy to pick up; and common sense tells why.

Managers can only buy three kinds of company—good, middling, or bad—and in only one of two circumstances—contested or uncontested (i.e., rape or seduction). The perfect combination seems to be the seduction of a truly beautiful company; but the seducer must usually overpay, since beauties are seldom bargains. He overpays still more in cases of opposed rape, which commonly results in an auction. Maybe, the companies to buy are the raped, bad ones—the only ones likely to be cheap in relation to their assets (if any are left), the only ones whose potential (if any) is sure to be underexploited. Even here lies no certainty: bad eggs make poor omelets. Inescapable logic stacks the odds against the purchaser—good companies come dear, bad companies are bad.

The Fifth Truth of Management also applies: *however high its level, management capability is always less than the organization needs.* The junior partner (or mergee) seldom brings in supercompetence. After all, the hotter its management, the less its reason for merging. So the mergee marvel has a broader management span, but even less management capacity in relation to need. Worse still, the overstretched management has the new, self-inflicted, and often chronic anxieties that come only with managing mergers. And human beings, when faced with more problems than they can handle (like rats in a psychologist's maze) do nothing.

Hence the familiar unconsummated merger—two companies that sleep together in name only. In Britain's Unigate, milk executives from two allegedly merged companies (United Dairies and Cow and Gate), glared at each other from opposite sides of the boardroom table for many years. At the food and drugs combine, Reckitt & Colman, a 1953 merger was still being consummated in 1970—partly because, as one wag said, "The Reckitts spoke only to Colmans, and the Colmans spoke only to God." And none of them ever spoke to R. T. French, the successful subsidiary in the U.S.

These virgin marriages are usually friendly mergers; and maybe they are doomed to relative failure. The senior partner, being amicable, can't pick up the mergee for anything less than a pretty price, which rules out any remote hope of financial bonanza. The pervading friendliness too means that nobody gets sacked, and no activity beloved of the mergee's managers gets dropped. So much for synergy. After a hostile take-over, unhealthy inhibitions are fewer. The opposing board of directors may even be forced to walk the plank without ceremony—and that, while crude, is not the worst way of making merger sense.

The general assumption (very British but also known in America) is that management upheavals are bad things. The trust-busting British Monopolies Commission was deeply impressed by the De La Rue executives' threat, or promise, to quit if a Rank Organisation bid succeeded, so it barred the deal. De La Rue profits subsequently plunged, the bid-time forecasts were missed prodigiously, the share price collapsed, and De La Rue looked much less of a management bargain.

But note the underlying assumption: the trustbusters worried little about the illogic of mixing Rank's Xerox, TV, instruments, cinemas (and that's not all) with De La Rue's Formica, playing cards, bank notes, and central heating boilers (and that's not all, either). The commission was far more concerned with having the status quo undisturbed by the merger. British bidders even give undertakings to this inexplicable effect. But you can't make an omelet, or sense of a merger, without breaking eggs, and the longer the egg breaking is delayed, the fewer the benefits will be.

Since mergers do bring problems that can't be solved without time, trouble, and sorrow, buyers should be doubly careful about price. But most bidders are doubly cavalier. They follow the advice of art dealer Lord Duveen to earlier American millionaires: "if you're buying the priceless, you're getting it cheap." For priceless, read desirable, and you have the formula for merger after merger. One avid finance director admitted that his latest buy had cost several millions too much. He explained that the overcharge had kept his dearest corporate enemy from picking the plum.

"We are paying far too much [it was nearly £16 million] for Cementation," said a Trafalgar House property man on another occasion, "but it fits into the pattern of our future development." If the second half of that statement was true, then the first half was false—and vice versa. In effect, the stockholders bet their money (or have it bet for them, willy-nilly) on the chief executive's judgment. He may be warped by vanity, or if a battle is on, by simple hatred of being beaten. "It became a personal matter" for one company chairman, "and he had to raise the bid twice before he finally won, the last time even against the advice of our financial advisers."

An expensive merger always exacts a heavy toll on the bidder's management, and mergers may expose the ghastly secret that the bidder has no management at all. The mighty Pennsylvania Railroad was popularly considered to be a whiz at running railroads, and at piling up money in side ventures. When it wed the New York Central, the Pennsy's Stuart T. Saunders said that the railroad was getting "a new type of manager." (He added, a little more realistically, "Our programs have pulled us back from the brink of disaster . . . but they have not rescued us from the financial danger zone.") Industrial logic was rapidly overtaken by the reality of two struggling managements that had to divert their inadequate energies to new struggles—many with each other, some with diversified nonsenses, most with the terrible illogic of trying to fit two distinct rail networks into one. By themselves, possibly, neither line would have gone bankrupt; together, they were doomed.

The Leyland Motor Company was famed for lean, keen efficient management when it united with the British Motor

Corporation. Since BMC had mislaid one fifth of its market share since formation (by another merger), its capacities for mismanagement were regarded with some awe. Leyland's high repute outlasted the merger by only a few months. The senior partner revealed many of the mergee's faults—in marketing, in middle management, underinvestment, one-man decision-making, aging product lines, and a vacuum instead of labor relations.

It takes a very bright executive to make a merger into a success; and a very bright executive often is too bright to try. The duller executive cannot see the problem (or solve it). When one large family-dominated, unprofitable beer company starts buying smaller breweries or wineshops, the rest plunge in pell-mell, paying higher and higher prices as the competition gets hotter: the same thing happened in British textiles and American computery, with the same indigestible results.

The tiny size of overpriced acquisitions against the bidder's own elephantine proportions is no excuse. A series of bad small buys rapidly reduces the chances of improving the return on a mass of capital—which is the prime object of acquisitions, or would be in an ideal world. In real life, power is a more compulsive force, conscious or unconscious. Just as few executives will genuinely delegate authority (for that robs them of their power and manhood), so few throw away chances to add new realms. And history and their contemporaries will applaud them for their power drives. The titan J. P. Morgan, a wheeler-dealer manipulator of James P. Ling proportions in his time, won eternal fame for his bloated, stock-watered creations, never mind that lesser figures had to make the monstrosities pay.

Of two British paper empires, Bowater and Reed, the first used to have the hero-figure: Sir Eric Bowater is remembered less for the management disorders he bequeathed than for the dynamism that built his empire, not by acquisitions, but by daring investments in North America. In the 1960s, the boot was on Reed's foot: its chairman, Don Ryder, won his management fame mainly by mergers that at last took Reed

100

above Bowater's weight. But on every measure save agglomeration, the performance of the two is very similar (and very moderate): Reed's net capital employed doubled after 1965, while its earnings per share actually fell. The only case for agglomerating is perverse: that the bigger a company gets, the more overburden, deadwood, or rubbish it accumulates for some future hero to cut away, elevating the profits and price/earnings ratio simultaneously, to the joy of all mankind.

The despised conglomerators once provided textbook theory in how to merge, if merge you must. Their only merger object was to enhance the capital value of their company; and they thought and bought big. A £200 million company rarely has any good excuse for a £2 million buy. The deal can't have any noticeable impact on earnings; and small companies fit uncomfortably into big pockets. Unilever paid several millions (less than 1 percent of its own capital) for a plastics growth company. The new business was unrelated to the rest of its oversized group; and the latter's weight soon crushed the golden goose's entrepreneurial character—and its eggs.

Before conglomerates were dreamed of, the British (always pioneers of technologies that others exploit) invented the very similar industrial holding company. The biggest, Thomas Tilling, took ten years and innumerable purchases to add £56 million to capital employed. Slater Walker, first of British conglomerates (and first to claim that it wasn't a conglomerate at all), added that much capital in the one year of 1968. Big guns shouldn't be deployed on too narrow a front. The conglomerates, of course, overplayed the logic of buying big: thus Jimmy Ling, eager to bust the billion dollar sales barrier by buying Jones and Laughlin's steel, virtually busted Ling-Temco-Vought.

It is easy but wrong to conclude that electronics companies have no business in steel, an industry that steel men themselves mostly mismanage. Ling's mistake wasn't made in the management, but in the original decision to buy. The weakness of most mergers is not that ignorant managers enter unfamiliar businesses; it is that the price was wrong, regardless. If the price is right, the synergy and the management can look after themselves. If not, it will take years to close the gap by the workings of "industrial logic."

This overworked phrase is usually no more than a post-humous justification. Cadbury and Schweppes, two generally healthy companies, one in chocolate, one in soft drinks, had very little in common; only the industrially logical lust to create a food combine capable of spitting in the eyes of General Foods, General Mills, and Nestlé. Neither company competed seriously with any of the three (except for Nestlé and Cadbury in chocolate). Their deal mixed up the high-premium, high-cachet business of Schweppes with a low-margin, low-growth bulk operation in confectionery. Either Schweppes paid dear to get into chocolate, or Cadbury paid expensively to move into soft drinks. Neither of the two American five-star food Generals, Food or Mills, lost a wink of sleep as a result. The corporate slumber lost through mergers is mostly within the merged company as managers try to put together what could logically have been left asunder.

It's industrially logical to buy a business that takes you into an entirely new market. Aha! But it's also "logical" to buy one in exactly the same market—hopefully killing two birds for the price of one. This is the only form of synergy actually proved to work, in the negative sense of closing down one of two factories or two distribution forces (not in the expansion of the mergee's business by the buyer's magic touch).

The conglomerates at their peak were much better at this negative synergy. In the game only for the money, they sold off everything surplus or movable on sight. One conglomerate executive even had a man standing by in Germany waiting to chop off a loss-making limb the instant the take-over was complete. This demonstrated absolutely sound tactics. Since deeper human motives than financial sense are always involved in mergers, you must start fast to make the best of what (more often than not) will be a bad deal.

The first step is to find out exactly what you have bought. When Saul Steinberg of Leasco uncovered the true contents of Pergamon Press, that discovery ended all further interest. Assuming that you do still want any part of the company, then decide what you want and don't want in assets and in managers. Mergees always have some seniors who shiver the spine, and some juniors worth their weight in silver dollars. Casting the former out (as generously as possible) and promoting the latter (at high speed) is the proper routine. As for unprofitable operations, close them, all of them, especially those where, according to the anguished cries of the incumbents, prosperity is just around the corner. These pets mostly go on eating profits forever.

Where the mergee's operations, brand names, distribution, and so on can be swallowed into the bigger company without any loss of business, do it, right now. When skeletons rattle out of cupboards, take the losses and write-offs at once. When executions have to be carried out, sooner is always better than later. Don't leave sentenced operations waiting interminably in death row. Of course, a merged company is no different in these respects than an unmerged one—executives are always putting off the evil day, especially an evil day that they themselves have created.

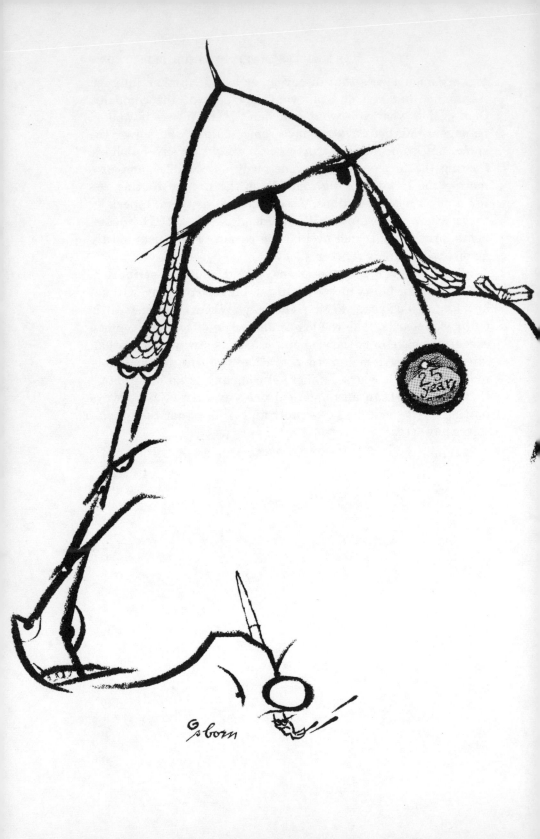

11 *The Badly Paid Executive*

MOST EXECUTIVES are badly paid, not in the sense that they get too little (many get far too much), but because they are paid in the wrong ways. Their take seldom has any true relation to their personal success or to the company's. Come rain or shine, their dinner pail stays full. This is less true in the U.S. than in Britain. But even in America linking an executive's efforts to his immediate rewards is more pretense than effectiveness.

The soul may be rejoiced by seeing that Lynn A. Townsend of Chrysler (and quite right too) suffered a pay cut from $630,000 to $200,000 in 1969 when the firm had one of its periodic relapses. (Some companies wax and wane like the moon, usually for some sound astronomical reason—such as that Chrysler's share of the U.S. car market is too small and always will be). But Townsend's case needs examining more critically. As a result of former lavish feeding, he should be full of wealth, so having to struggle along on $200,000 (which is something more than small potatoes) for a year or so would hardly have stimulated his executive glands.

What really determines any top executive's pay is the size of the organization in which he works. A law invented or discovered by the nineteenth-century Italian economist Pareto explains practically everything about business. (Roughly speaking, it says that 20 percent of customers account for 80 percent of turnover, 20 percent of components account for 80 percent of cost, and so forth.) His law shows that all organizations build a pay pyramid. The broader the base, the higher the summit of the pyramid. I learned about Pareto's law on pay from research inside the personnel department of Rolls-Royce. Maybe this work had some connection with the pay raise, of £9,000, which the chairman got in 1969, shortly before his company completed its crash: one of the weirdest illustrations in history of the poor correlation between pay and performance.

Another oddity is the way multimillionaires tie their rewards to profits. Sir Allen Clarke of Plessey gave himself a contract, before the war, for a slice of the profits. By the time he died, when his electronics business and own fortune were huge, he was entitled to around a quarter of a million pounds in pay—all promptly taxed away. Henry Ford II (whose salary slumped all the way from $600,000 to $515,000 in 1969, poor fellow) and Thomas Watson, Jr., of IBM are others who, though their fortunes Yo-Yo around in the stock market in one day by greater amounts, go through a solemn charade of pretending that their annual salaries in some way affect their performance as profit earners.

Are lesser (or less flush) executives made more efficient by dangling financial carrots in front of their twitching noses? The mythology in Britain is that superior U.S. corporate performance is greatly stimulated by stock options, cash incentive awards, and the like. But in the 1960s, among the top one hundred companies in the U.K., there was no distinction in results between managements that granted themselves every financial stimulus under the sun and those tiny few that bumbled along on straight salary—except that, by performing no better than the straight salary managers, the carrot danglers got much richer. Surprise, surprise: the stock option and its associated goodies are now all but universal in the U.K.—because what executive in his right mind will work for a company where the loot is less?

The American situation is even more bizarre than that. By 1968, fully seventy-three of the one hundred had both stock options and incentive awards; another seven had incentive awards only; seventeen had stock options only; and three languished in the outer darkness of straight old-fashioned pay. Fewer than two fifths of the goodie-stuffed seventy-three bettered either the median performance of *Fortune*'s five hundred largest companies for ten-years' growth in earnings per share, or the median for profitability in that particular year. The seven companies with incentives, but without stock options, did barely better. The less directly a management's pay was tied to the company's profit performance, surprisingly, the worthier the performance became. Stock option companies with no incentive awards did very well on growth —88 percent were above the median, and 59 percent beat the median for profitability. All three of the benighted straight pay companies, however, outdid the ten-year median growth rate; and two of these three were abnormally profitable.

Some of the possible conclusions are too obvious to be true. For instance, growth-hungry investors would be rash to charge into straight stock option companies before discovering which came first—the option or the performance. Often the executives, finding themselves on a good thing, smartly arrange to share the bonanza. But incentive awards, unanswerably, seem to have no discernible incentive effect. The reason lies in the logic (or illogic) of incentive schemes. Honeywell, which employs greedy, hot computer salesmen as well as the average executive, has found that 30 percent of pay has to come from incentives before "other guys get the driving go of the fellows in the Brooks Brothers' suits"—but what would the other 70 percent be paid for? Occupying the office space?

Management by objectives looks like a solution: work out an executive's objectives with him, then relate his pay to his success in hitting the target. But here, too, there is logical trouble: the man gets much of his pay for *not* meeting his objectives. You pay him for failing, and reward him with more for doing what he was hired to do in the first place. A manager is hired, and should be paid, to do a job that *includes* meeting a set of objectives and producing profits that can be reported to stockholders without sackcloth and ashes. If he excels himself, he is enriched, anyway, in a sensible company. If he fails, through a fault of his own, you may not want him at any price.

Incentive schemes have other snags, notably making sure that profit-linked bonuses really do reflect managerial merit. Head office can contain a bundle of superannuated dodos whose main contribution is, by all means in their power, to prevent the divisional directors from earning large profits. If the latter triumph against the odds, guess who collects the largest bonuses. And how do you distinguish between an executive who shuts off a £1 million loss and his luckier colleague, who, given the company's plum division, raises its profits by £500,000?

Until you near the Lynn Townsend level, what's more, you can rarely cut an executive's salary. A British managing director earning £10,000 a year can't take much of a slash— not so long as he has a wife, three children, and a mortgage to support. The incentive system tends to be all rewards and no penalties; that being so, it doesn't work. Systems of genuine incentives do exist; however, few boards of directors would dream of imposing this kind of straitjacket on themselves.

Pay in a deadly serious scheme starts from a base enough to cover ordinary living expenses and no more. Part of pay above that level is linked to profit performance; part is tied to stock performance (which executives can fiddle less easily than the profit figures). The stock-linked element, moreover, carries a downside risk. The money is either in deferred earnings, or in stocks held in trust. If the stocks fall, so does the money in the executive's hope chest. Contrast this with the typical salary position in a large company. Pay is determined by rank and rises gratifyingly year by year with time and seniority. With it, up and up goes the pension entitlement. The executive knows at the beginning of the year what he will earn over the next twelve months, which will be more than his juniors get and as much as his peers. Given a choice between this security and the razzle-dazzle uncertainty of true incentives, ninety-nine executives out of one hundred will plump for security.

As for the one hundredth, he won't stay long in a big company, anyway. For all their talk about the entrepreneur, about risk taking, and about the golden lure of profits, the majority of executives are staid by talent and temperament. Their instinctive, silent reasoning must be, Why expose myself and my family to financial risk, when I can always find secure employment of much the same kind in a noncommercial bureaucracy? Because of this, pay systems in all companies—including stock option schemes and incentive plans—gravitate, or degenerate, toward bureaucratic stability.

Executives have great difficulty in recognizing this desire for financial peace and quiet in themselves. When the Conservatives cut taxes on top British incomes in the 1960s, and again in 1971, a clinching argument was that reducing the tax bite would give executives greater incentive to take risks, win export orders, and generally sweat harder. The unexciting record of most big British companies after the first surtax cut dismayed the incentive advocates not at all. Obviously, the cuts were too small. Reduce top taxes to the American level, and British management would *really* show what it was made of.

In reality, tax rates seem to have little effect on effort. The Dutch economy, just as highly taxed as the British, has grown faster. And the tax argument cannot explain away the yawning gulfs between the performances of different managements whose members all pay much the same tax rates. You can't of course blame executives for arguing that they would work harder or better if taxed less, even though they lie. What they really want (and who doesn't?) is to pay less tax. High taxes, again, are blamed for the lush fringe benefits with which many British executives are cosseted—the chauffeured cars; the personal Rolls or Jaguar; the house and gardeners; the expensive public schools for the children; the executive dining room, butler, and wine cellar; the trips to South Africa in the winter; the flats in Mayfair or Belgravia; and so on.

We don't actually like having all these presents, runs the argument—the tax system forces them on us. Before the war, however, and before taxes became so penal, British companies had their grouse moors and their private trains, as well as today's popular treats. A survey by Shell once established that most of its executives pined for the life of a country gentleman—and among British chief executives today country sports are far and away the most popular pastime. The British company traditionally provides its leaders with life as their more leisured grandfathers might have known it; and if American executives live lower off the hog, at company expense, that too is more a matter of social tradition than of the tax system.

Not that the American hates using company money for his own creature comforts. That soaring skyscraper in Wall Street, Park Avenue, or Westchester County, that chairman's office festooned with rare art and furniture, may be good for the corporate prestige. But they also do no harm to the executive's own ego. The Germans are more frank: they admit that the depth of floor carpet matters almost as much as the size of a German director's salary. Stock options have become roughly the same thing in the U.S.—part of the furniture, which the executive expects to find there, but which doesn't motivate him recognizably. If fortune shines on the company, he pockets the profits. If the stock slumps to the floor, that's the way the cookie crumbles—believe it or not, there are even stock options in United States Steel, that deadest of corporate giants.

Over a certain level, pay always loses its importance. This

is the weakness of commission systems. Once a salesman has earned what he reckons to be adequate, he is much less interested in earning more for the company. That level of adequacy varies between individuals and between cultures; in the United States the cutoff point is very high. But even one of the world's all-time selling champions, Roy Perot, after shattering all IBM's records, stopped selling computers. (With his own software company, he made more money in less time—on paper—than any man in history, and then lost more in less time—on paper—than anybody, when his stock market bubble deflated).

The general theory of remuneration is to pay people their market value, pay them still more as their responsibility and contribution rises, and not to keep expensive deadwood around the premises. Only executives who are themselves incompetent keep on at $30,000 a year men whose services are worth half; only a misguided management congratulates itself on getting senior executives for $8,000 a year when the going rate is $16,000. For some reason, the proprietorial company finds this lesson hard to master. One British multimillionaire took enormous exception to paying his new managing director, in a billion-dollar company, more than a marketing whiz-kid would get elsewhere.

The fact that a laborer may not know his hire is no excuse for paying him less. In Britain, where people are traditionally more secretive about money than sex, executive reticence has helped to keep executives' pay before tax far below European levels. Over the 1960s Europeans worked up to between 20 percent and 60 percent more, depending on country, than their British executive counterparts; and both groups looked sick beside American standards; it is a sickness that European and British companies can afford to cure.

Giving some pay, somehow, in the form of stocks is one right antidote; but not because it will produce superior corporate performance (it probably won't), and certainly not because a capital stake will make the manager more forcefully independent. A craven who won't argue with his superior because he's afraid of losing his job won't argue any more

111

readily because he has a stock option. Executives should be deeply invested in their company's stocks for two different reasons: first, a man who devotes much of his life to a capitalist concern deserves capital himself; second, he also deserves to share the sorrows as well as the joys of the stockholders— when the stocks go down, it should hurt him, and preferably more than it hurts them.

But the corporate bureaucracy is most unlikely to reward its executives unfairly; and the unfairness is certain to get less and less the nearer the executive gets to the top. For top executives are in the happy position of fixing their own pay. Their bliss was perfectly summed up by a great *New Yorker* boardroom cartoon, in which the table is surrounded by smiling faces and the chairman is saying, "Gentlemen, I think we can congratulate ourselves on voting these large increases in salary, thus ensuring to the corporation our continuing loyal services."

III Menaces

12 *Who's in Charge Here?*

THE MODERN principle of decentralization makes enchanting sense. Simply split the corporate leviathan into big lumps of homogenous activities, then break down the homogenous lumps into individual morsels. Each lump and morsel has its responsible boss, and each boss has another boss upon his back to bite him. Gone, or kicked upstairs, are the functional directors of production, marketing, engineering, or what have you—jobs so loosely defined that nobody could tell when they were mangled. In their place stand the divisional executive and his subsidiary executives and their subsidiary executives, each in charge of a distinct business. If the arrayed subordinates all perform according to plan, the chief executive and his summit sidekicks have little to do, except pat backs, collect pay, plan the future and wait for a rich retirement.

With all this going for it, the decentralized company should have soared into new orbits. It hasn't: decentralization has often meant deterioration. Du Pont is the daddy of all decentralized and financially motivated managements. In the 1960s, its sales growth lagged behind that of other chemical giants. Its earnings per share growth was negative—a decline of 1.79 percent a year. Its net profitability fell to 9.1 percent. Yet du Pont had decentralized down to the last digit long ago: British rivals even used to gibe that du Pont's board members were just a bunch of chemical bankers. Difficulty in recovering adequate loot from decentralized divisions is not confined to the bankers of du Pont.

Some companies are starting to wonder whether they should reverse engines. "Recentralization is the word now," said one American executive gloomily. "But I haven't met anybody who's actually done it." The decentralization theory has no fatal flaws in itself. It just doesn't fit the real-life way in which companies work. The conglomerates fell foul of the reality. Some of them (some by accident) collected quite good companies in their stamp albums. But decentralization was their essence. The conglomerator sat at the center of the spider's web, while, all around, the new acquisitions, separated by distance, organization, and the different natures of their trades, spun away. Very few big black spiders, however, could leave well enough alone for long—and the lust to interfere became still more irresistible when "well enough" turned to terrible.

The ur-conglomerate, Litton Industries, seemed to discover perfect decentralization. It kept the head office small; broke big units down to minimum, more manageable size; exerted strict financial control by fast, frequent, and elaborate reports, including weekly cash statements; placed able sharpies in charge of operations; and promoted them swiftly when they succeeded. And the top duo, Tex Thornton and Roy Ash, held strategy sessions at which, with the unit managers and the latters' group bosses, they belabored the questions at the core of any business—where it was going and how it was going to get there.

But even at Litton the system failed, not because of an

act of God or a national economic crisis, but because of mis-calculations and plain mismanagement in two of the new decentralized joys, shipbuilding and office machinery, which it had added to all. No structural device (and "strategy sessions" are only gadgets) exists by which the head office can both manage and not manage. A clear choice has to be made, one way or the other—and you don't have to guess which way the head office manager will jump: into interference, with both feet.

Managing directors or presidents are possessed by ambition, power drive, and vanity; they have climbed many miles, over long years, to reach the top. Once arrived, they won't breathe in, dock their highly polished brogues on the desk, and drop any desire to manage actively. The motivations that propelled their rise are just as powerful once they have risen. The decentralized corporation, with its profit centers, its corporate plans, and its group executives, becomes a labyrinthine mechanism to let the head office heads play at being executives—for in the end they cannot manage. Decentralization, even in quite small companies, is not a theory, but an inevitability.

Some executive, somewhere down the line, is in personal contact with reality—the customer who won't buy, the product that won't work, the machines that won't produce. The longer the rope between that man and the summit, and the more the men on Everest seek to know and influence what is happening in the far foothills, let alone in the valleys, the more the company becomes an expensive device for generating unused information. But modish decentralization rides over this truth, in the opposite direction. Turn everybody, it says, even the salesman, into an executive. Push responsibility further and further down the corporation ladder. Substitute individual initiative for central initiative. Achieve coordination through a common corporate philosophy plus common controls and common corporate systems.

Inhabitants of this wonderland should consider a letter written in blood by one employee of an American group which is alleged to be a rare example of successful big-time management of diversity. Like most corporate fames, this one crumbles slightly if growth is assessed after deducting inflationary increments, or profitability by knocking off near-monopoly markets in the U.S. But still, it is, relatively speaking, a good company and a lesson to Europeans—or is it?

The letter from its humble son, well down the scale, out on one of the European limbs, reads:

> *We have a very able sales manager who in turn reports to New York, but he is not able to see us very often. I have been told that I must be responsible for everything to sell my product—marketing, sales forecast, advertising, mailing campaigns, etc.—everything to enable me to sell my product better. I am completely inexperienced in how to do this.*

Every day some decentralized employee, like this victim, is told, in effect and sometimes in so many words, "This is your business and your responsibility. It's all yours—off you go and run it." But the man may not have the resources to run the department or the true independence that alone makes sense of the policy. The more important his operation, the more hotly his superiors breathe down his neck. The less important, the more likely he is to be strung up in that salesman's position—left alone, to hang himself, or to be hung by some offended superior.

The organization chart won't reveal that somewhere in darkest Germany, Stygian England, or murky France is a sales manager whose boss is three thousand miles away in Manhattan, and whose own subordinates have all but forgotten what he looks like. That boss on Park Avenue is too remote and too busy with his own bureaucratic spawning of words and figures to understand the local business. Even if there is enough time to explain the business to him, is there really any point? The Sixth Truth of Management lays down that there are only two possibilities: *either an executive is competent to run the business or he is not.* In the first instance, leave him

118

alone. In the second, move him. In neither case should another executive try to run the business through the subordinate by remote control.

Often the besetting preoccupation and sin of the distant

superior is to demonstrate that he really is superior. The inferiors in turn become too preoccupied with the pressures from on high to avoid stupidities themselves—such as giving impossible responsibilities to unprepared salesmen. When the victims fail, the calamity is demonstrably not their fault; it's that of decentralization carried to its usual centralized excess. The whole idea stemmed from the exact observation that businesses had grown beyond the scale and scope of the center's ability to command. But responsibility can be pushed too far down. The Peter Principle seeks to prove that eventually all executives are promoted beyond their abilities. But incompetents are manufactured more often from above, by demoting responsibility below the critical point—the level at which it can reasonably be carried.

Many large groups commit the sins of centralization and decentralization at once: they condemn their lesser executives to failure by this sure-fire method, while the abler executives waste oceans of time, initiative, and energy in preparing and discussing plans and reports and budgets with the allegedly detached center. Every westbound transatlantic flight transports the boss or subboss of a European subsidiary of an American multi-national to Des Moines, or New York, or Pittsburgh. Briefcase bulging, he is on his way for the monthly or quarterly confrontation with his superiors. A common supplement is for the parent's senior management to go on a grand procession, like the doges of mediaeval Venice, around their satrapies; and nobody stops to query all this travel (which is easier and more enjoyable than work).

Yet the multi-nationals have the perfect setup to decentralize truly—if they want to. The local business is geographically remote and clearly marked out by national frontiers, often by national market characteristics. Its management too is largely separated by nationality and language. And the overseas businesses, mostly starved neither for capital nor marketable products, are substantial economic powers in their own rights and own lands.

The parent's only vital functions are to watch and count

its money, to coordinate (i.e., stop any one subsidiary from slaughtering the others), to soup up its baby's growth by providing any riches that the locals request from the American cornucopia, and to change the management if it fails. But the overwhelming tendency is to absorb the national company into the parent, until decisions in Scotland, France, and the Midwest are homogenized into one bland whole.

Once, Henry Ford II's British *pied-à-terre* was brashly independent, with a large minority of British stockholders, a self-consciously tough Irish boss, and a creaking but tolerably successful product line. Then the Americans from Dearborn descended on Dagenham. The minority stockholders were bought out, hundreds of millions were poured in to reequip the plants and revitalize the products, and American executives arrived in droves. At first their control lodged in a popular watering place for American executives, Brussels. Then the outfit, Ford of Europe, was removed to the same lush Americanized executive block as Ford of Britain, which came under the direct managerial control of the Americans, for ill as well as good.

The first, but not the last, ill was the choice of an American-style replacement for its largest Zephyr-Zodiac range—long bonneted, wide wheelbased, gas guzzling. It flopped, and one British director of the time believes, rightly or wrongly, that its mismarketing was compounded by production faults, in part because the local executives had no real faith in a project that wasn't truly and wholly theirs.

The Ford company still argues that it is really, honestly decentralized and even maintains (and possibly believes) that the British directors (who had four managing directors in six years) are still the captains of the subsidiary's fate—as they should be. The Sixth Truth of Management still applies. If the locals say they know best what to produce, they should be left to prove it, and to pay the price if they fail. If they can't be trusted on that, how can they be trusted with anything else, except the key to the executive washroom?

Cars are a special management problem in one respect—as

trains used to, they turn almost any adult into a schoolboy. (A minor problem with middle-aged rail executives is their passion for drawing up timetables.) But even if the products are less compulsive playthings, the urge to fiddle is omnipresent—partly because the chief executive likes to take personal credit for any successes (the failures he leaves to others).

Effective decentralization, however, means no fiddling and no meddling, except when mismanagement occurs. True, by then damage has been done, but, as Litton teaches, the center never has an early enough warning system, however elaborate. In Litton's case, its Hull factory in England was expensively geared up to manufacture typewriters that it could neither produce properly nor sell; this became evident from reports only when the company was already locked into disaster. The mistake was not lack of reports; it was the original, strategic decision, in which the Litton bosses had "participated," to use their word.

In any big American corporation, the top executives participate all the time; that is, they hold endless meetings to second-guess the executives who are supposed to be in charge. Once you decentralize, you become more investor than director. You should act like a sane one. It's interesting how old saws of stock market investment apply to decentralized direction—Cut your losses, but let your profits run or reinforce success, and never invest in failure.

One old-line English board ignored both wise saws. It was notorious for inability to influence its largest subsidiary, which had decentralized itself right out of head office orbit. When the offshoot's ideas and those of another part of the empire overlapped, both projects sometimes, ludicrously, went ahead. Both even developed their own computers. The correct answer, since the child went around the track much faster than the parent, was to back baby. But this would have meant downgrading another business over which the main board actually did possess day-to-day control. Only when senior managements change their entire life-styles, abdicate the interfering habits of a managing lifetime, and substitute the fair but demanding standards of a hungry investor, will decentralization be more than a myth—and often an expensive one.

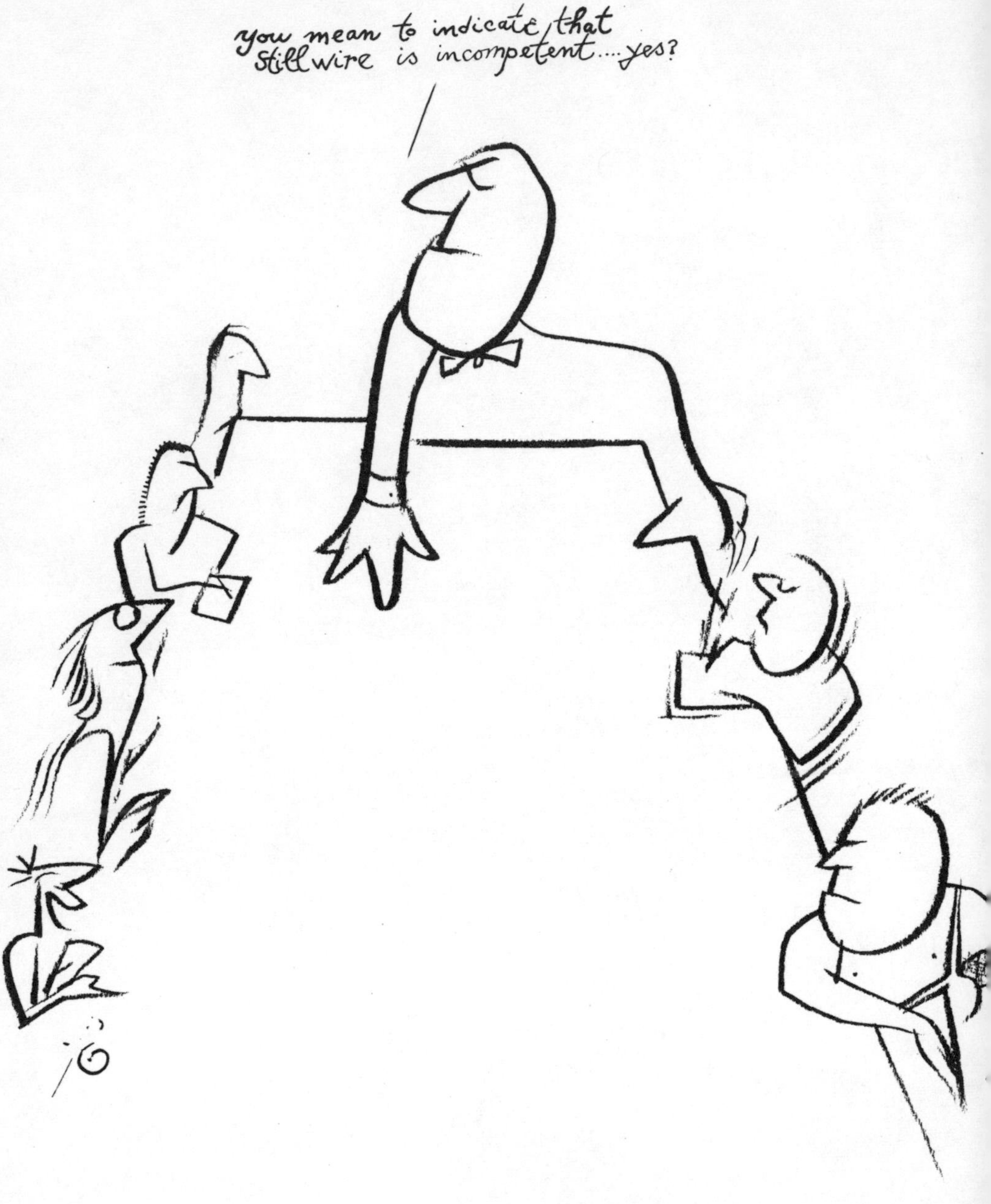
you mean to indicate that
Stillwire is incompetent....yes?

13 The Boardroom Mafia

BOARDS OF DIRECTORS have an aura of sanctity roughly akin to that of the College of Cardinals. The law sees them as they see themselves—guardians of the stockholders' rights and the company's long-term future. A pungent *New Yorker* comment, at the height of the Valachi revelations about the Mafia, is more accurate. The cartoon showed a board chairman snarling at his youngest and brashest director: "Perkins, will you stop calling this company *Cosa Nostra*." Perkins was perfectly right. Since senior executives in most corporations are both the dominant directors and the controlling executives, the business all too readily becomes Our Thing.

The board elects itself, reshuffles itself, congratulates itself. The directors are supposed to call the executives to account —and possibly did in ancient times, when the general manager of the business was a lackey, like the doorkeeper. Today

125

the general manager is either chairman of the board, or managing director, or president. His first loyalty is not to the board as such, and certainly not to the unseen stockholders, but to an amorphous body of no legal standing, the upper management.

The Mafia-like aspect of top management coziness raises large, well-aired, but unresolved, questions about the relationship between stockholders, directors, and companies. One question, at least as important, seldom gets any air: the relationship between the management Mafia and the efficient conduct of the business. This issue is most transparent in Britain, where the all-executive, all-supreme board has reached its apogee.

A U.S. giant such as Honeywell had only four current working executives on its fourteen-man 1970 board, a British colossus such as Courtaulds, only two nonexecutives out of thirteen—the rest are all working directors. Honeywell's ten nonexecutive titans too, are all businessmen, some of them former Honeywell executives, which follows standard U.S. practice; British companies in the local tradition, favor out-of-work politicians. The American system looks more sensible, safer, and less Sicilian; but, as usual in American organizations, first glances do not reveal last truths.

The outcome, on both sides of the Atlantic, is remarkably close, despite the apparent contrasts. The most obvious of these differences is the position of the *capo*, the boss. In Britain's corporate families, the chairman, who is also chief executive and managing director, surrounded only by his disciple deputies, enjoys double strength. In the U.S., the chairman's job of presiding over the company is normally distinct from directing its operations. General Motors has both a chairman and president (plus a raft of more or less powerful committees, which needn't be chaired by either potentate); but British Leyland, the local GM, after brief dual control, settled into the standard British pattern, with Lord Stokes alone at the wheel.

Keeping the chief executive in his place—one rung down —has its virtues. Or rather, the lonely summit has its vices.

First, nearly all the capo's boardroom colleagues owe their careers to him and are used to his command, so they are less likely to challenge his policies—no matter how terrible—and when the emperor's clothes fade away, it takes them far too long to see him bare.

Second, the chair's formal and ceremonial obligations eat up hours. Any portly fellow can cut the ribbons and show around the visiting firemen. Running the company requires talent and time. Like everybody else, the capo has only twenty-four hours a day. After sleep, ceremonial and publicity distractions, he's lucky to find more than twenty minutes to attend to a reasonably important division—and this assumes that he is well-organized. He is far more likely to devour available time with trivia that suddenly grab his emotions. Somebody should stop him, sure—but who?

Hugh Parker of McKinsey in London pointed out that the managing director's job is to press good performance from his subordinates, while the chairman squeezes the managing director. But if the latter doubles as chairman, is he going to put pressure on himself? The board can't do it collectively, since the members are largely those other executives whom the chairman is pressuring in his managing director role, and they stay squashed. One major British company has a mighty capo who loves flying kites—making and half-believing outrageous propositions. In the cold light of day, he leaks stories about how his fellow directors (none of whom would say boo unless ordered) have rebuffed him. The technique is that of the Dickensian lawyer who was always willing to agree but whose unseen partner (actually entirely somnolent) would have none of it.

Within the Mafia too a form of *omerta* applies: the code of honor lays down nothing but good about the capo until he is dead—or gone. After departure, the stories of the great man's weaknesses, foibles, and gross errors flood out. Not even Khrushchev telling tales on Stalin exceeds the relish of a successor executive recounting the sins of a predecessor (in which the successors were as deeply implicated as any Khrushchev).

The more collective the leadership, the more collective the

clinging. The code is only broken when the leadership structure itself is cracking under extreme pressure; its breach is a sign of corporate disintegration and the first stage in the battle for power. The pressure has to be intense. Executives will dance the gopak for the boss, submitting to all manner of indignities—public rebuke, being kept waiting all day outside closed doors, even (in one case) writing out copies of the chairman's thoughts—and still they won't protest. Their submission is an inevitable part of the system when a Stalin has emerged.

The business can then become more His Thing than Our Thing—but only if he too obeys the unwritten law. He must preserve the continuity of the corporation, by which is meant the senior executive roles within it. The upper management's desire to perpetuate itself collectively isn't easily distinguished from devotion to the company: the directors' rewards and their powers rest on preserving and defending those of the corporation. If the capo threatens the survival of the management family, therefore, he is as doomed as Joe Colombo or the late, bullet-riddled Albert Anastasia.

Both Shell and ICI, which had dominant one-man control prewar, now have explicitly collective management—Shell with a bevy of managing directors, ICI with an array of executive directors, most of whom have no direct power over operations. A rigid written code actually seeks to ensure that the ICI chairman never will exercise the powers of chief executive, and ICI's directors resolutely opposed a McKinsey suggestion that somebody else on the board should.

For a glimpse of the self-protective, self-perpetuating instinct at work, take this passage by Sir Peter Allen, then chairman of ICI (the capital letters are his): ". . . in a Company as complex as ICI, it is extremely difficult for anyone, however able, to come in as Chairman and be an effective head of the Company. Inevitably, his lack of knowledge of the Company's affairs would mean the appointment of a Managing Director, who himself would have to be so well-informed of the Company's business that it would be just as well to make him Chairman and have done with it." This neatly glossed over the fact that ICI had no intention of having a managing director in any shape or form.

It is almost as if the management Mafia, after bruising and unsettling experiences of a one-man past, had collectively breathed Never again. Making collective managements work is no picnic, either. The company tends to move at the pace of the slowest director. But this drawback is less unpalatable to some corporations than the insecurity of a capo-dominated regime—especially in times when capos (just as in the real Mafia) are getting worse at their jobs. Today's American trend toward "a president's office," with three or more persons forming a multiple chief executive, reflects this lust for collective security. It springs from the sheer difficulty, in the system, of developing the supermanager necessary to run, single-handed, corporations on this scale. There seem to be few human giants in U.S. business today, simply because there are few.

Try as it may, the cult of personality cannot hide the fact that the typical U.S. executive is interchangeable and disposable. There is nothing wrong with this absence of idols. Business management in the supercompany is not an individual, but a collective process. It must operate on the assumptions that somebody other than the leader may make the best contribution; that everybody's ideas are open to criticism, especially his; and that the leader is not a giant among pygmies, but a first among equals.

But executives won't take actions that are inimical to their own interests; they will always be tempted by decisions that directly benefit them, never mind the corporation. When one British company proposed to merge fully with its own foreign subsidiary, a minor consequence was that the parent directors would no longer sit on the Paris company's board. At the meeting that discussed the merger, five and one-half hours out of six went on this issue. One director protested that if he lost his regular lunches in Paris, "It will be the beginning of communism in this company."

On the Continent the system of dual boards (with the supervisors appointing the executives) is meant to purify this

impure relationship. But the German supervisory board is just as feeble as the annual general meeting in Britain or America. The supervisors meet infrequently; nearly all promotions and appointments are from within the existing management; and the upper management of big German companies forms as heavy, impregnable, and self-respecting a body of men as an American pro football lineup.

Even at Krupp, where otiose mistakes ran the company into a horrible cash predicament, the top management echelon was hardly affected by the removal (through political pressure and the still more certain accident of death) of the last of the Krupps. By the nature of things, the upper tier of a two-tier board is seldom more than a gold-handled rubber stamp.

The Americans, technically ingenious as ever, have a two-in-one-tier system. The chairman, supported by the nonexecutive numerical majority on the board, is supposed to safeguard the long-term interests of the corporation (meaning, to establish corporate policy) as well as to cherish the stockholder. A finance committee, usually chaired by someone outside executive management, often grips the purse strings—especially the fixing of the directors' pay and prerequisites, which is the most Cosa Nostra-like activity of the British boardroom. (One U.K. boss maintained that a small nonexecutive knot on his board likewise ensured that executive fingers didn't wander into the money box. Since the nonexecutives included his father-in-law, he may have been right.)

The U.S. system seems to recognize and regularize the fact that a company's executive officers develop a vested interest in their own actions and their own status. The American board is in theory designed to guarantee that the vested interests don't jeopardize the interests of the company as a whole. Except that it doesn't work that way. In the first place, the chairman is often a full-time executive, previously president of the company, a charter member of the Mafia.

At least he knows and understands the business and the men who run it (which is more than can be said of most nonexecutive chairmen). But poachers seldom turn gamekeeper. Bitterness can creep in; but the president is usually the chairman's boy, his protégé; and a president turned chairman won't challenge the entire basis of the upper management's operations and plans—after all, he was the genius who formed them.

Nor are nonexecutives, however expert in their own rackets, in much of a position to question the wisdom and integrity of the managerial elite, represented on the board by its senior group. Realism dictates that nonexecutive directors—as the City of London's one-time ornamental bank and insurance company boards found out—are in the hands of the top executives from whom all information comes. Any moderately astute executive can fend off a nonexecutive outsider (half of the latter's questions are likely to be silly, and the outsider never knows which half).

This assumes, anyway, that the American company chairman or president, serving as a nonexecutive on another board, wants to make life uncomfortable for the other boss who (very likely) asked him to join. The invitee isn't a fool. He has a board of his own, with the same situation, and he doesn't want to be uncomfortable, either. Consequently, the you-scratch-my-back-and-I'll-scratch-yours philosophy gets built into the corporate system, or you-serve-on-my-board-and-I'll-serve-on-yours. A wider management conspiracy, the presidents' and chairmen's club, gets superimposed on the narrower one of the company.

Managers only get blackballed from the club and cast into outer darkness for gross transgressions against the rules—and even then it takes time, and too much of it. Chrysler had a boss who wasn't very successful at running Chrysler and got involved in scandal about his own business transactions with the company; it was a long wait before he was expelled. But really bad behavior is not the problem, since appalling misconduct will eventually break up the management Mafia, which (again like its criminal counterpart) can sometimes be exceedingly inefficient.

The real trouble lies in the self-perpetuation of the mediocre: of executives who are never brilliant and never atrocious, but whose use of the assets is less effective than the dumbest stockholder could manage for himself. There is no easy escape. The company is the upper management, and the upper management is the company, for so long as executives maintain an acceptable level of competence (or incompetence). Pressure rarely comes from inside because of the rare emergence of individuals outstanding enough to apply it. It can only come from outside because of a change or incipient change in ownership—mostly in the form of a take-over bid or, in other words, from the injection of insecurity.

Human beings clustered in any group will always seek security, and that is the enemy of dynamic business management. Fairy Blackstick in Thackeray's *The Rose and the Ring* wished the princelings "a little misfortune" as her christening present. It made them into excellent rulers. A little insecurity might do wonders for managements everywhere, for the idea that business life is short and nasty is an illusion sponsored by the Hollywood dream factory; most executives, though they talk and even think differently, sleep safe enough in their nests.

Executives who want to be insecure can easily arrange it. No contractual hiring, no compensation for loss of office, all nominations to the board entrusted to a committee of investors, salaries submitted for approval to the same committee before ratification by the annual general meeting, executive directors' stockholdings (and their families') held in non-voting trust while they remain executives, and no chief executive allowed to double as chairman. Such conditions wouldn't guarantee the breakup of the management Mafia, but they would increase the chances of Our Thing being managed as Their Thing—"they" being the outside stockholders.

14 _The Risk-Taking Delusion_

MANAGEMENT THEORY IS obsessed with risks. Top executives bemoan the lack of risk-taking initiative among their young. Politicians and stockholders are advised (by directors) to make directors rich, so that they can afford to take risks. Theorists teach how to construct decision trees, heraldic devices of scientific management; and how to marry the trees with probability theory, so that the degree of risk along each branch (each branch and twig representing alternative results of alternative courses of action) can be metered. But the measuring is spurious, and, anyway, the best management doesn't take risks. It avoids them. It goes for the sure thing.

The greater the risk, very obviously, the smaller the case for embracing the project at all. Risk taking holds its pride of place among the management virtues only because it's a sin of which most managers are guilty. They need no urging to

135

take chances. The most purblind old buffer in the boardroom will cheerfully approve ventures of total insecurity. The monstrous chances that directors take with other people's money are often unwitting, but they are still risks. And executives who take great risks, whatever folklore says, are as dangerous to a company as a crooked accountant.

The great and fabled business empires, with hardly an exception, were built, not on outlandish risks, but on irresistible ideas of elemental simplicity. This is not just hindsight. From the Model T and the chain stores to semiconductors and instant photographs, the great entrepreneurs have taken available methods and married them to burning market needs. A peddler named Michael Marks decided to sell every object on his stall under one slogan—Don't ask the price, it's a penny. From that moment, the main lines of development of the Marks and Spencer chain were fixed: simplicity (the price limited the merchandise); control over supplies (if you wanted to sell everything for a penny, you had to buy everything for under a penny); value for money; and a uniform trading policy. Risk hardly came into the idea.

A marvelous, risk-free whim, such as Henry Ford's mass production to serve a mass market, can survive grotesque mismanagement. Ford lost $8.5 million in the 1930s, as Henry I bungled the challenge of Chevrolet, fell into the toils of the gangsterish Harry Bennett, and tortured his son, Edsel. He still died richer than Croesus—because sales went on proving, in their millions, that it takes a genius even more perverse than Ford's to ruin the commercial career of a great idea.

Terrible disasters (such as the oversized, overpriced and monstrously designed Edsel car put out by Henry's son) likewise result from gross and elementary errors of concept, not from marginal mistakes in abstruse calculations like discounted cash flow. Yet intelligent men plump for one project rather than another on the strength of a difference of a few decimal points in the rate of return calculated over the next decade. All such mind-stretching calculation comes under the lash of the Seventh Truth of Management: *if you need sophisticated calculations to justify an action, it is probably wrong* (the sophisticated calculations, anyway, are all too often based on simple false assumptions). A rider to this is, Shun any project that, if all goes according to plan, will just earn its keep. In real life, hardly anything follows the script. What sensible executives seek is the project whose margins are so wild that, if it actually works out, they can all retire to the Bahamas.

Most businesses meet only three classes of major investment decision—the inevitable, the optional, and the make-or-break. Only the last involves risk in the classic sense. The first category includes embarrassments such as new steel, paper, or cement works. Nobody interested in profits would build these expensive encumbrances today; but failure to expand in step with the competition guarantees slow atrophy in a business to which (because of its deadly concentration of fixed assets) the company is bound in perpetuity.

Factory extensions, modernization of machinery, even important product changes are usually fixed by market forces, not by managerial choice. The risk here is to do nothing—like Gillette when first confronted with the Wilkinson blade—or to do the inevitable at ruinous cost and delay, at which British steelmakers have proved adept. Gillette's forlorn hope that the stainless steel blade would rust away was matched by the resolute conviction of Detroit car makers that small-sized imports were a passing fad. The fad passed, all right: it passed into a permanent feature of the market, one that cost Detroit billions in lost sales, and billions more in a belated effort to catch up. Part of the effective executive's armory is a sense of when the rape of his profitability is inevitable.

The second category is where the company has a choice, and the decision, either way, will leave a viable business. This is where rashes of big mistakes are made—installing a computer, extending a product range into new markets, diversifying into new fields, merging with another company. The basic mistake is often not to recognize that any risk exists —for instance, in mergers, one of the most promising disaster areas. The error is usually compounded by refusal to cut losses. Sir Alexander Maclean, the toothpaste king, knew better. One of his associates recalled, "Maclean tried all sorts of things, but he exploited those which were successful and cut out those which were not." It's hardly a difficult technique.

By making really addlepated decisions in these optional matters, a corporation can even and very quickly disprove the original assumption—that the viability of the company will be unaffected. The International Publishing Corporation, which prided itself (inaccurately) on being the world's largest publisher, built a brand-new printing plant in Central London that piled trouble on existing agony. It installed a computer in the books division and paralyzed the business; diversified into computer services and computerized ticket sales at a cost of millions more; and, by adding a color magazine to the *Daily Mirror*, dropped another £4 million. By the time all these and other foibles had been paid for, IPC had moved gratuitously from viability to teetering.

More commonly, calamity follows from failures in the third main area of decision making, the make-or-break variety, where the entire company hangs on success or failure. In most of these cases, a compelling truth lies behind management's mental processes. Rootes had to widen its penetration of the car market to survive as an independent. With defense business in long-term decline, only civil airliners offered Lockheed a growing market for its talents—just as, in the same game, Handley Page needed a new civil plane to survive. Power Gas had to win a large refinery contract to figure seriously in an American-dominated market. (Power Gas didn't know what it was doing; the customer, Continental Oil, thought that Power Gas did; and the result was a £10 million overrun.) In computers, English Electric had to come up with a new range or else get out of IBM's way.

Rather than do just that—get out—the executive, despite his alleged caution, goes for all or nothing; and nothing is often what he gets—like the British shipbuilders who modernized expensively, when they had neither markets nor management, and mostly went broke. The finest economy of scale, from the executive's point of view, is that size can bury monumental mistakes. Divisions of Ford and General Dynamics both survived the two greatest commercial errors up to then, the Edsel and the Convair jetliner, because even losses of $400 million (especially after tax offsets) can be absorbed within empires whose assets total $9.9 billion or $1 billion. The stockholder pays the tab: Ford's earnings per share over the 1960s rose by little more than 2 percent annually.

Even in big companies, executives don't take brave risks. They make foolish errors. Like politicians, executives have a genius for compounding bad policies with worse execution. The Eighth Truth of Management is: *if you are doing something wrong, you will do it badly.* The reverse of this truth is that, if your decision is blindingly right, you will execute it well—or appear to do so, which is much the same thing. But any executive can massacre his own nonsensical project. The correct decision for Lord Rootes—feudal lord of his company —was not to struggle for independence, but to seek a partner (the firm plopped into Chrysler's lap, anyway). Instead, he chose to build a new mass market car. This wrong decision was compounded by building the Imp in the wrong place (Scotland); in the wrong price/size category, competing at the static and least profitable bottom end of the market; and with wrong production engineering that finally undermined the tottering Imp economics. Rootes never got near break-even, though its directors continued to pursue the impossible like knights after the Holy Grail.

Similarly, nobody in the air industry believed in the original specifications of the Handley Page Jetstream, or in the fabulously low cost of its development, or in massive orders promised by an American distributor. This little dreamboat was supposed to carry up to two dozen passengers. "Sure it can," grunted one competitor, "if they're all gnomes." Ironically, the company had some real-life American orders, from the ever-ready Department of Defense, for the greatly changed, far more expensive Jetstream with which the company eventually and inevitably crashed.

Make-or-break risks can make it. Rover, another of the last

British car independents, poured £11 million (equal to total net capital employed at the start) into the 2000. A sharp increase in car output, based on an entirely new model, was the only way to ensure, not its independence, but its future as a factory. In this case, the answers to a host of subsidiary questions were golden. Was the Rover name and image saleable for an "executive" car? Could the company finance the project? Was the two-liter, under £2,000 executive market a growing sector? On reasonable assumptions about demand, would the 2000's price, in this expensive area of the market, yield a profit? These were not computer-bending problems. But the greater the primary risk, the safer and more careful your secondary assumptions must be—a project is only as sound as its weakest assumption.

Companies only reach true make-or-break points because of past risky errors. Rootes had a long history of expensive engineering, bad model planning, and family-dominated management; Rover hadn't developed its car range for years; Handley Page had refused, out of stubborn pride, to surrender its absurd independence; Lockheed had to go for broke, and in much less favorable circumstances, with the Tri-Star because of its flop on the Electra; English Electric, with no experience in business machines, should never have gone into computers, especially against a background of poor profitability in the rest of its cornucopia.

Even with technology imported from RCA (another company that had no business losing money in computers), English Electric saddled itself with a project based on implausible assumptions—first, that it could win, largely on the merits of advanced technology, a juicy share of the British market from IBM and International Computers, which owned two-thirds of U.K. sales between them; second, that the machines would get into production on schedule and even work when produced; third, that if the first two assumptions were wrong, the company could afford the cash drain. The computers didn't steal anybody's market share; they were late, and didn't work. Something like £20 million was lost, and that is a principal reason why English Electric was digested by GEC, a company whose new management got out of computers as soon as look at them.

If you seek to eliminate all risk, you risk something else— eliminating all enterprise and innovation. Nine times out of ten, this may be to the stockholders' benefit. But what about the tenth time? What about those unsung ghosts of American business—the IBM man who turned down the Univac computer, the du Pont executive who showed the inventor of

xerography the door, the Kodak man who turned up his nose at Polaroid? Right back to the men who thought the horseless carriage had no future, business history is haunted by the memories of missed opportunities. But the unsung ghosts weren't frightened away by risk; like bureaucrats everywhere, they couldn't see the opportunity.

General David Sarnoff, English Electric's remote partner in its computer disaster, certainly gambled, by the standards of his time, when he pumped $50 million into commercial TV. He took an equal gamble, apparently, in backing color TV in the 1950s, for $130 million more. But the odds were much shorter than they looked. Sarnoff's RCA was the only set maker that could take the gamble because its NBC network could transmit (at a loss) the color programs without which, clearly, nobody would buy a set. And was color TV really a gamble? Color had taken over the cinema screen, and was as certain as anything in life to take over TV. Sarnoff's only risk was of being too early—as he was, both technically and commercially. RCA still made a mint. Note, however, what happened in a virgin market where Sarnoff was not building on his know-how or his assets—those computers again. Just like GE, RCA had to throw in its hand: all its risk-taking had bought was a $500 million loss.

Faced with a decision, always ask one implacable question: If this project fails, if the worst comes to the worst, what will be the result? If the answer is total corporate disaster, drop the project. If the worst possible outcome is tolerable, say, break-even, the executive has the foundation of all sound decision making—a fail-safe position. Heads I win, tails I don't lose, may not sound madly adventurous, but that way, the executive always wins. As played in many companies, the game is Heads I lose, tails I don't win—and that is a pastime for idiots.

The catering tycoon Sir Charles Forte, a believer in wearing both belt and braces, kept his trousers up brilliantly, until an unwise merger with Trust Houses lost him personal control for a time. He bought up his companies, hotels or restaurants, in great quantities, expecting a satisfactory income return, but making sure that the property value covered his investment. His one major exception, a soft ice-cream business, proved a soft mistake. Directors should stick to their maxims. In any business, remember that the object of good management is not just to maximize profits, or growth rates, or market share but to maximize them at minimized risk.

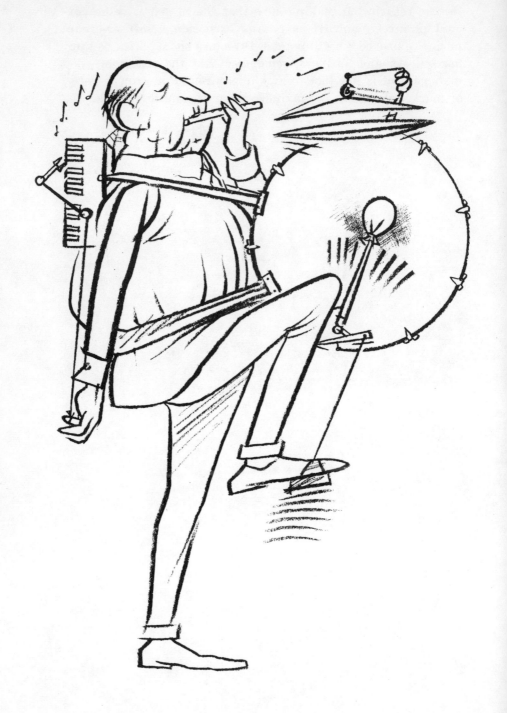

15 *The One-Man Band Plays On*

CALL AN industrial chieftain incompetent, and he won't love you. Tell him he has laid a Grade A egg, and he will argue. But call his company a one-man band, and he will be furious —especially if it is. The natural tendency for powerful men is to dominate, and the natural instinct of those who serve them is to be dominated. One-man bands, moreover, are quick to spot each other—what they can't recognize is themselves. They are blinded by the received idea, in a democratic age, that one-man bands are a particularly heinous form of bad management.

When the ideal is the nebulous team, nobody likes to admit that he personally makes every decision—major, minor, or minimal—that his senior disciples, after years as yes-men, could never rule independently; that he lusts for supreme authority and would wither away without it. One such chief executive, whose brilliant dictatorship was as emotional as *Wuthering Heights,* maintained less a headquarters staff than a court. The courtiers sat on long into afternoons or evenings listening to monologues that, while fascinating at first hearing, palled by the ninety-first. Yet the tycoon would never admit that his company had little top management, just him.

One day, when the master's behavior became too erratic to bear, the worms turned. Looking back on the debacle, the ousted chieftain philosophically admitted the truth. "The trouble was," he said, "that the company was a one-man band." In any company, and in any area of management, it's better to face the truth at the time when it hurts—and possibly helps.

There happen to be real managerial advantages for the one-man band, but self-deception can lose or offset all of them. The advantages are not in any textbook, because the reasons that make them great also make them nontransferable —they harness the working forces of a corporation to one highly personalized and identifiable driving power.

In logic and in fact, one man can't run a group of ten thousand, or thirty thousand, or eighty thousand, or two hundred thousand people—though some do try. There are chief executives who pass on *all* capital expenditure, right down to electric typewriters; others who approve all foreign travel; and others who operate a private KGB to discover what's happening before their underling bosses know it themselves. All this is totally illogical. But management is not logic. One unusual man can impress his personality on a gigantic organization, not only so that he knows, controls, and influences everything in the present, but so that for years into the future the company will live in his shadow.

This happens outside business. The British Broadcasting Corporation is still within the aura of its first boss, Lord Reith. The FBI won't escape from J. Edgar Hoover for decades after his final, final curtain. In business, the great founder-entrepreneurs have the same supernatural impact—Henry Ford; the first Lord Leverhulme, creator of the British half of Unilever; or Thomas Watson, Sr., builder of IBM. The company is run as their personal property. The continued exercise of their property rights is founded on business genius, personal charisma, and family stockholdings. Such one-man orchestration is perfectly acceptable, up to a point.

If a mighty entrepreneur can raise the earnings and the stock price year after year, it hardly matters to stockholders that he also plays the dictator. It probably doesn't matter to his executives either. Many people love having every decision made for them, and executives are no exception. At least, the one-man band makes the decisions, and usually at high speed. Delay makes a good decision worse and seldom improves a bad one. If the dictator is a genius, the decisions may even be right. The odds favor him more than the rest of mankind. He, after all, is the company, absolutely identified with its purposes and potential. And he has, by creating the empire, shown the energy that makes a good decision work—and can sometimes save a bad one from its badness. But no man's genius lasts forever, and the longer he reigns, the more seeds of decay get planted.

Few really able men will work indefinitely under an autocrat. Those who do either lose the habit of making decisions, or never get the experience: either way, there's no adequate succession. Anyway, dictators dislike having strong men behind their backs—though most, for some deep psychological reason, have an *éminence grise*, a long-time, shy associate, whose special expertise, usually technical, keeps him out of power's way. (One tycoon, in a verbal use that would have delighted Freud, called his eminence his "day wife.") Another harmful quirk is that many one-man bands are also bullies —though, again, many executives like to be bullied. But victims won't turn into heroes after the bully quits; they are more likely to be punch-drunk.

The timing of the succession is decisive. The presiding genius may be the last to understand that his best days are over, and terrible erosion can follow while he blindly hangs on. Many companies have known what it felt like in Nero's Rome: the decaying emperor fiddles while the city burns. In one case, the other directors were just alert enough to take evasive action. They got the founder-chairman to agree that a new executive committee would make all decisions before matters reached the main board. The committee was identical to the board—except that the chairman was left out. But mostly the decision to relax the iron fist has to come from the dictator himself, and this is the one decision he will not make.

It will eventually be made for him, if not by palace revolution, then by illness, fatigue, or death. Then comes the moment of truth. The autocrat has to pass the same test as any director (dead, deposed, or departed); does he leave behind an organization that—like Marks and Spencer after Lord Marks—shows great continuity, flexible strength, and regenerative powers? Or does he—as in Ford Motor after Henry Ford—leave behind a shambles, capable of losing $22 million in a single quarter?

The key is that men like Simon Marks, for all their pervasive personalities, are so deeply interested in organization that their bands are orchestras. They express their egos through the systems they build; they have their eccentricities (Marks was described posthumously by one long-time associate as a Stalin of the retail trade), but they don't manage through eccentric egos alone. The one-man band, in contrast, rarely has organizing ability. He convinces himself that he is an organizer, and easily convinces others—for arguing with success is even harder than admitting to failure.

But what looks like effective organization is the working through of that tremendous personal urge. Remove the drive, along with the person, or bring the drive up against some unexpected obstacle, and the apparently well-organized company tears apart. Maybe this is legitimate if the company really is the dictator's personal property. What a man creates, he is presumably entitled to destroy. But a great industrialist's empire can rapidly transcend the scale of one ego. Henry Ford I retained the power to destroy Ford Motor; he no longer had the right.

This applies far more to the professional director. The man who doesn't own the business has a particular obligation to follow the footsteps of Alfred P. Sloan, who created order out of primeval chaos at General Motors, not Ford. As the paid servant of the company the pro has no property rights. He must expect to be judged severely on short-term results (though he isn't) ; he must also demonstrate that he is *not* indispensable (which he isn't). The professional executive has no excuse for one-man bandmanship. But powerful forces push him that way; precious few countervailing forces hold him back; and who can resist an invitation to play God (the internal nickname of many a chief executive) ?

The difference between proprietors and professionals is not really understood. The pro is expected to play the part of the founding genius, without having the latter's mystery ingredient X, which is his two-way identification, as owner and creator, with the company. True, the pro identifies with the upper management and with his own ego, but that's a different matter entirely.

The public can't tell this difference. It lionizes the management hero by instinct; it dangles before him the front cover of *Business Week,* or a knighthood, or membership of the president's blue chip panel of business leaders, or a life peerage. The public does this because it dearly loves a leader. This is the one argument in favor of the one-man band that its critics will accept. Everybody believes that leadership is a supreme human attribute—it even gets praised in school reports. But in management terms, leadership is a greatly overrated quality.

The British, with their long tradition of war, kings, aristocrats, and empire, have an innate tendency to fall down in worship before chairmen, headmasters, prime ministers, royalty, and commanding officers. The Americans are blinded by their recurrent desire for "a man on horseback" and by simple refusal to believe that anybody who has made millions, floated to the top of a large corporation, or both, can be an idiot. But at least Americans used to be quicker on the draw when the leader failed. The British often don't shoot until they have been staring at the whites of a failed capo's eyes for years, and sometimes they never fire at all.

A sad sign for American business, however, is that the bul-

letproof executive vest became more common wear in the
1960s; even the authors of unprecedented aerospace disasters
failed to bite the dust in the requisite numbers at the requisite
time. In such high technology traumas, British or American,
lack of leadership has seldom been the agent of fate. If anything, the companies have suffered from an excess of being
led. Under the one-man command of leaders who could have
charged the Light Brigade into suicide, these companies too
have headed straight for the enemy's guns.

The story goes that one ennobled, embattled, and really
leading leader of British industry was persuaded to spend
three hours with an American, a great and wise guru of real

management. The guru emerged, shaking his head, and told the other directors, "It's up to you boys. I can't do a thing with him." One of them ventured in and asked the peer how it had gone. "Very well," he replied, "he said the way I manage this company is perfect." As the highly led company gets bigger, and the high leader gets more heavily laden with outside activities and honors, he loses contact with reality. (Founder-entrepreneurs are more reluctant to take on outside commitments than professional one-man bands—another vital clue to the difference between them).

Very easily, the dominating concept, the informing element, of all managerial work in the company becomes not what is right, but what will Sir This or Mr. That agree to. This is only acceptable if the boss himself is consistently correct; but in eight cases out of ten, he will at some point become consistently wrong, and the consequences will show in the company's figures—not in calamity usually, but in mediocrity.

In the two exceptions, so long as the one-man bands are fit, in form and in situ, the company will run surprisingly, even magically, well. But even here their refusal to admit to their solitary power means that no action gets taken to prepare the corporation for their inevitable departure. This danger can only be countered by a simple rule: compulsory appointment of a new chief executive when the old one is sixty, compulsory final abdication of the old buzzard at sixty-five, and stick to it. Don't be like J. Lyons, once Britain's greatest eating chain, where the retiring age of sixty-five was theoretical and "the older anyone was, the more theoretical it became."

Never mind that the towering tyrant is still doing ninety situps every morning and can outrun, outtalk, and outdeal any man in the room, the earlier he has to go, the more likely he is to think about the succession with an unwarped mind and to create some kind of organization to go with it. At Beecham, when the tyrant Philip Hill died, "All the performing seals got down from their barrels and began to fight," remarked one executive of the time. At Associated Electrical Industries, when the elderly colossus Lord Chandos finally came down off his plinth, there was no scrap—Chandos had brought in a hand-picked successor from outside. This too broke a simple rule: the more dominant a man is, the less he should be allowed to name his own successor.

For subconscious reasons, great men select successors who will not surpass the great one. Proprietorial one-man bands usually have this guaranteed for them by nature. Most have sons, nearly always inadequate copies of the master design, ready to step into father's oversized shoes. There is an immortal (and doubtless unfair) remark about Robert Sarnoff, boss of RCA in succession to founder General David Sarnoff. The son, said some jester, joined the company at the bottom—but then his father took a fancy to him.

Men cannot bear the idea that others will say of their successor, "Of course, he's done much better than old Lord ——." A Stalin chooses a Malenkov to succeed him, a Churchill picks an Eden. The man most likely to succeed is the man least likely to disturb his predecessor's legacy; yet counterrevolution, no matter how brilliant the past, is almost certainly a necessity at the moment of inheritance.

This is true even where the ruler genuinely created a superb organization. Counterrevolution was needed—and badly—at Marks and Spencer, where in the last days of the father-figure expansion of lines and stores was seriously retarded. It was probably needed for years, but not provided, at Sloan's General Motors, where the corporate constipation as the 1960s ended was already causing bad outbreaks of spots in overseas car operations (the Continent and Australia) and in the small car market in the U.S.

The ideally wise one-man band would know these risks. So the third simple rule for producing discord-free corporate music is gradually to disengage—to reach the point of domination from a distance. You don't have to emulate the ghostly manner of a Howard Hughes (who, incidentally, was for long a highly effective director, even though he never saw, and seldom spoke to, any of his executives). But it is possible to animate a company brilliantly without day-to-day interference. The most successful mid-century oilman in the U.S., some believe, is Robert O. Anderson of Atlantic Richfield, who only comes near the corporate headquarters twice a month and is sometimes incommunicado for weeks. Unfortunately, self-control is rare in self-centered successes; and absolute power tends, just as Lord Acton said, to corrupt absolutely. The essential weakness of the one-man band is that it establishes a closed circle, in which only the one-man leader can act against his vices. There is no way round this: his ultimate privilege is to be the first Gadarene swine over the edge.

Osborn

16 The Eighteen-Hour Menaces

THE ETHIC OF Western society dictates that to work hard is good. By extension, to work harder than anybody else is, therefore, to be better than everybody else. Since the only measure of an executive's work is the time spent, the hardest working executive is clearly the man who puts in the longest hours: the eighteen-hours-a-day paragon. No normal executive would boast that he worked only three hours a day, no matter how superlative his performance. But corporate annals regularly feature the tycoon who (in the words of that great business musical, the *Pajama Game*) can hardly wait to get to work at eight. Hardly anybody worries about the abnormality (and sheer physical impossibility) of the eighteen-hour business jam session.

Once upon a time, it made sense for the boss to get in first and leave last—then he could keep a constant eye on the till.

But in the great modern corporation, without a till to its name, the boss keeps shopkeeper's hours for one reason only—to satisfy his ego. In itself, there is nothing wrong with this hobby. A man who has clambered to the top of a business empire deserves some pleasures. But the pastime has unpleasant and sometimes serious consequences for the company and its other executives.

The eighteen-hour chief executive is unlikely to fancy working all alone in an empty office: he wants company. So secretaries and subordinates have to appear at the same unearthly time, but for less good cause. One dynamo regularly employs two young management recruits as personal assistants. In theory, they are being groomed for future stardom; in practice, they serve as early morning and late evening acolytes at the great man's altar, and their later starring roles are rewards for the service.

Young men are resilient and probably suffer little ineradicable harm; but older men, including the dynamo's directors, also get sucked into the same maw. If the chief executive summons a divisional manager to a breakfast conference or a 7 A.M. meeting, the subordinate may be man enough to refuse, but he will quail in his boots. Gradually, the whole working life of the executive suite revolves around the eccentric timetable of the perpetual motion machine at the top.

One personnel consultant felt obliged to tell a company chairman that the corporate organization could not survive in the same form after he stepped down. No conceivable successor would work the same punishing routine, starting before dawn had even cracked. Nor, judged by the recent results, would anybody want to. That chief executive was Daniel B. Haughton of Lockheed, which was about to sail into the Galaxy, Cheyenne, and Tri-Star disasters—the greatest triple threat in the troubled history of aerospace.

It doesn't follow that, if Haughton had worked on a saner regime, the company would have got its sums right. But equally, it didn't follow that, because the chief executive was a glutton for hard hours, the company would win success, avoid error, and fly into an ever-golden future. In management there is no correlation between effort and effectiveness: a fact so obvious as to be trite. But there may often be a correlation between excessive effort and ineffectiveness. This is foreign to the puritan ethic. Yet everybody knows the symptoms of ineffective effort lower down the management slopes—the departmental head whose desk is littered with pieces of paper that he endlessly shuffles as, piece by piece, he mentally sinks beneath them.

The eighteen-hour chief executive is the same breed of cat. Only, because of his power and because he has bursts of real effectiveness, the disease is not recognized by its symptoms, by its progress, or by its results. No man in any important executive position can find enough work to fill even ten hours a day, day in, day out, unless his operation is badly organized and/or he wastes time in what looks like work, but isn't.

The prodigious worker who heads one of Britain's genuine growth companies garners most of its growth (and most of its profit) from an operation jointly owned with an American partner, a joint goose that lays its golden eggs with little attention, apart from an occasional pat on the head. The rest of the company consists of diversified interests, most added in recent years, which, like all mixed corporate baskets, include some rotten eggs. The company created its own problems by buying them; and its chief executive creates his own work load by sending out a stream of memos, manufacturing at one stroke two pieces of paperwork—his own inquiry (which may or may not be relevant) and the reply (which may not be relevant either to the inquiry or to the business of the division).

In consequence, his in-basket is always one of the most heavily loaded in Britain. Vicious circles of this kind are hard to break. One merchant bank in the City of London, notorious for long hours, adds to the burden on its bankers by the chief executive's memos: one director alone found an escape—he refused to answer the memos on the grounds that he never knew what to say. The longer an executive works, the more time he has to dispatch unnecessary pieces of paper—and the more work he makes for the subordinates and superiors

157

who have to deal with them. Some of the documents may be worth reading, but Pareto's law undoubtedly applies—80 percent of the useful transmissions will arise from 20 percent of the corporate paper flow, 80 percent of which will contribute virtually nothing.

But the paper proliferation is only a symptom of the disease. It usually reflects a deadly underlying situation: the executive who gets into too much detail of another executive's job is filling his own hours at the expense of the other man's effectiveness. There are other ways of achieving the same miserable end than flying paper darts around the corporation. The best-known and most heavily used device is the meeting. Nearly all executives spend a large proportion of their time in meetings (just as their secretaries say).

Simple logic dictates that the more people attend a meeting the less effectively the time of its average member is used. If four people meet for one hour and talk for an equal amount of time (an unlikely story), each is active for one-quarter of an hour and passive for three-quarters. If eight people fill the same time span, the active-passive ratio declines from one to three to only one to seven.

In practice, the time taken expands to accommodate the numbers present, rather than the subject matter. So eight managers take two hours where four take one hour, and so on ad infinitum. It hardly matters whether the meeting is formally called a committee, or that the theoretical model is spoiled by all manner of incidentals, such as the proportion of those attending who are asleep (or wish they were). The principle is always the same—the more people present, the more managerial time wasted.

The eighteen-hour menace, however, introduces a savage twist as chief executive. His long hours and his detailed interference with subordinate operations imply that he is the dominant personality. The decisions taken at any meeting he attends will, therefore, be the ones he would have taken on his own. The other executives are only present like a claque in a Viennese opera house—paid to applaud the performance.

Actually, the only effective meetings are those in which one personality does dominate and which in effect simply endorse what he proposes. Hence the desultory nature of board meetings (a board is nothing but a committee) with nonexecutive directors present. Etiquette forbids dictation, so the conversation rambles on without direction, and the chairman often has to resort to standard strategems to get his way (like leaving the only important matter until ten minutes before lunch, or referring contentious issues to a pliant subcommittee).

Probably a company that pretends it is managed by committee, but isn't, is more effective than a company that genuinely is committee run. Du Pont has the longest-running multiple top management, a nine-man executive committee that passes collectively on all matters of importance down to $500,000 investments (a bagatelle in the context of multinational chemical giants). The du Pont committee even votes. A very strong chief executive could operate this system as a rubber stamp; but if the president is both very strong and very good, what's the point of wasting time on endorsing his decisions? If he is neither strong nor good, there is even less point in continuing his employment.

Even the best and strongest executive needs advice and double checking. But not all the time. Part of a chief executive's essential equipment is to know when to scream for help and when not to; part of his duty is to be as sparing of the time of other executives as of his own because time is the one irreplaceable corporate asset. Physical assets can be replaced, financial losses can be recouped, lost production can sometimes be made up, but time passed can never be regained. No company is short of executives. The shortage is of effective executive hours.

Unfortunately, executives have marked regressive tendencies in the use of time. Several studies have proved that, if the executive day is analyzed, large fallow periods pop out that, by self-discipline and changed methods, the good manager can promptly fill up with productive labor. Any follow-up, however, would surely show steady backsliding—probably to the point where as much time as ever slips away like sand through the fingers. Possibly, in some cases, the eighteen-hour executive, by spending twice as much time as normal in ostensible work, gets twice as much effective time. But this is the wrong answer: the ideal of summit management, and of delegation, is to reduce the job content at the top to the bare minimum. The boss who keeps his desk bare and his calendar empty, for one thing, is certain to be available when somebody really does need him.

Sir Arnold Weinstock comes close to this ideal. He turned a near-bankrupt GEC into the only profitable company in the electrical industry's Big Three (and finally turned the Big Three into a Big One) without any outward appearance of effort. Mythology has it that between mergers Weinstock could be found wandering around looking for something to do—and the myth contains some reality.

The blissful state of always having time is easily achieved. First, the executive must avoid outside entanglements like the plague (most big-time executives, not content with squandering time on internal obligations, itch incurably to serve on outside committees). Second, attend internal committees only when strictly necessary, except for board meetings, which should be purely legal formalities anyway. The test of strict necessity for other meetings is whether the chief executive will save more time by being present than he will lose. The most important step, however, is to delegate—and mean it.

The dogma of delegation is simple—the Sixth Truth of Management again: either the delegatee is capable of running the operation successfully by himself or he isn't. This handy formula relieves the top executive of any responsibility except that of finding, supervising, and (at the appropriate time) moving the men who are doing all the work. He can then truly manage by exception: he does not get worked up over operations that are going well, but concentrates on the plague spots, where everything, including the management, is going badly. But human nature is such that, the more wondrously smooth and rich a business, the more the head office wants to meddle; and the more dreadful and backbreaking a problem seems to be, the more prepared the head office is to abdicate to any potential savior.

Many years ago, a British board was well along the course of its rake's progress toward American intervention, ending with take-over by one of its own customers. In this emergency, it turned over its northern interests to a bright young director, who, in his own words, rang down an iron curtain between head office and the factories. Left to itself, without interference from London, the business turned around smartly; but as soon as profits were again respectable, the board started boring holes in the iron curtain.

The director quit, and the company rapidly relapsed into its antigrowth trend. This tale is repeated again and again. The former boss of what is probably the fastest-growing big company division in Britain estimates that he spent half his own time insulating his executives from the interference of the multi-hour work glutton who chaired the holding company.

There are plenty of other ways to fill the workday of a management positively determined to get in eighteen hours— such as travel. First-class jet flights across America and around the world rapidly consume time; and the operation of the biological time clock, which gets thrown out of gear by even the small transatlantic shift, guarantees that few useful results will follow. Another device that combines maximum consumption of time with personal gratification is the business lunch or dinner. Hours can be eaten away in expensive restaurants or lush corporate lunchrooms on the excuse of conducting business that might take a brisk ten minutes on the telephone. Often there is no specific item of business to discuss, anyway —the engagement is purely social. But it still contributes its stint to the eighteen hours.

Work in these corporate circumstances is more realistically defined as absence from home. If real work is effective application to the purposes of the corporation, nobody has ever worked an eighteen-hour day. To the extent that they try, they merely create an artificial situation that can't possibly endure, and shouldn't. One American oil company prided itself on the superhuman hours its senior executives worked seven days a week. They argued that as they were no brighter than their rivals in other companies, they would outdistance the competition simply by putting in more mileage. In fact, the company did grow faster than any other outfit in the industry. But to what end?

Any corporation, looked at from one angle, is a club of senior executives who all have lives outside its frontiers. A breed of zombies can always be created; but the corporation is not an end in itself. The sensible company organization operates successfully within the framework of human (and humane) hours. In *Up The Organization*, Robert Townsend tells a revealing tale: "One of my colleagues once spent a twelve-hour night working on an undated document that turned out not to be the current draft." Townsend's point was to always date a memo; but the better point is that twelve-hour nights indicate gross organizational failure somewhere along the line.

If a man has this strange inner compulsion to spend the maximum time in the ego-boosting security of the office, there is no harm in letting him indulge the urge, provided that, first, he is effective, and, second, that he doesn't force saner men to adapt to his rhythm. The second trap is hard to avoid, if only because underlings will be tempted to emulate their boss (and grab his attention) by showing equal enthusiasm for the office. More often than not the maximum-hour leader explicitly expects to see effort matching his own. The corporate boss who calls the break-of-day conference, or who rings around on the squawk-box in the evening to tell the executives they can go home, is asking for inferior performance: it takes an inferior executive to submit to what is little more than bullying.

Outside the entrepreneurial foundations (whose founding bosses often have a touch of monomania, or megalomania, in their genius) the eighteen-hour boss is a rarity. The corporation man seldom has this lust for self-flagellation. Yet he tends to work longer and longer hours as he gets older and more senior, as if the corporate executive's ideal was somebody like Harold B. Geneen of ITT or Haughton of Lockheed. The first named has probably been the most successful of the conglomerate makers. But neither his record, nor Haughton's, says anything for or against masochistic hours. Nobody would dream of modeling a corporation after the life-style of a lazy genius, and there is just as little point in building the company in the image of an obsessive worker. But if you have to choose between the ant and the wizard, pick the latter every time.

17 *Every Executive's Secret Vice*

NO MANAGEMENT SCHOOL runs courses in mendacity. They aren't needed—executives are to the manner born. Not the deliberate lie: that is reserved for occasional denials of financial deals or other forlorn suppressions of the truth. Not, usually, deception on the criminal scale, like that of America's convicted electrical or plumbing price fixers. No, the kind of untruth that is endemic in management, and potentially fatal, is self-deception. For example, it is well-known that if five firms compete in an industry and all five are asked to give their market shares, the resulting figures always add up to well over 100 percent.

The American boss of a GM outfit in Europe was once asked about the miserable sales of his new family car. "We don't think it's done badly," he replied. "It has 70 percent of its market." "Market" had been defined to exclude practically everything else on four wheels, except a few imports. Car makers are prone to wishful futility; the GM man was eventually moved, or removed, as the company slid further down the scale of reality. This habit of gilding the lily, or the weed, is every executive's secret vice, and often his last protection. Executives usually quit after a "policy disagreement," or "for personal reasons," or even because of ill health—seldom for the real reason, such as that they have been sacked for incompetence. (One departed chief executive, said to be at death's door by his successor, turned up right as rain in an even tougher chief executive spot the very next week.)

Deciding when the secret vice is conscious or unconscious is for psychologists. When a Ford of Britain man says, "we don't believe they can sell the same car in Germany as we can here," when the company is about to do precisely that, is the untruth deliberate or instinctive? (Or did the American overlords simply forget to tell him?) Men who apply more or less uniform private standards of morality divide their commercial lives into areas of honesty and other areas (such as future product plans) of total untruth. Lying in the cause of commercial secrecy does little managerial damage (and little good for that matter, as competitors mostly know what you are trying to hide, without benefit of industrial espionage). But damage comes when the truth, the whole truth, and nothing but the truth doesn't govern every aspect of the company's internal affairs.

The secret vice can spring from virtue. Enthusiasm is an essential component of the executive's survival kit. He has to believe in the product: if he doesn't, how can anyone else? But enthusiasm shades over easily into obtuseness. A top British shipyard executive once denigrated Japanese competition as that of "little yellow men with vacant minds," and his company objected violently to being told in public that the little, vacant yellow men built ships far faster and much cheaper than the British.

That same shipyard later on boasted that it would sign only profitable contracts, then promptly signed several that made losses in the millions. The excessive patriotism and the gross commercial error are two sides of the same coin. There is no ultimate escape from reality. The executive eventually must come to terms with his real blessings and curses. The longer he delays, and the further his fantasies drag him from the truth, the worse his danger.

The crash of John Bloom's Rolls Razor was a tale of self-deception on its usual journey to self-destruction. Bloom hit on two blinding truths—that the established washing machine manufacturers, led by Hoover, were keeping prices artificially high, and that selling door-to-door was a marvelous way of undermining the big boys at top speed. This great commercial notion swept all before it, swamping less savory truths, such as that Rolls Razor had virtually no management; and that the door-to-door method, paying greedy men great commissions to drive around ringing doorbells and backing them with heavy advertising, is nasty and (worse still) expensive.

Stock market enthusiasm for Rolls was fed by profit figures that were about as conservative as the Black Panthers. But Bloom, a multimillionaire of incredible youth, had concluded that he could sell anything, from Bulgarian holidays to rickety home movie kits. Bloom's management aura even inspired the most intelligent financial journalist in Britain to call the shares "a must for every portfolio." But behind the razzle and the dazzle, Bloom had just one thing: a precarious hold, becoming rapidly still more insecure, on the U.K. markets for nonautomatic washing machines.

Price competition from the majors was now intense as non-automatics were nearing saturation point: Bloom had no automatic to fill the hole, and the door-to-door suckers were also near exhaustion. Bloom neither admitted to reality, nor reacted to it. Instead, he stepped up advertising and give-aways in an inept bid to restore flagging sales. Each sale made a still greater guaranteed fat cash loss; and Rolls slithered off down to financial ruin.

The minor conglomerators have had to learn the same hard lesson. Their only talent was to stick together lucrative paper empires and personal fortunes by using fast, fancy, and modish financial glues. They couldn't manage anything or anybody (except Wall Street patsies), but they pretended otherwise. Even some major conglomerators managed to get seduced by their own myths. Jimmy Ling, who owed his apotheosis mainly to success with the military, had no aptitudes for most other businesses he shoved into Ling-Temco-Vought. All he knew was how to buy them (and sell them all over again to a doting public). Litton Industries, also basically a successful Pentagon contractor, kidded itself and everybody else that the corporate genius lay in civil high technology.

Just as Goebbels persuaded most of Germany, and the rest of the world, that Hitler's mugs and murderers were statesmen, so corporate publicity men, or external hired hacks, have often convinced the public (and the man himself) that a lucky wheeler-dealer is a superexecutive. The misrepresentation needn't be deliberate. Goebbels genuinely believed in Hitler and company, and this real faith made him a fearsome propagandist. Very likely, even Bernie Cornfeld sincerely believed in Bernie Cornfeld.

Self-deception flourishes in more respectable surroundings than the Sybaritic château of the IOS mob. The public relations directed from the Litton office in Beverly Hills (a former movie palazzo, furnished with low technology antiques) cost plenty, but it worked wonders. Of all postwar companies in the U.S., Litton was the most flattered and followed. Its emphasis on converting expensive space-age technology into commercial products summed up the ethos of the moon age; and its speciality of "systems" introduced a new and magical phrase into the salesman's sample bag.

Litton raised the pursuit of higher earnings per share, with the aid of heavy debt gearing, to an art form, starting off a nationwide chase that only ended with the 1969/70 market crash. Its stockholders got their dividends, not in cash, but in stock; its executives too got their kicks in stock options; the top two, Charles B. Thornton and Roy Ash, achieved their higher rewards in the rise of sensational paper fortunes. The whole Litton legend was built around the constant rise of the share price, though Ash said, predictably, in a 1968 interview, "It is not an essential or even an important part of our growth for the price of the stock to go on rising."

In fact, the bounden duty of the publicity machine was self-evidently to keep a high head of steam behind the stock price. Yet the truth, as opposed to the untruth, is that Litton as a company is very like an old-line mastodon such as General Electric. GE, like Litton, pioneered any number of new management concepts; its resources in high technology leave Litton lagging; and it too is heavily decentralized, with 50 divisions and 170 departments (observers see this as a weakness in GE, although it was hailed as a strength in Litton). This similarity extends even to normal measures of efficiency —except that GE comes out better. In 1970, Litton earned 2.9 percent on sales, GE 3.8 percent; and net return on stockholders' equity was respectively 8.9 percent and 12.3 percent.

The real difference between the companies is the behavior of the two stock prices. Litton was for long a glamour stock, GE mostly an off-color blue chip. In other words, because people believed in Litton's story, they made it believable. After all, isn't any company that increases its stockholders' wealth tenfold or twentyfold in a decade a marvel of management, technology, and diversification? It's not necessarily so. Litton's sheer growth in sales volume, half at least coming through acquisition, was formidable, but its profitability (the name of the real game) was never up to much.

Litton has gone on living its myth. Interviewed at the end of 1969, Ash said, "I regard what happened as a stumbling in the search for growth." The stumble lasted so long that it qualifies better as a crawl. In 1970, earnings after pooling of interest were only 20 percent higher than in 1964 (on doubled sales). Would Litton's management have operated any more successfully over this period if the myth had not been believed, internally and externally? If Ash and Thornton had not persuaded themselves (presumably) and the public (certainly) that there was some meaningful connection between building ships and making portable electric typewriters?

Since history can't be written backward, questions like this can never be answered. But when myths swell up in such huge bubbles, their eventual bursting makes a far louder bang. Even in 1971, with the Dow-Jones index pushing up to the magic 1,000, Litton shares dragged along the ocean floor, at only a quarter of their one-time glory. And yet in many respects—such as the quality of its managers and ex-managers (the so-called LIDOs, or Litton Industries Dropouts)—Litton was truly admirable. Its trap was pretending to be something it wasn't.

Inside every fat bubble there lurks a truth, sometimes even a big one. Bloom went straight through a real gap in the washing machine market; Cornfeld saw unerringly that nobody was using American sales methods to tap the oceans of non-American savings; John King of King Resources, another battered hulk, noted that an entirely new (and ignorant) class of investor could be lugged into oil exploration by mutual fund techniques. All these ideas (like the inertial guidance systems with which Litton first made its way in the world) were strong enough to make fortunes for anybody who exploited them with vigor, whether the men were corruptible or incorruptible, organizers or hucksters, captains of industry or con artists.

Because of a basic myth of management (that success equals skill), the public makes no distinctions. But as the wonder idea pays off the wonder boy's competitors—the big corporations who missed the beautiful force of his idea—run scared, act jealous, and retaliate. Their Cassandra-like carping, however, is always discounted by everybody, including the wonder boy. This is sheer folly. Hoover really does know the washing machine market down to the last spin of the drier; and once the company was over its humiliation and was competing effectively, what Hoover said about Rolls Razor and John Bloom—that he was taking a loss on every machine he sold—was dead right.

However, the hero is now so rich, so successful, and surrounded by so many flatterers, that he is convinced of his genius at management, as at everything else. He has a lovely growth record, a managerial myth, and money. Money has a magnetic attraction for other money; so the wonder man, bit firmly between his teeth, typically strays (just like Litton) into businesses of which he knows nothing, such as oil lands and banking (Cornfeld), or steel (Ling), or encyclopaedias (Maxwell). The new areas rapidly strip bare the wonder boy's shortcomings, organizational and personal, in short and horrible order.

Organization-man types will protest that they aren't a bit like Cornfeld, or Bloom, or Ling. Then they shouldn't behave like it. Don't deceive anybody, especially yourself. For a start, listen to what competitors say about you, your company, and your products: eight times out of ten it is more accurate, and, if used properly, more constructive (and much cheaper) than the findings of a management consultant. What you believe about your own products and performance, eight times out of ten, is untrue.

Second, never trade solely on a personal reputation: observe that entrepreneurial stayers who leave enduring empires are usually as close with their mouths as they are mean with their money. And never seek to manufacture a myth. Mythmaking can fuel a stock boom, making it much easier to raise money and buy up other businesses. But if the record of achievement is genuine, the stock price looks after itself, there are no cash problems, and acquisitions are optional. If the achievement is spurious or inflated, the stock price will collapse one day, the borrowed money will strangle the corporation in its inevitable downturn, and most of the buys, being compulsory, will be bad.

Third, never misrepresent the financial facts, internally or externally. If an old, old product is expensive to make, but looks cheap because there is no longer a depreciation charge, the management which keeps churning it out is being misled just as dangerously as the investor who thinks that a change in accounting methods produces a real gain in profits.

Fourth, act on the truth about products, services, and the caliber of colleagues. As a rough rule, if nobody tries to hire away a company's executives, they are not as good as they or their superiors think. A top executive who starts praising "the team" is usually concealing the fact that none of the players is of much value by himself. As for the product, it is not a world beater unless it is demonstrably beating the world. Moreover, every product and every service (like every management) could be improved, usually to a marked degree, and should be.

Fifth, never believe your own advertising (after all, nobody else does) or your own public relations (even if everybody else does). The public relations chief for a Swiss giant said firmly, "Our top officers would like to get their names in the paper, but I say no." He could be doing them a wonderful service.

Sixth, don't lie gratuitously. When asked, on leaving a secret conference with a company you want to buy, whether a merger is on, don't deny it with your hand on the Bible. When a new product line moves from losing £1 million to dropping £900,000, don't say it's nearing break-even. When you fire an executive for failure, or having his hot little hands in the till, don't say he is resigning for personal reasons or after a policy dispute—just don't say anything.

Finally, discover what the company is really good at, and remember that there are no such things as technological strength or management depth in themselves. If these claimed assets are not being applied to useful purposes, the company is good at nothing. And if the company really makes its money, not by any real merit, but by fooling the suckers, forget it. You *can* fool all of the people, but you can only do it for some of the time.

IV *Methods*

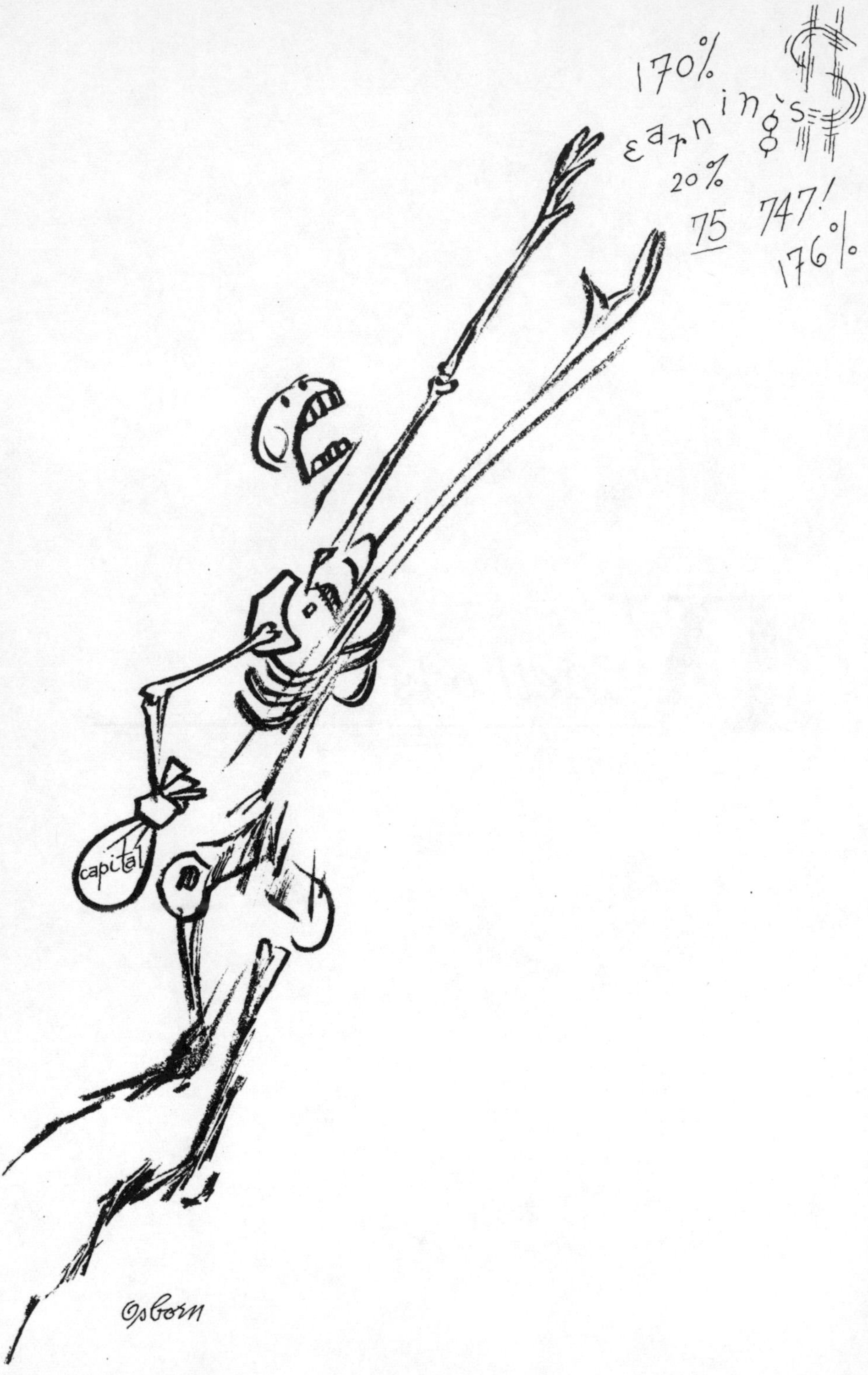
170%
earnings
20%
75 747!
176%
capital
Osborn

18 _Death in the Long Run_

IN THE 1960s big business found a new religion of planning that, with many subcults, culminated in the long-range corporate variety. This ultimate in techniques had to wait for its moment; earlier managers needed the long view, all right, but they lacked the computers, or the men to feed them. When a new breed of hardware and soft humans was born, corporations could at last cope. Before the computer, the task of gazing into the chasms of the future, and juggling with its endless permutations would have chained every manager to his slide rule for eternity. Thanks to the computer, companies can now do their sums—and get them wrong—in comfort.

The long-range corporate plan goes hand in glove with the compulsively reasonable subcult of management by objectives. Of course, directors should know what they are trying to achieve; of course, it's fair to judge them by how far they reach their own objectives. Provided that the aims are realistic, and the man isn't proposing to outsell Chevrolet with a three-wheel mini-car this wraps up in one neat parcel the messy problems of appraisal and direction.

The trouble starts with the misplaced hope that the formality of the dance—in which boss and subordinate go through a fixed waltz of setting mutual objectives, and then assessing performance together—gets rid of the dreaded interpersonal conflict. You no longer give your subordinate orders: he gives them to himself. You no longer have the painful task of whipping him for his failures: he flogs himself before you. And if this smacks somewhat of the confessional, so be it. The Catholic Church hasn't found the guilty conscience of the faithful to be a useless management tool. But if a manager hates his boss to distraction, he will hate him no less because they have worked together on his objectives. The second pious error is to hope that all management tasks can be turned into objectives, or that all objectives can be described precisely. The great entrepreneur, for instance, doesn't manage by objectives, but by instinct, and by riding his luck. He doesn't, above all, work on a system.

In the objectives system, the corporation's aims, or plans, are broken down into a hierarchy of lesser aims or plans; and the grand total of all those objectives adds up to those of the corporation. Then all the executives have to do is meet their planned and agreed objectives and—presto—the corporation does the same. Perfection in management, at last, has arrived, except that it hasn't and won't.

The last few years have seen errors of planning and missing of objectives on a macabre scale. Massive overordering of airline equipment had jumbo jets crossing the Atlantic more than half-empty; only the despairing support of their bankers kept the airlines aloft. Steel and chemicals have likewise veered between undercapacity and overcapacity the world over. In industry generally, plant after plant, computer after computer, has come in late and at grossly excessive cost.

Even the electricity industry in Britain and the U.S., whose only business is to balance supply and demand, has run short of generating capacity at critical times. Annual growth targets have been missed by so many miles that companies have wisely forgotten all about them. One U.S. conglomerate, which in 1967 had the sensible-seeming, fashionable objective of 15 percent annual growth in earnings per share, by mid-1971 needed a 170 percent jump in one year to get back on target. That's some objective.

None of this has disturbed the planning industry one whit. The long-range planners have been striving to establish themselves as a separate breed—technicians as essential to the corporate future as a competent accountant is to its present. Some American companies already have brilliant vice-presidents who spend half their year planning and the other half converting the plan into an action program for the next year. Which conveniently leaves them no time whatsoever for managing.

Since taking action is where painful mistakes may be made and jobs risked, merely thinking about what to do may be nicely to an executive's taste. Nobody is to blame for a plan that is falsified by events—for nobody can foretell the future, can they? After five or ten years nobody will even remember who drew up the original document. Like Lord Keynes and everybody else, the planner and the executive are both dead in the long run. The long run, however, is only a series of short runs added together—and this is vital, as the directors of John Thompson, Britain's biggest boiler company, should know. Self-described as an unrepentant planner, its former boss said, "The real benefits of reorganization will be tested in five to ten years' time." Within just two years, the company had run into a brick wall and disappeared by merger.

The first responsibility of the executive is to the here and now. If he makes a shambles of the present, there may be no future; and the real purpose of planning—the one whose neglect is common, but poisonous—is to safeguard and sustain the company in subsequent short-run periods. Every executive should go to bed happy that no omission of his will leave successors with no new products in the pipeline, with no cash

177

in the bank, and with an inadequate production plant crippled by crazy labor relations, as actually happened at BMC. This kind of planning is only intelligent anticipation extrapolating the trends of the business to determine probable needs for capital, cash, new plant, product replacement, and the rest, with a massive allowance for contingencies thrown in.

What goes wrong is that sensible anticipation gets converted into foolish numbers: and their validity always hinges on large, loose assumptions. After the first Suez crisis of 1956, the world oil industry, stacked to its eyebrows with planners, concluded that, without a major new pipeline across the Arab world, built at stupendous cost, Western Europe would run dry of oil. For the first and presumably last time in history, every oil company boss who mattered (and many who didn't) met, blessed by the U.S. trustbusters, at a London hotel. As soon as the moguls got back to their desks, they found that, because forecast growth in oil demand hadn't materialized in a single year, Western Europe was oozing with excess oil, a condition in which it has remained, with odd interruptions, ever since.

The British fertilizer company, Fison's, plunged into ambitious corporate planning. It ended up with huge overcapacity and tiny profits. Its basic figures for the growth of the British gross national product were rashly taken straight from the Labour Government's National Plan, whose figures were not forecasts, but targets (missed abjectly, at that). This confusion appears in most planning. An exercise that starts in simple prudence—ensuring that you have the resources you need —becomes another gung-ho device for achieving superlatives of growth and profitability. Executives take their eyes off what is going to happen and think about what they are going to *make* happen—they manage, in other words, by objectives.

In the long-range passion, they even ignore real short-run happenings. Commonly executives start playing with their "rolling five-year plans" in the spring of the preceding year. At that point, they can only guess the outcome of the current twelve months. Anything from cocoa blight in the Congo to a strike in Wichita or Upper Tooting may be about to hit them;

yet they plunge into documents of immense volume and tiny detail. The translation-into-numbers defect smartly takes over. Once the basic assumptions are made—just as the corporate objectives can be split into atomized individual aims—the entire future of the business can be sliced up, right down to the usage and price of raw rubber in four years' time, or the sales margin on light bulbs in three.

This is tricky enough when executives are simply trying to predict. Better to heed the experience of the Beecham drugs to foods group. "We found a five-year forecast was pie-in-the-sky and it tended to encourage excessive expenditure. The forecasts were nearly always way out because one cannot legislate for failure." When executives are attempting to achieve, as well as forecast, the corporation has a potential tiger by the tail. Since the mercy of God is infinite, however, there is a self-correcting device. The executive soon catches on to the notion that, if he is being held to a plan or objective, the plan had better be one he can meet.

The Russians, though they lag behind Western management technology in every other respect, have pioneered in this subtle art. The only yardstick of a Soviet executive's performance is whether or not he makes his plan. So, not being a complete idiot, he spends most of his ingenuity on getting an easy plan. One Communist executive whose screw factory's output plan was set by weight, switched, clever lad, to making heavier screws. When the boss of a plan-happy American corporation such as Honeywell says, "The numbers are getting better all the time," he cannot know whether the executives are improving as planners or as timeservers, Soviet-style. (Honeywell's own plans, anyway, can't have envisaged the merger with GE's computer side, which threw everything back into the melting-pot—making Honeywell fight for its hard-won computer happiness all over again.)

Locking executives into detailed plans and objectives, self-fulfilling or not, has a saving grace. At least, the executive is made to think about what he supposes himself to be doing and what the consequences will be. Companies part at the seams, not because executives don't plan, but because they don't think. Planning and management by objectives has its point as a device for compelling thought, so long as executives don't forget that any plan worth making is inaccurate; the longer a plan takes to write, the worse it is—just because of its consumption of time; and the more they change plans to suit events, the better they will manage—if you've made a mistake, you had better admit it.

Even businesses into which the long-range planners have not burrowed need these three lessons; even in such firms, unless they are stuck fast in prehistory, annual budgeting (really a one-year corporate plan) and capital spending approval (the crunch part of any planning activity) are bound to crop up. Even annual budgets are a postwar fashion, at least in Britain, where many companies still have no controls on costs and none on revenues, and where quite large firms still strike the profit at the year-end. The surprises are only occasionally pleasant, just as capital spending plans do sometimes pay off according to schedule.

This isn't for lack of sophistication. Investment appraisal is now advanced enough to generate worthy tomes on discounted cash flow, net present value, and internal rates of return. All of these sets of numbers rest on anticipations of the future that are so dubious that the use of the technique, according to some statisticians, is little more effective than picking projects with a pin. This won't worry most executives —for expansion projects are all but unstoppable. Boards of directors are always claiming that performance will be "greatly" (or "significantly" or "substantially") improved when the new wonder factory starts producing, in March, or August, or whenever. In case after case, it doesn't produce then. When it does, for month after month all that pours out is trouble and loss. The only thing that doesn't emerge is the promised rate of return.

If the board sets 20 percent or 25 percent as the minimum return on investment, the managers cook the futuristic figures to fit the target. Every company has beloved projects on which if prices had held up, if the contractors had finished on time (or finished at all), if the plans hadn't been altered, if the

thing had actually worked, the planned return would have been earned. But since some or all of these calamities usually happen, any manager who neglects to allow for them is not planning—merely thinking wishfully. Desire for the project has, as usual, overtaken desire for profit.

Letting the wish be father to the accomplishment is only one route to a false objective. Another is to start from a false premise—say, that the company really can achieve some dazzling growth rate or return on capital. Like setting a subordinate a "stretching" objective (i.e., one he can't reach), this guarantees failure. Managements regularly survive many years of missing announced targets without much damage, even to their self-esteem.

The whole game of picking on arbitrary figures and then working back is defective. Take 15 percent annual compound growth in earnings per share; and forget, for the moment, that since earnings per share is a very funny number, it can be manipulated to produce "growth" from the wild blue yonder. Even if the 15 percent is translated into real, honest growth, what grounds are there for expecting this jacket to fit the corporation? And if it doesn't, what then?

The saner executive would surely plan and develop each component business according to its potential and settle for whatever group growth turns up. Then, so long as the business can coin the requisite money, growth will look after itself. If only it were so easy. That's the du Pont way, and the net result is that ICI, from its bogged-down base in the British economy, drove past du Pont for the heavyweight lead in the world chemical stakes. Du Pont has reaped no harvest in profit terms, either: net earnings in 1961–70 rose by only 20.5 percent, which compares (almost unbelievably) with 176 percent for sleepy old ICI.

How executives plan or what numbers they choose doesn't count: what does is the standard of performance they are ready to exact. The essence of any objective is that reaching it should be reasonable. The precondition is that you expect it to be met. But corporations settle on plans and targets with little idea of how to react if the objectives are missed. If the whole company undershoots its targets by the width of the Atlantic Ocean, the directors are unlikely to take the extreme step of firing each other. This weakens their position when it comes to firing others for the same offense—which consequently rarely happens, except in time of earthquake, when the system has already (and long since) broken down.

Every executive has one double objective, to do the most possible with the least possible. Don't concentrate on the first —the earnings—to the exclusion of the second—the capital. An executive who is being tyrannized by his boss into raising return on capital from 10 percent to 15 percent grows ulcers trying to lift profits by half. He can get the same effect by reducing capital employed by one third. Don't start from statistical objectives and work backward. Begin from the premise that whatever the company is doing could be done better, and start moving forward by making the improvements that are always waiting to be grabbed.

All companies use more capital than they need. Like the Pentagon or the army, they hoard stocks that are too hefty and slackly controlled; they let unnecessary fixed assets pile up; their forgetfulness about cash flow leads to regular and

182

excessive borrowing; they tie still more money up in businesses that never have produced a worthwhile return, never could, and never will. Anyway, all capital generates costs, so cutting out capital must eventually cut expenses. Other things being equal, the capital cutter will improve profitability simultaneously on both sides of the hallowed ratio of return on capital employed.

The process, while as near as anything in business management to ranking as a golden rule, is less thrilling than planning a five-year future. The future, however, is pure uncertainty, limited only by the constraints of possibility. The manager must understand those constraints, and he can limit that uncertainty by thoughtful anticipation. But, above all, if you want to master the future, you have to find out what is really and truly happening right now—and to make sure that it is happening right.

6.

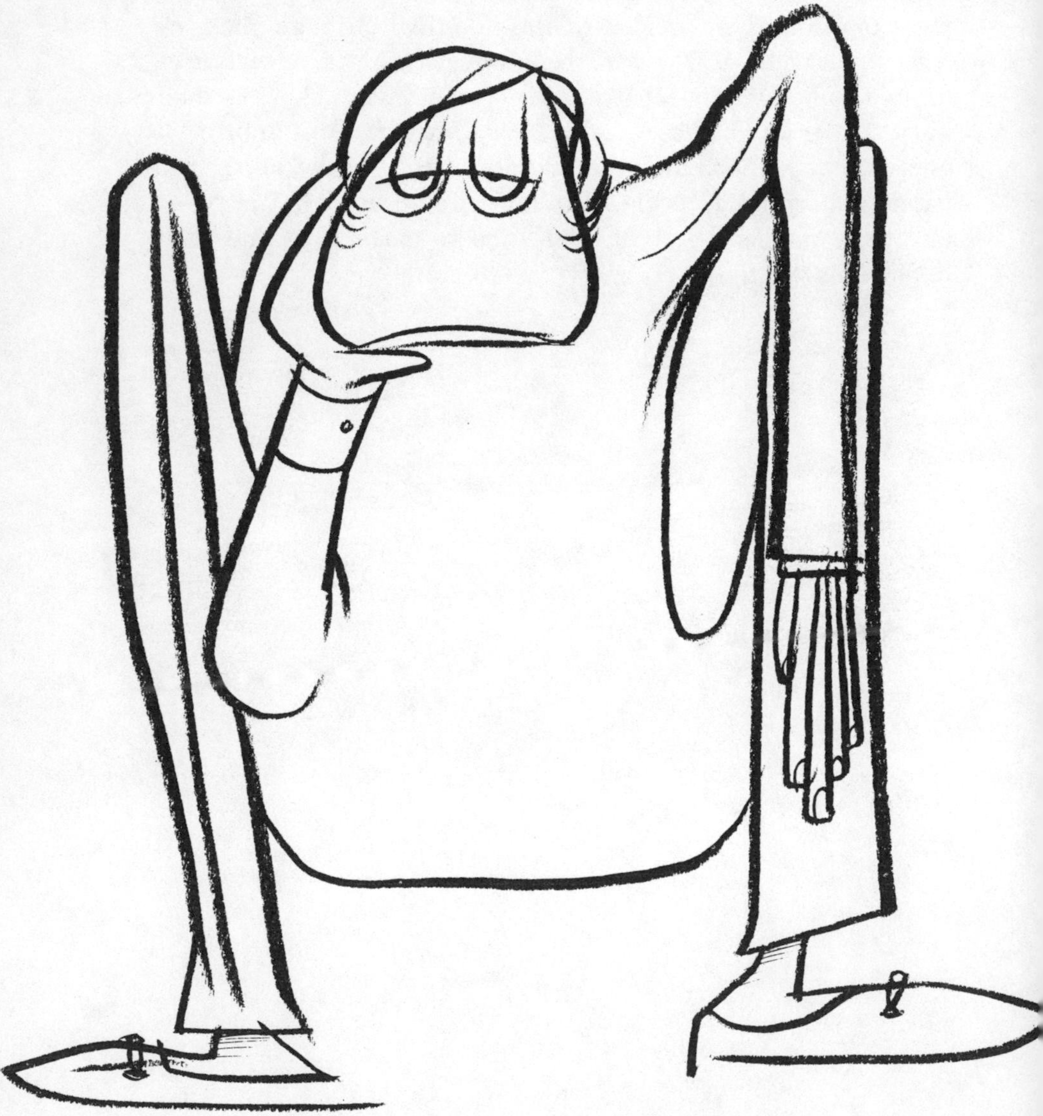

19 _Please Motivate Me, Someone_

THE MOST emotive word in today's management vocabulary is motivation. Those four syllables motivate boards of directors so powerfully that they shell out £200 a day or more to have Saul Gellerman, or some other high priest, elucidate the mysteries of motives. And Gellerman doesn't even claim to be the original hot gospeller: the original is Frederick Herzberg, an academic consultant, who (as a founding thinker) is reputed to pull in £1,000 a day from some corporate admirers.

Motivation—like all spiritualism—contains its fair share of truths, or rather truisms. Its blue chip acolytes basically get an insight that they could obtain as easily (and much more cheaply) from peering into their own interiors: that money is only one of the forces that motivates people to work effectively. This truism burst upon United States and British companies like a blinding light because of their deep yearning for a universal key to unlock their everlasting problems. The "behavioral scientist" offers a kind of philosopher's stone, an explanation and solution rolled into one, with which to attack the irritating refusal of men to act in the best interests of the corporation.

The mid-twentieth century executive feels his pains more than any predecessor. He is also more convinced, after being inundated by a Niagara of business theory, that cures exist for any corporate condition. Man, he believes, is a perfectible animal. So, if the management is not developing marvels of entrepreneurial initiative, drive, and speed, or if the workers, instead of churning out untold productivity, are militant, grudging, and alienated, the solution is plain. They all want (because all normal men do) to achieve: they are just not properly motivated. Press the right motivating buttons, and the machine—at last—will whir off into beautiful action.

Even the language of business has begun to change. Companies don't "employ" executives anymore. In the now standard phrase, you "attract, retain, and motivate" them. In this Holy Trinity, motivation must loom largest: it's no use having a splendidly attracted and retained executive who won't work. The behaviorists can show, which is easy, that management's approach to employees has been misguided and muddleheaded for decades. Better still, they can apparently show— "scientifically" too—how to get elevated results by amending the approach.

But anybody with elementary human insight knows that the question What are your motives? is embarrassingly subjective. The answer varies wildly from person to person and day to day, and men lie about their motives, even to themselves. In the days when British scientific brains were draining across the Atlantic in flood proportions (just in time for the great aerospace and computer recessions), the deserters never admitted that doubling or trebling or even quadrupling their living standards was a prime reason for going West. No, the confessed lure was always the wider scope, the richer research and development budgets, the more lavish scientific equipment.

Those disinterested scientists who would have emigrated to the U.S. for unchanged standards of living could have been comfortably hijacked in one small executive jet. But Western society considers it shameful to admit doing anything (even something perfectly respectable) just for the loot. How often does a multimillionaire allow that making still more millions is his dearest hobby and most pressing motive? That he simply loves to roll around in the green stuff? On the contrary, the money, he will say, is just "figures on a piece of paper." The man clings to those pieces of paper like a starving octopus.

Self-made tycoons are highly acquisitive and retentive: the proprietor with millions in the bank gets wild over wasted paper clips or secretaries paying for cabs with his cash; the professional executive, with little more to his name than a big mortgage, never minds at all. Greed is a great motivator, in all its forms, and you can't disentangle greed, for money or anything else, from nonfinancial motives of equal force, such as ambition.

The boy who sets out to be president of the United States is motivated by personal ambition, desire to better mankind, lust for power, and other drives. He also ends up rich, with a fine white pad on Pennsylvania Avenue, an army of servants (and a real army too), two private 707s, a fleet of cars, a high salary, and after these delicacies are removed (by the voters or the end of his second term), a huge pension and rich sales of his ghosted memoirs. The corporate man who wants to achieve is a bundle of powerful motives, which include desire for the personal benefits, in wealth, prestige, and their companions, that await those who reach the top. But that man's motives are of little interest or relevance. Motivating an ambitious, able executive isn't the problem: the difficulty is to retain him. The real agony of the corporation is motivating the vast majority—people who don't have any particular wish to achieve.

The large corporation is structured more for timeservers

than as a springboard for the ambitious. Big companies adore to offer a lifetime career to those they hire, still moist behind the ears, straight from the universities. Lifetime hiring means a steady progression on grounds of years alone from one rung on the ladder to another. The ladders would all come tumbling down if the corporation became a gymnasium for the ambitious, all vaulting over their seniors in a mad dash for the top.

If a company opts for a board of go-getting, high fliers under forty, what age will the next tier of management be? If that is thirty-five (allowing five years before they high-fly onto the board), the next rung down will be thirty. What does the great and good company do with everybody over forty? Shoot them? And what about the forty-year-old whiz-kid directors when they in turn reach the rotten old age of forty-five? The big organization needs its medium fliers and even its earthworms: it needs them so that the relatively few high fliers can have somebody else to manage.

But there's bound to be a leakage; some of these low-voltage managers will seep through into the highest levels of the company. Arrived at the top, panting and unprepared, they seek more motivation for the company, when they really need it for themselves—and the man who has to ask for motivation is not the most suitable case for treatment. Every force in the organization presses him into the conservative mold that his own temperament prefers. This long-service, low-volatility element dominates most large corporations: at General Motors, the chairman and president of 1970, James Roche and Edward Cole, had soldiered on for eight decades of service between them. The photographs of GM's Praetorian guard of vice-presidents are captioned, like a citation, by their long years of loyal service. At du Pont, in 1971, only one executive director had come in from outside—and he was hired as a lawyer twenty years back.

In this pattern of organization, mere survival and the submerging of personal ambition into the corporate ethos set up the motivational norms. Managers such as Roche and Cole at least have their public exposure and awesome responsibilities to stimulate them. But how does anybody motivate the equally long-toothed managers who lie secure lower down in GM's bosom? As the behavioral scientists have said, money alone won't do it, partly because these men earn too much, too easily, anyway. But nothing else will ever change them into human dynamos; dynamism isn't in their character, or in the corporation's prescription for their behavior. If a man is disinterested in money, he can't be made to be interested. If a man is unambitious, he can't have ambition thrust upon him.

The corollary is that, the more highly motivated a man is, the easier he is to motivate. If he loves money, he will try twice as hard to get twice as much. One danger of the motivational movement, however, is that the cardinal motivating importance of loot can get mislaid. James Thurber tells how Harold Ross, his great editor at the *New Yorker*, tried in vain to hire the old *Herald Tribune*'s star writer. Finally a new managing editor snagged the prize by offering the man three times his *Tribune* salary. "You're a genius," said Ross, "I never thought of offering him money."

Every man may not have his price. But corporations customarily pay the price irrespective of what, in performance terms, they are buying. If an executive is paid adequately for being adequate and loses nothing by being inadequate, money has very little chance to show its power. Don't think that material bribery will get you nowhere. Rather, unless the bribery is skillfully calculated, or the bribee (like some IBM salesman) is highly bribable, it won't get you far enough.

Herzberg ("I am an achievement bug. I think the most rewarding thing is achievement.") distinguishes between the "hygiene factors"—a curious phrase, which suggests brushing the managerial teeth—of the environment, such as pay, and other factors to do with the content of the job itself. The latter, according to Herzberg, are the motivators: achievement, responsibility, recognition, advancement, the nature of the work. But what if the manager's idea of achievement is to earn $100,000 a year by the age of forty? What if the recogni-

tion he seeks is a fat pay increase, a lavish stock option, or a more profoundly carpeted office? One man's hygiene is another man's motivation.

The motivation prophets also preach, "You don't hire a thumb, you hire the whole man." But you can't activate one motivating factor, you hire the whole lot. You can only motivate the entire man, which means the whole complex of his personal drives. Equally, you cannot motivate him beyond the potential of the organization. Put a rapacious, ruthless egotist into GM—the kind of man who becomes a millionaire by thirty—and the organization will squeeze him out before he is twenty-five.

The key to motivation is not only the man, but the company. Place an executive in a well-found company with whose objectives and style he can identify, and whose growth and drive create personal opportunities and challenge, and where the executive feels secure, appreciated, properly rewarded, and constantly under fair test: there you have the conditions for marvelous motivation.

190

The number of corporations fitting this definition is small, partly because the two elements are in continuous conflict: security and appreciation in one corner, contradicted by challenge and testing in the other. Most top managements concentrate on providing the first couplet rather than the second; they have their own security and comfort at heart and they hate the psychological traumas of demanding good performance.

The typical executive, myths to the contrary, hates firing, does it rarely, and usually after long and pointless delay. He can't face the terminal interview, even though most candidates for firing know they deserve it, feel guilty in consequence, and can only have their guilt expiated (to their enormous relief) by being fired. If companies don't fire when firing is essential, they do injustice to their other employees. They also lose a motivator almost as powerful as money: the stick, as opposed to the carrot.

Apart from firing, a company has very few canes in the cupboard. Cutting a man's pay or demoting him is tantamount to firing; he may quit and he is unlikely to be an effective servant of the great company after the act. The corporation is like a dictator who has only one legal penalty to control the rabble—sudden death—the difference being that most dictators are less namby-pamby than directors when it comes to capital punishment.

Hire-and-fire companies, in contrast, are run by neo-Nazis, not by namby-pambies; and their malevolent dictatorship usually has to be balanced by high pay. Too much benevolence and too little money are the worst motivational combination; but malevolence and too much money can work wonders. One company boss surrounded himself with well-paid weaklings who periodically had to be fired for their weakness. Over a long-drawn-out dismissal, the boss would sadistically strip the victim of his last vestiges of self-respect. Rebuking a man violently and cruelly in front of others never fails to demolish the current target and soften up later candidates. Finally, the victim would yearn for dismissal as a condemned man longs for the scaffold. The irony for humanitarians is

191

that investors in this company have multiplied their fortunes tenfold over the last decade.

As a rule, and for a time, hire-and-fire companies have disagreeably good growth and profit records. At first sight, this seems to prove that the stick can motivate more magically than the carrot; and it is true that, used alternately, the two produce a positively Pavlovian response to stimulus. The chief demon of one growth company, for instance, found this technique highly effective: he would wait at some highly paid subordinate's desk and go through the latter's papers; the sight of the dreaded boss metaphorically laying bare the executive's soul was correctly calculated to produce a quivering, malleable subordinate.

Even Saul Gellerman has called the carrot and the stick "the oldest management theory in existence," adding ruefully that "the rationale of the carrot and the stick is not altogether unrealistic . . . some people are motivated by the lure of wealth or the fear of being fired all of the time and all people probably are so motivated at least some of the time." But don't conclude from this that the neo-Nazi corporation has an advantage. That's the same mistake made by prewar commentators who ludicrously thought dictatorships were more efficient than democracies, because Mussolini made the trains run on time. Hire-and-fire companies grow, not because of their addiction to carrot-and-stick management, but in spite of it.

The carrot guarantees that they attract mobile, hungry managers; the stick, however, also produces a large quota of murderees, born victims who lust to be whipped by those to whom they act as yes-men. The sadism of the corporate führer eventually motivates his better managers to leave, as soon as they can match his pay in some more benevolent climate. And the sadism doesn't generate the growth; that's done by the sheer personal drive. Part of the drive is expressed in the autocrat's despicable personal behavior, but the two are not inseparable. Both the man and the company would be better off, if possible, to keep the drive and lose the whip.

192

The most you can say for carrot and stick is that a good executive heading into this variety of company has the self-confidence to accept risk, welcome insecurity, and be judged on his results. The standard corporation operates on a different philosophy: carrot and comfort. The executive who makes it to the top makes it financially and in every other way; the executive who misses still has few material complaints—except that, if his last two working decades coincide with a periodic spring-cleaning or national recession, he may be gently (but still shatteringly) put out to grass.

The issue always comes back to the motivation of the firm. How individuals respond to treatment depends above all on the behavior that is the organizational norm. Where the bland are leading the bland, all the behavioral scientists in the American universities will not improve performance. However, those scientists have obtained impressive-seeming results below the managerial line, by allowing workers to plan their own operating schedules or salesmen to organize their own selling. They should try persuading a few more corporations to allow their executives actually to execute; then the behavioral geniuses will really earn their fabulous fees, though it shouldn't require a posse of expensive professors to teach chief executives how to suck that particular egg.

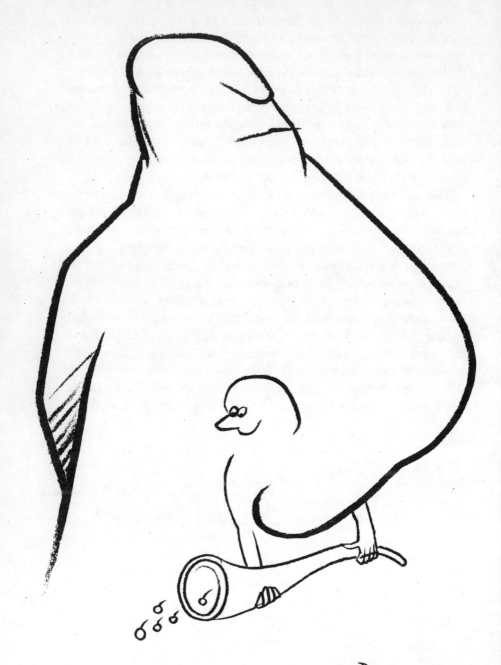

20 A Business Like One's Own

THE IDEA OF the profit center, of slicing a business into the maximum number of accountable components, has taken its time to work through. In 1971, it was just penetrating the nether regions of du Pont, the first bastion of American capitalism and of decentralization. Many large companies have missed the message entirely. In a way, the benighted can't be blamed, because many (perhaps most) profit centers don't make any profits, and they aren't centers. But the device satisfies a great managerial yearning to imagine that every cell of the corporate body is a business like one's own.

Top executives in profit center companies brag that they want every junior to run his center as if that were truly so. It's an answer to corporate flatulence, a medicine to revive the flow of entrepreneurial blood in stiffening arteries, a means of ideal progression for the executive—earning his spurs in

195

his very first little profit center, moving on from center to center until he arrives at that big profit center in the sky, the chief executive's suite. This ideal hankers back to the golden past when the business was small enough for one man to run and the founder in his buggy could supervise his first clutch of salesmen from the end of the road. The profit center, with its one man and his show, is a spiritual snub to corporate bureaucracy.

But the profit center is no more a manager's own business than a self-drive car belongs to the customer. Like Hertz or Avis, the company leases out a piece of its property; but it retains full possession, and it exacts a heavy toll. The center can't be run like one's own business because the real owners (not the de jure ones, the stockholders, but the de facto ones, the managerial Mafia) don't want it run that way, whatever their brags.

The small businessman must answer only to himself, his family, his conscience, his professional advisers, and his tax collector. Nobody makes him submit an annual budget, plus his plans for the next five years, for scrutiny and approval. Nobody tells him how much he can take out of the business or put in. Nobody vetoes his bright new ideas or his choice of staff or his business proposals. But the powers kept by top management include all this—and more.

In any event, the profit center can be so arbitrary a creation that it isn't a business at all. In chemical companies this little fact is at its nastiest. Much of the work in chemical companies is for a sole customer—the company itself. Profit Center A sells all its output to Profit Center B, which sells all its output to Profit Center C, which finally off-loads the stuff on the public. At this stage, the company at last makes a profit.

The game is played to well-known rules such as, Never make anything inside that you can buy cheaper outside. Philips Lamp of Eindhoven plays the game more than most, since it has diversified into almost every component under its sun. But what happens if Philips satellite A, buying component X from satellite B, finds that Xs are a drug on the outside market and selling for peanuts? Will B give up its Philips business?

Not on your life: it will cut its internal "transfer" price down to the outside level, and the stockholders will be left with yet another unprofitable chunk of turnover (earnings per share at Philips fell by 22 percent between 1961 and 1970).

Any striking of profits down the line is merely an imaginative hobby, at which corporation executives pass many an idle hour, day, and week. What's more, A, B, and C are all lumbered with charges for central overhead—basically the costs of the head office, over which they have not an atom of control. So even their accounts bear very little relation to those of an independent company, especially since A and B largely depend for their sales growth and investment projects on how those bastards in C make out in the market.

The consumer markets see the most contorted attempt to slice up the corporate cornucopia—the concept of the brand executive. His "business like his own" is a brand, and the lucky man (normally young) is responsible, in theory, for everything from its packaging and pricing to its advertising and distribution. If the brand is a proud and treasured heirloom, however, the company will tie the brand executive to its apron strings so tightly that he can hardly breathe.

The only brand executives allowed real freedom are those with products on which the corporation has given up; and then, if the bright young man puts real management muscle behind his baby, he comes up against the sound barrier—the corporation won't provide any more spending money. It's all earmarked for Duz, or Maxwell House, or some other boring product without which the whole corporation would cease to be a center of profit.

The total profit center (the corporation) won't genuinely atomize itself, for mechanical and emotional reasons. This hard fact matters most to those who share the ideal of the small business. The theory is that the large business breeds inefficiencies out of its size (true), and that small businesses are therefore more efficient (false). Most small businesses are just as incompetent—that's why they stay small, and why so many go bankrupt, passing unnoticed and unwept over to the other side. Every now and again the true course of events in a small business gets known outside, and the picture can be quite fantastic.

There was one modest-sized, fast-growing company whose boss demanded only one management accounting statistic— weekly turnover. So long as turnover was rising, this happy entrepreneur was tickled pink. After all, he knew his percentage profit, didn't he? He didn't: in any case, the turnover figure was inflated by double-counting whenever (as it largely did) the sales division sold to the hire side. The company duly descended into bankruptcy, turnover figures still bounding upward, as the result of infantile errors that any competent accountant, if allowed, could have eliminated in an afternoon.

Small firms are always publicized as the backbone of the economy, especially in the United States, where the image of the little entrepreneur is as strong as that of the pioneer frontiersman. But neither, in point of fact, made the United States economy what it is today. The small firms dominate only numerically. In qualitative and quantitative terms the clumsy mammoths lead. Without them, America and Britain would still be stuck at the Spanish level of economic progress.

The record of one small British textile company is representative of the way that little firms merely cling to life like limpets on a rock. After fifty years it was earning less profit and making fewer sales, in real terms; its investment in new plant had been negligible; what there was had been wasted; and much of the energy of its management had evaporated in internecine disputes that made boardroom politics seem like cosy parlor games.

No big corporation would want any segment of the business managed as a small company really runs; and it is stupid to moon over a nonexistent ideal. The profit center cannot work as a way to make managers think like individual businessmen. It is only another good, vain try at resolving the conflict between the corporation as a decision-making entity (i.e., head office) and the corporation as a business (i.e., the sharp end, the places where the money is made).

As H. G. Lazell, now chairman of Beecham Inc., and president of the British parent, once said, "That's the struggle all the time, the battle between head office and division, the battle for power." The profit center is a fiction to give the divisions the idea that they are winning the struggle. But the divisions know the real score; and they resent the millions that (as they think) they shell out for central expertise, control, and direction, which in divisional eyes seem more like expense and interference.

This is why ICI executives jest about the Millbank headquarters in London as "Millstone House," or why an aggressive divisional boss in Unilever says about central charges, "You have to pay your club subscription . . . but there are few operating skills of our sort sitting in the middle." There does, in fact, seem to be an uncanny correlation between the size of the head office and the ineffectiveness of the company.

A large company's stock price often nosedives when it moves to spanking new offices in town. Vickers, which put up London's most ambitious office skyscraper, and whose stock promptly halved between 1959 and 1965, is one awful example. Union Carbide's 1958 collapse was even more immediate; the Park Avenue skyscraper had to stand in suspended animation until earnings picked up again. Both Shell and BP ran into profit constipation and organizational purges after they moved houses; and there is clear managerial logic involved.

Overhead always shoots up, because the new building invariably costs much more, and it's temptingly easier to add more central staff, more central departments, and hence still more central cost. So it was a good omen for the Vickers stockholders (and divisional managers) as occupancy of the tower shrank from the original thirteen floors to a mere half-dozen. It was a bad sign for the owners of the British steel industry (the Labour government) when their newly nationalized British Steel Corporation moved next door to Buckingham Palace. The same offices had housed one of the most notorious cost centers in Britain, headquarters of the defunct AEI (its 800 central employees compared with 160 in its purchaser, the three times larger GEC). The U.K. steel industry promptly lost some £140 million in four and a half years.

None of these moves and expenses are undertaken at the request of the profit center. The head office, the cost center par excellence, imposes its levies whether the divisions like it or not. And the levy is never light. In modern times only a brilliant giant has pretax profit margins of 10 percent; so incurring £1 million of extra central costs, in effect, cancels out at least £10 million, very possibly £20 million of profitable turnover. Yet the onus is never on the head office to prove itself; the onus is always on the divisions and that onus is to pay on demand.

The profit center practice finally breaks down here. Executives shouldn't be held to account for expenditure that they can't control. They can never run their bit as if the business were their own, because it isn't. The recipe, however, is to let them run it as if the *money* were their own. The money isn't theirs either, and don't let them forget it, but it can be made to look that way. Start off by imposing no central charges except for specific services (such as market or product research), which can be charged for specifically. After all, the head office ultimately collects all the loot, anyway, and it can afford to pay its own expenses.

The counterargument is that excluding the central overhead gives a false view of divisional profitability; but so may the arbitrary allocation of that load around the joint. The most remarkable operation of this kind is at du Pont in Wilmington. There the theoretically decentralized divisions share the same monumental offices as the headquarters. Elaborate apportionments of the central costs have to be made continuously, as if the divisions were headquartered in distant places like Nome, Alaska.

Du Pont, moreover, acts on the typical big company principle. Because a division is making a bundle of money, it doesn't mean that it can spend a lot. It follows, of course, that even though a division is making no money at all, it may be authorized to invest like wildfire. In logic, a high earner should cash in on its luck; an unprofitable unit should suffer the pressures of its own misfortunes. The notion of running a business as if the money were your own demands no less.

What hurts with your own money is not the earning of it but the spending. Profit centers are strictly speaking cost centers, and it's costs that executives should agonize over. But in real life the detailed head office control is over one kind of spending only—investment. A divisional director must line up, cap in hand, to get permission for a £100,000 extension while, out in the sticks, a factory supervisor is incurring extra current costs of exactly the same amount, without the head office even knowing.

That problem is supposed to be dealt with by the budget. But nobody can accurately predict all costs for a year ahead. Targets too are seldom set in cost terms, and managers are not assessed on their cost-cutting ability; witness the sluggish acceptance of value engineering, which expresses the devastatingly true idea that no product is ever designed for manufacture in the most economic way possible.

Executives are natural spendthrifts with other people's money. One great company chairman excused his company's total lack of control over a trade investment—this "profit center" had to be saved from dire losses and bankruptcy—because the pounds involved were only a few million, compared with, say, £300 million for sales of a major division. This is a man who would be hurt by a personal expenditure of a few hundred. If he had been taught to think of the company's money in the same way as his own, that few million might never have been lost. The relative amounts are irrelevant—it is all money, and other people's too.

When the big corporation director starts to think of millions only as numbers, the termites are in. The head office's prime duty is to remind executives that money is real, which naturally means that the head office must take the same unpalatable view. In fact, directors do customarily treat the corporation's money as if it were their own—but not in the proper sense. They spend as if in recent receipt of a rich uncle's legacy.

Few firms reach the opulence of one British company that kept three kitchens for the directors, each offering a different national cuisine; owned a grouse moor; provided two houses for the chairman; and hired private trains for the board's annual pilgrimage to its Midlands factories. But few companies follow the austere standards of one chief executive who bars all fringe benefits and all padding of expense accounts, even with tiny sums. (He somewhat spoils the picture by refusing to work for a company that won't provide a decent car—meaning Rolls-Royce all round.)

How the director in the profit, cost, or loss center down the line behaves is a function of how the executives at the top behave and of what they expect from others. They should start from a known truth: that head office is an unnecessary evil unless proved otherwise. They should confine headquarters functions to those central areas that are central by definition (patents, law, finance, and the like). The executive directors, kept as small a band as possible, shouldn't attempt to duplicate in any way the operating functions in the divisions. They shouldn't spend their time second- or third-guessing the operating directors to no good effect, or waste money providing services that the divisions either don't need or can perfectly well, and much more cheaply, supply for themselves.

And the head office shouldn't become a luxurious, free men's club for the chosen few, nor should expense accounts be high-class pocket money. Nor should the inhabitants pretend that central expenses are low because only a few people work in the West End pad or Manhattan glass mansion. Many a company has a tight headquarters only because all the central staff are stacked up around the main factory site. But that is where staff should be wherever possible—not in the company's Taj Mahal, but close to where it's all happening, close to the factory, or to the market, or to both.

In this recipe, the head office functions as banker (you can't leave cash lying around all over the corporation) and almost as an independent investment trust whose business is owning operations, taking in dividends, and reinvesting the money. But this banker has the unique advantage of being able to demand performance from the executives running its investment. If the profit center concept really meant anything, this would be the only role reserved to the head office. By minding their own business, the management Mafia would in truth be able to run the company as if it were their own. But they want passionately and insistently to manage, and to manage the wrong things. Consequently, the executives under their authority feel that nothing is their own and they manage just as you would expect.

21 *I'm Selling the Future*

AN ENGLISH tycoon, famed as an emperor of automation, hated to be told that he made and marketed hardware. He would retort with heat, "I'm selling the future." His firm later became more and more unprofitable until it was sold (at too high a price) to an even larger and equally troubled seller of futures, which duly disappeared in exactly the same way. Those who sell the future, like those who buy it, face a heavy risk of being sold a pup. No law, economic or moral, holds that all technological advance must provide rewards. In many industries, technology not only advances slowly, but its significant moves exploit innovations that are scientific ancient history.

The larger the advance, the greater the chance that the executives will end in the most uncomfortable, exposed, and expensive posture of all: sitting well ahead of the market.

The postwar history of the aircraft industry should disabuse executives who believe that if you look after the future, the future will look after you. The jet engine saw action in the last war. Large pure-jet bombers were flying in the late 1940s, but Boeing's 707, itself a development of a military tanker, made its first flight in 1954. Yet to win orders, Boeing felt it had to price the plane to the bone. When the wide-fuselaged jumbo (embodying even less significant technological advances) flew along, this sad history was repeated, with much the same financial results.

The aerospace industry's troubles stem partly from the conviction of its executives that, like Everest, the next technical peak must be scaled, because it is there. The aerospace managements love their technology more than their money. That being so, nobody (including their financial backers) should be surprised when technological effort ends in financial failure. What's more, disaster strikes even though the companies are largely spared the bugbear expense of research and development. Fantastic largess has been invested in this group by governments, especially by the U.S. government, all because of their importance to national defense and technical prestige.

Europeans commonly cite the American figures with anxious awe as the most unfair disadvantage under which European competitors labor. But the so-called spin-off from military work is small both in absolute terms and in relation to the total U.S. federal spending on research. The military is a highly specialized customer; and, in any case, executives are incompetent at transferring technology from one market to another, even within the same company.

The men making missiles and lunar modules are not interested in machine tools or refrigerators, even if the advanced technology is cheap enough to be of any use (which it isn't). Rockwell, big maker of automotive components, had the hilarious notion when it bought North American that the latter's aerospace know-how would help Rockwell itself. Al Rockwell later sadly admitted, "We did overanticipate that there were some products at North American that we could tool up and take off the shelf and manufacture."

The most advanced technology is often worse than expensive—it may not even work. The record of electronics in weapons systems supplied to the Pentagon, with six out of eleven major systems begun during the 1960s achieving 25 percent or less than specification and only two coming up to snuff, does not inspire faith in applying defense goodies to mass-produced goods. The spin-off from civilian industry into military technology is probably much greater than the reverse spin: for instance, all the du Pont products in the Apollo program had originally been developed for down-to-earth sale. Those industries (data processing and electronic components, for main examples) that have been utterly transformed by advanced technological developments are exceptions. Those apart, there is no evidence, so far, that the rich economic prizes go hand-in-hand with technological preeminence.

West Germany's record in high technology is about as inspiring as its performance in management education: nil. Yet it has the world's second most successful economy, the most brilliant being a Japanese economy led, not by space age whiz products, but by supertankers (which are nothing but floating boxes), motor bikes, cameras, and portable radios. And how about hovercraft, carbon fibers, metal oxide semiconductors, fluidics, and glass transistors? All of these are technological marvels of the 1960s on which, as late as 1971, any investor would have lost most of his shirt.

None of this will stop a director from bragging about his research and development spending, as if the money itself promoted something beyond the continued employment and well-being of scientists. The latter's executives are sure that research and development is intrinsically good and absolutely essential; yet its results in big companies are generally disappointing. Rather than conclude that there is something wrong with the management of the whole company, directors decide that the fault lies with the specific management of research and development. Consequently, quantities of intellect and trouble are now going into attempts to make research and development live up to its billing as a fountain of profit.

The most discredited of these pastimes is "brainstorming,"

in which the participants are encouraged to throw in every idea in their heads, however asinine; and that's what you get —asinine ideas. The most intellectual game is known as technological forecasting. The object is to show companies where, given the likely developments, they should concentrate their own efforts. The names of the technological forecasting techniques (Delphi, morphological research, relevance trees, and the like) are a poem in themselves; their weakness is that, by the time the forecasts are proved right or wrong, it's too late. If you back a wrong horse (for instance, if you happened to choose the steam engine in preference to internal combustion), excellent research and development will inevitably go to waste. Technological forecasting won't solve the problem that makes research and development genuinely baffling to the directors: that its results are so hard to predict and to measure that the directors cannot quantify what they want.

This vagueness has its charms—the executive can (and usually does) merely avoid making any sensible calculations at all. Investors have the same entranced rapture in face of the future. The case of Viatron can stand as their monument. The hot technology idea was to apply MOS (metal oxide semiconductors) to LSIC (large-scale integrated circuits). Investors who couldn't tell an MOS from an MTB, or an LSIC from LSD, rushed to buy the stock on issue—even though the prospectus said candidly (as U.S. law insists) that the management had no reason whatsoever to suppose that it could make anything but a shambles of the business, which it duly did.

Under the banner, Never before have mass production methods been applied to the computer industry, Viatron offered to lease its System 21 wonder terminals for $39 a month. This low, low price, in a typical hot technology gambit, was not justified by economics, but by the necessity to get high orders, without which the price of the MOS magic could not be lowered from sky-high levels. The inevitable end was a collapse all along the management line, a switch to selling the terminals at much higher prices and a bankruptcy that stranded all the stockholders high and dry—and nobody could say they didn't deserve it.

The moral of Viatron is that greed is no substitute for intelligence. The company's own statements made it clear that Viatron was a monstrous gamble, which in any context save that of high technology and buying the future would have been shunned like Central Park by night. The Viatron backers got mugged. Any attempt at purchasing the future can be reduced to figures, and all that Viatron's known statistics showed was loss, loss, and more loss. Against this known chasm, its executives and supporters set the prospect of entirely unquantified Xerox or Polaroid-style gains—if the technology, marketing, general management, and following wind were all set fair. That's like jumping out of an aircraft without a parachute.

But sums fly out of the window when the future comes in the door. At a prosaic level of technology, the International Publishing Corporation launched a color magazine, a free giveaway with the *Daily Mirror*, to protect the latter's black and white flanks in a color-dominated future. It was supposed to attract £7 million of advertising revenue to break even. Even supposing that the cost estimate was high enough (it wasn't by £3 million), how could the sums be squared with the experience of IPC's own mass-circulation women's magazines? The best made only a modest profit after charging a cover price. So how could IPC make money by giving away a similar product for nothing? It couldn't, and that was the end of IPC's independent future.

Similar lessons should be engraved on the hearts of all futurologists, high and low. In estimating costs, work out an honest number and then double it. Nor is the future priceless: there is always a point where the price becomes too high. Whether the cost lies in research and development or in operating losses in a new business, the question is always the same. How much can current earnings be sacrificed for future benefit? In this context the only sensible (and often only too accurate) way is to treat research and development as pure loss. The minute a company starts to kid itself that scientists' wages are an asset, it is writing its doom on the wall.

How much a company shells out depends on personal taste and the quality of its research and development staff (a quality that nontechnical managers, being ill equipped to judge, are prone to exaggerate). Given that research and development is a game of chance, it is dangerous to spend less than the other players; you may as well have the same number of throws. The research and development write-off can also be regarded simply as a firm's subscription to the industry club, as the license fee that entitles it to stay in business. Whatever the firm spends, however, executives must do the kind of back-of-an-envelope sums that far too many managements either fail to scribble down or else ignore. It's no use putting big money into a transistorized combination electric toaster, tea maker, and radio clock: the likely demand for such a toy will never generate the needed earnings. (One firm actually did produce a combination portable radio and camera, which is just as weird.)

If a company is going to lose £1 million this year—or spend it on research and development—the financial pain is only worth incurring for a sure *extra* £250,000 profit after a five-year wait. "Anyone who enters the Continental computer market must be prepared to stand a loss operation for five years," said a Honeywell man sagely. He didn't add (because he didn't know) that the five lean years would not be followed by the five fat ones that would have made the losses worthwhile. Obviously the longer the wait, the larger the return has to be. Any executive who lets money drain away today without knowing which tomorrow will bring the payoff, or even what size that bonanza will be, is leaping into the dark with somebody else's cash.

Expensive research work can be sorted out by a simple question: If it succeeds, what is the maximum potential financial benefit? Once the spending has passed the point at which the return is worth having, the answer is equally simple—halt. A new and potent danger sign pops up at this point: the just-around-the-corner complex. Just as prosperity was always around that next bend during the Depression, executives persist in believing that the loss-making business, the failed new venture, the great research and development program, is going to pay off—any moment now.

The complex has a subsyndrome: "We've spent so much already that it would be silly not to go on." If $100 million has vanished without trace into a project, and "only" $10 million more will bring the breakthrough to a $5 million return, the investment seems marvelous: only $10 million for a $5 million annual pay-off! Gee! But the return on the total outlay is still hopelessly inadequate. Even supposing that the latest forecast turns out to be right (and it won't), simple payback will take twenty-two years. The result is a permanent drag on the business, or when the same argument gets applied to some prestige aerospace venture such as Concorde, a heavy permanent tax on the national economy.

The Beecham group learned how not to research, and how to, in the most telling way, which is the hard one. Its former chairman, H. G. Lazell, believed in the goodness of research. For years he defended and sustained Beecham's research effort single-handed, with no valuable results at all. Then Lazell saw his error. Nobody had decided what Beecham wanted from research; therefore, the company could neither concentrate its efforts nor define them. A chastened Lazell chose to concentrate on one of the lush pharmaceutical markets; taking his expert adviser's expert advice (another rare virtue), he put all Beecham's research money on fermentation chemistry, and came up with a well-bred, wealthy family of synthetic penicillins.

Beecham could still have failed. Its research was still undiluted risk: rumor says that a rival penicillin fan was only narrowly beaten to the tape. But Beecham knew that it could easily survive the loss if the project failed. Just as important, the reward, if success came, was certain to return the research and development investment many times over. That is much more intelligent than spending money you haven't got to achieve an objective that is either not worth reaching or impossible to attain.

The Ninth Truth of Management is: *if you are attempting the impossible, you are bound to fail*. Worse than that, you will fail abjectly, because the Eighth Truth—as shown in the saga of Lord Rootes and his Imp Car—also operates its malevolent magic. Because what you are doing is wrong, it will be done badly. The implausible, if not the impossible, can be achieved. But the process is essentially romantic, random, unplanned. No big corporation, being prosaic, routinized, and formal, could have contrived, say, the extraordinary encounter of two Hungarians and a German, who created Syntex and the birth control pill business by processing progesterone from the barbasco root, a yam grown wild in the Mexican jungle (into which the shy German has since retreated as a recluse).

The pursuit of the impossible explains the fiasco record of British airliner manufacturers. The back of an envelope says that projects only coin money at a production rate of eight a month, with the break-even somewhere around three hundred copies. Because no British manufacturer, given the predilection of U.S. airlines for buying American, had any hope in this world of that kind of orders, all their projects were doomed to economic failure, either relative or absolute. And there was no margin for the errors that, exemplifying the eighth truth, duly arrived—the icing up of the Britannia, the drag on the VC 10, or the crashes of the BAC 1-11 (which was also true to British airliner form by being too small for world markets in its first shape).

He who seeks the most advanced, sophisticated, versatile, and technically interesting product reaps enormous development costs and a heap of trouble. He who wants the most foolproof, rugged, purpose-built, and technically boring product can make it more cheaply and sell it on those humdrum qualities alone. Old-fashioned, small-sized, turbo-generators have been giving the British electricity supply industry nearly 100 percent service. The newfangled high technology mammoths—such as New York State's Big Allis—are the ones that work half the time, with luck.

The real edge in U.S. technology always lay more in

improving established commercial technology and production techniques than in genius in the labs. Europeans have been wise to whip across the Atlantic to see what new productive wizardry the Americans have wrought. Great fortunes have been built in this elementary way—such as that of the electronic knight, Sir Jules Thorn in Britain. Thorn benefited enormously from taking and improving Sylvania technology, while deftly sidestepping two traps. He kept Sylvania's parent, General Telephone, firmly under heel as a minority stockholder, and he shunned the pursuit of homegrown, high-flying innovation, thus avoiding either American take-over or financial collapse.

The ultimate blessing of technology is that you can buy what you cannot invent. So do it. The Japanese have developed this to so fine an art that they now license back to America products and processes originally brought from the United States. Steel's basic oxygen furnace is a wondrous illustration of today's real technology race—invented in Austria, applied widely in Germany, taken up late by the Americans, perfected by the Japanese, and adopted last by the British. There can be virtue in coming first. Like everything in management, however, it depends on the price, and sometimes it is better, richer, and safer to come a very good second.

Your technologists will oppose bitterly your refusal to allow them to waste your money by trying for firsts. They will also oppose any new idea that didn't spring from their own brains. Don't let them get away with either idiocy. Technical experts are always wrong until they prove themselves to be right; and it's the layman, not the scientist, who is most likely to spot a market opportunity or sweep aside some technological roadblock put up by well-educated blockheads; as did one executive who made his name by refusing to believe that drop forging couldn't be made continuous. You're not after a Nobel prize, but an innovation that is useful and thus commercial. Remember that the zip fastener has made far more money than the nuclear power station ever has and possibly ever will.

22 *The Conglomerate Complex*

THE CONGLOMERATORS were convinced (and boasted of it) that they were experts in management itself. Never mind whether the product was cornflakes or computer memories. The conglomerate executive could manage whatever you gave him by applying his expertise in his real business, which was management. Since management does not exist, however, neither did the conglomerates, not in the sense in which they sold themselves to a fond public. Even the conglomerate makers seem to have suspected their image: at least, some affronted aces in this hole did their best to escape the name.

They coined futile phrases such as "multi-market company," though conglomeration described their activities rather well. All conglomerates, the respectable and disreputable alike, used financial techniques to pile together unconnected businesses. They managed the results in the way of all holding companies since their time began (which was long ago). The purchases were shoved into common accounting and reporting systems and left to paddle their own canoes, leaky or buoyant, subject to varying degrees and forms of helpful and unhelpful head office intervention.

The basic financial technique was no more a business innovation than the management method. Financiers have been able to work out simple sums for a long time, and few sums are simpler than the one by which $1 million Company A, earning $1 million a year and valued in the market at $20 million, buys $1 million Company B, earning $1 million, but valued only at $10 million, and so neatly boosts its own earnings per share from $1 to $1.33.

This performance should not have fooled the management professors. But very few foresaw, as Peter Drucker did, that the red-hot conglomerates of the day would become the corporate hulks of the next. There are transferable management skills, and there are transferable executives. But it doesn't follow that all management skills transfer, or that one central team can possess all necessary skills, or even that all conglomerates had management skills of any kind, or that all executives can shift easily between all businesses.

Companies are only effective at managing in a certain line of business and some of their skills are nontransferable, intrinsic and essential to that racket. Because this is so, large corporations are bound to find diversifying less diverting than it seems. But at least diversifying is extraneous to their main activity. For the conglomerates, diversifying was their only business, and in the long run, that's a bad business to be in.

The sharp practices of the sharper conglomerate makers naturally offended the industrial Establishment. Like the senior conglomerate citizens, Litton and Textron, the nonconglomerate members of the billion-dollar club hated being tarred with the same brush. But just as conglomerate makers lied in claiming to be a new form of business, so did the established companies who swore they were anything but conglomerates. All but nineteen of the two hundred largest

U.S. companies were in at least ten different manufacturing categories as long ago as 1968. No avowedly multi-market company has such multiple markets as General Electric. And even staid old citizens such as du Pont see no reason why they should stick to chemicals; like the conglomerates, and with no more reason, they think their skills and resources are universal. After all, didn't they build the atomic bomb?

Large companies mostly decide to diversify at the moment when their profits from the businesses they really do understand are wilting. New sources of profit are the standard prescription at this juncture. But relative failure in fields you know is no great qualification for success in strange pastures. General Mills was the world's largest flour miller when it decided, under the stirring leadership of an Air Force general, that milling was a no-good, low-margin business, and that it would shift to emphasis on growth in earnings per share by risk-taking diversification. After costly purchases of food companies and European businesses as far afield as fashion and toys, General Mills is no longer the mightiest miller. But its earnings per share in the 1960–70 period rose by precisely 69 percent. Fuddy-duddy old Pillsbury, the other Minneapolis flour giant, more than doubled in the decade.

The best business is the simplest: a firm that markets one product in one market and lives happily ever after. Any executive in full possession of his self-interest would trade an Avon for a GE any day. Avon's elementally simple idea of door-to-door cosmetic selling by agents yields almost one-third of GE's profits on one-eleventh of GE's sales with a tiny proportion of GE's anxieties. Yet even a champion one-marketer eventually gets nervous about the golden eggs sitting in that one beautiful basket. It begins to diversify, to spread (i.e., to increase) its risks.

The more bets you have on a race, the more bets you are likely to lose. True, because the industries are widely spread, if some components are down, others will be up. But executives seldom spot the opposite truth—if some parts of the company are up, it follows inexorably that others will be down. The company is condemning itself to mediocrity, and to more conglomeration; for one diversification (like the first step on the primrose path of sin) leads to another.

Before top management knows where it is, its preoccupation has ceased to be thermostats, or tires, or computers, but is the management of diversity. A brilliant Harvard Business School team, primed to the ears with accurate information about U.K. companies, came to the conclusion that British management's prime failure lay in mismanaging diversity— as if the Americans have proved any better. The confessed conglomerates and the diversified nonconglomerates have discovered alike that management doesn't work in the abstract. In practice, the many eggs in many baskets corporation either has to fall back into today's typical rut of unhappy compromises, or to abdicate a management role on classic lines and settle for a banker-investigator function.

Effective diversified businesses do exist. Even though most businesses make odd bedfellows, strangeness doesn't rule out a happy sex life. Clothing companies shouldn't even dream of going into food. But after the war, Marks and Spencer, second only to Sears Roebuck as a textile retailer, did so, and with more success than in its basic business. The company had abilities, premises, and policies that fitted both lines, and it capitalized on those genuine strengths, not on its mythical abilities.

Tobacco companies, in Britain and in America, had reason (a la Levitt) to think that their strength lay in marketing packaged and branded consumer goods. They were truly adept at selling cigarettes, a very different commodity, being neither necessary nor competitively priced, from food. Imperial Tobacco discovered this painfully in Britain, even though in many ways its diversifying job was tackled in textbook manner.

You can crash in from scratch, as IBM did with electric typewriters, and get away with it, but that depends on having a decisively better product and a transferable asset such as IBM's immovable indoctrination of office bosses (and secretaries) with its name. The further out a new line is (Rolls-

Royce once even tried making saucepans), the less chance there is of making it succeed (Rolls couldn't even get the thing to stand up. Another giant military contractor, Vickers, started unpromisingly on its dismal peacetime trail in 1919 by investigating the market potential of "boy rabbits (squeaking)" and "girl rabbits (nonsqueaking)."

Imps had a little subsidiary making its first chosen food, potato chips. But the name of Imperial Tobacco, or any of its cigarette brands, was even less use than the company's distribution expertise, because potato chips are not sold in the same proportions in the same outlets as cigarettes. Still, Imps' Golden Wonder had a toehold in a market dominated by Smiths Potato Crisps. Now a subsidiary of General Mills under a different name, the company was then an example of old-line British management in so peaceful a dotage that its factories could subsequently be cut from fifteen to seven without any loss of capacity. Before long Golden Wonder had half the market, but only won at the price of enormously heavy promotion costs, and of driving the competition into American arms.

With merger barred by U.K. trustbusters, Imps was locked into a fierce market, which for various external reasons, turned suddenly sour, landing General Mills with a $13.5 million write-off along the way. Food has attracted more diversifiers than any other dreamland, on the unsubtle argument that people will always eat. But even in inexhaustible markets a rule of thumb applies to all companies in all fields: only the two largest competitors and one specialist make big money.

The price of becoming number two, let alone number one, is so ruinous that executives merely run their legs off to budge not one financial inch. It cost chocolate expert Cadbury £400,000 to launch an instant potato nationally: the stuff chalked up sales of £2 million and has since doubled, it still needs over $500,000 of advertising a year and that sounds none too attractive a bargain. In a virgin, or *demi-vierge*, market, the diversifier has to buy his management experience. The lack of this asset, which can only be acquired over time, ensures a costly initiation.

Some work by the Boston Consulting Group suggests that

the greater the market share, the richer the accumulated experience, and the more profound the ability to extract the highest profitability from a market. So buying a small unit to get your feet wet—or developing one—may not be such a masterstroke after all. Don't rely on something your company doesn't have, transferable management skills, to develop something else it lacks, a worthwhile share of the market. But the purchase of companies with a lovely plump market share comes no cheaper. One American diversifier has kept its nose reasonably clean by refusing to pay more than fifteen times earnings for any purchase. On that none too demanding criterion (it means a payback over seven years, assuming, as you must, no increase in profits because of your own brilliant management), many diversifications by acquisition would never have been made, to the eternal benefit of the stockholders—and even of the executives.

Company executives seldom reflect that nobody forces them to diversify. They can afford to be greedy, to wait for opportunities where the criteria are all satisfied—rate of return, degree of risk, use of real existing strengths. That last criterion almost certainly restricts you to vertical acquisition —buying firms that fit onto existing interests. In a study of mergers by John Kitching, no vertical amalgamation failed, but 42 percent of the conglomerate mergers went phut. And while executives wait for the right buy, they can concentrate on their central assignment—making the most of existing major markets.

These foundation businesses—the data processing of IBM (still a highly specialized company), the textile fibers of du Pont or ICI, the instruments of Honeywell—in the end make the accidental conglomerate a better bet than the deliberate multi-market, whiz-kid creation. The basic, solid sectors, however, bore executives. They want to pioneer new commercial frontiers. They love to quote the progress of new businesses, to boast how acquisitions have blossomed under their gardening—though a one-point drop in margins on the bread-and-butter business would wipe out the profits of every new jam tart in the group.

220

This gross disproportion encourages executives to hang on to their errors, in the forlorn hope that some miracle will avert the admission that they have boobed with stockholders' funds. Something about losing money warms an executive's entrails. It proves that he is doing what executives are supposed to do —building for the future. Capitalist mythology holds that all great businesses start by losing money, until the tide turns, the risks pay off, and the risk-taking company or entrepreneur finally gets his just glory.

Since most great businesses started small, this must be untrue. Small businesses can't survive years of loss—or couldn't until the mid-twentieth century. The bull market of the 1960s saw the American invention of the perpetually loss-making potential growth star: one hot Wall Street tip was an electronic tape firm that had lost money for fourteen successive years. The truly great and good product pays off early and piles up wealth incessantly. Where the payoff takes years, only a handful, like RCA's color TV, are genuine gambles against time. Mostly simple management mistakes spoil a perfect setup. Just as Boeing underpriced the 707, so did du Pont originally sell and manufacture Orlon for the wrong uses.

Neat little financial tricks are used to ease the pain of diversification losses. If managers buy companies, they don't calculate the return on the actual capital expended. Standard British bookkeeping practice allows writing off the "excess over book value" of assets purchased (the difference is laughingly known as goodwill). If managers start new ventures, they work out returns only on the capital spent—the current losses made before that elusive corner is turned are forgotten as if they had never been. The exception comes when the firm's current profits aren't big enough to bear the strain; then the losses are "capitalized" as development spending. According to British government inspectors, the International Learning Systems Corporation "capitalized" any shortfall from its encyclopaedia sales targets, territory by territory in this enchanting way.

One American giant whose bold geographical diversification had at long last broken into profit, kept its prodigious pride unmarred by memory of the losses incurred over the past years. Asked when accumulated profits would exceed accumulated losses, i.e., when the European push would finally yield a clear cent, the corporate treasurer said, "I wouldn't know what to do with that number if I had it."

The secret of being conglomerate (after first confessing that you are) is to be far more exacting and sharp financially than that—and to insist that money is paramount. If an operation justifies itself in money terms, you have an executive there who clearly knows his business. Don't bother him so long as he goes on proving it. Save top management time for operations on which the group prosperity really swings, and for those that are going wrong. The easiest way of dealing with sour apples is to throw them out, but that means taking the easy route, when executives much prefer to have dramas and excitement instead.

The fatal error is to diversify because deep strategic thinking convinces the board that diversification is essential. That approach converts a respectable shipping and commodity company such as W. R. Grace, or a cheerful enough dairy firm such as Borden, into problem areas in the chemical industry. Any fool can end up with a corporation that has nothing for anybody—its backers, its stockholders, or its employees— except the ability to grow bigger and broader like a fat lady in the circus. Wide industrial spread is a misfortune that piles burdens on managers as they struggle to achieve genuine expansion in earnings. The irony is that, for a spell, the conglomerates set about the management of agglomerated multi-market companies in a realistic, demanding, and financially alert style. Their tragedy was that they came to share all the follies of the established and conglomerated nonconglomerates, including that of believing their own myths.

V Medicines

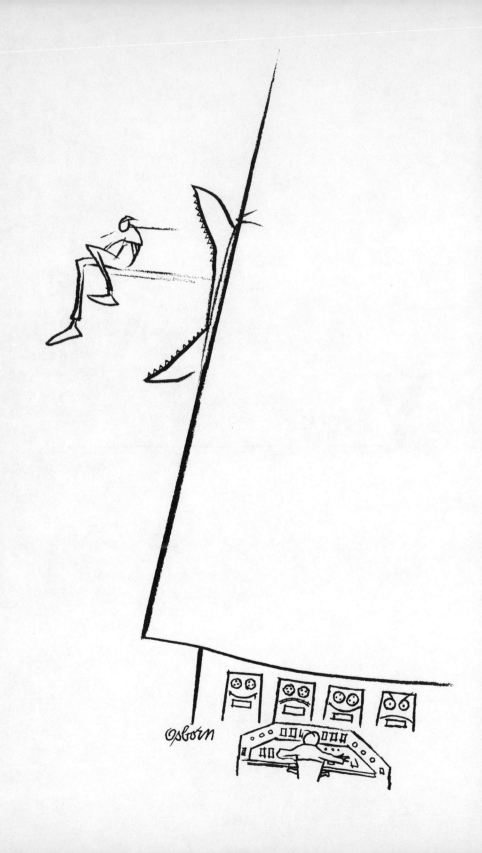

23 _The Computer Says Jump_

THE COMPUTER has scared more managers stiff than any other invention—even the allied myth of automation. Business throughout the West ran into its worse postwar troubles with human labor at the end of the 1960s, which was about the time when, according to the more eager prophets, advanced mechanization would be making the two-legged factory staff redundant or servile, or both. The computer industry likewise ran into its first recession around the same date, when managements, according to the less realistic pundits, were already supposed to be recasting their entire corporations around the machine.

The computer robots were to allow chief executives to recentralize their corporations, to reduce middle executives to mindless functional roles, and to concentrate the information flows of the company into one glorious "on-line, real-time" system, in which to know was to obey—with the computer issuing the orders. But if computers were such marvelous management machines, why did computer companies make such mighty losses? Honeywell, by no means IBM's worst managed competitor, took ten times as long to break into profit as it planned, at a cost (supposedly $500 million) ten times as great as it expected, and broke into the black only shortly before the non-IBM industry as a whole turned sharply toward the red. Control Data seemed to have the business of fighting IBM taped. "We had and have the best strategy in the industry," it boasted. "We didn't hit IBM in the hardest part of their big belly." But choosing the softest part, the large computer market, didn't save CDC from coming seriously unstuck in 1970, only five years after an earlier setback.

All the miseries of IBM's competitors, called the seven dwarfs before they shrank to five, were causing pain when the dwarfs, like IBM itself, were trying to sell customers on so-called management information systems—huge, ambitious complexes designed to take the guesswork out of management and, incidentally, to sell rich quantities of computer hardware.

Never mind that the few commercial examples of these wonder complexes were unconvincing—such as the automated MIS at the California Department of Motor Vehicles, a masterpiece that in 1969 was not expected to break even until 1978, and which provided absolutely no information for management. Never mind that the experts themselves, when formed into "software houses," dreamed up monster projects such as Speedata (for automating grocery movements), which proceeded to collapse—in this case for $20 million—because time and cost were underestimated.

Univac even sent some hardy pioneers to Europe to publicize its achievement at a plant in Marietta, Georgia. The Georgia customer, too, added some of its men for the ride in its pride over this ultimate in management control systems. The wonder was designed to reap extra profit from tight control by, among other things, giving a running account of actual expenses and updated estimates of production costs, keeping the program on schedule and even building in automatically the financial results of any change in specification (the plant's major product was a gigantic complex job whose costs history was critical).

The Georgia company was Lockheed Aircraft, and the project, the C5A monster transport, overran its budget by $2 billion, worked none too well at the end of the process, and would have sunk the company without trace in 1970 but for a Washington rescue act. It was a spectacular demonstration of the truism that any computer is only as good as the assumptions and information fed into it. A human being determines what results his marvelous machine can produce: more than that, he determines what use to make of the results. The common complaint of executives that they are "disillusioned" with computers is bathetic—the executive is really disillusioned with himself.

Computers have been bought that didn't match each other, or match the purpose for which the management wanted them, and have stood around forevermore, idle, costly, unloved, and unmated. One British group had four main subsidiaries that opted for four separate, incompatible sets of hardware. As a result, one executive found his overhead up by the equivalent of three research chemists or four salesmen because his payroll had been computerized—to fill up computer time. Companies that badly needed the improved systems that a computer can provide have poured huge sums into computer setups but not into the systems. Rolls-Royce, Lockheed's partner in crime, had £5 million of IBM computers (with its usual eccentricity, it had forty-six of the things, all bought instead of leased) and spent £2 million a year on running them: yet its cost control was painfully weak.

Computer manufacturers themselves have grandly announced new giant machines that never came anywhere near specification—IBM gave away its abandoned STRETCH machines at cut price, and followed that fiasco by dropping the big 360-90. The size and complexity of the big idea in computers defeats the big thinkers themselves. Feeding forty thousand instructions into a computer is a Herculean chore, and the poor overstuffed electronic whiz-machine then has to spend most of its own expensive time on "housekeeping"—working out how to work.

Back in 1967 one giant computer setup was the glory of its creators: it had got up to 30 percent efficiency. Two others, when used by several people at once (the so-called multi-access mode), could only manage 5 percent, breathing hard. Teething troubles (i.e., the machines don't work) have afflicted all manner of computer installations, big and small. IBM hit difficulties with the components and the software—the paraphernalia that operates the hardware—on the 360 range, which replaced its entire product line at a cost, and risk, of $5 million. Any company with a less heavy stranglehold on the market might have crumbled.

But IBM, for all its computery and management reputation, has failed in public view at other times—its pricing policy, designed to hold its returns aloft, formed an umbrella under which leasing companies could steal IBM's own customers. The setup was so obvious that Saul Steinberg, a business school student, spotted the opportunity in an academic thesis and made his Leasco fortune as a result. Executives were slow to wonder why, if computers were such fabulous aids to better management, their makers had benefited so little from the aid; although a few sage skeptics said they would not install a "total management information system" until a computer manufacturer had done the same.

The executive's mind has boggled before the computer because it is mind boggling. It can spew out data and calculations at speeds infinitely faster than any human mind can cope with. Not only do most executives (being stuck personally at the hi-fi stage of electronics technology) fail to understand how the machine works, they can't address it or work it except through human intermediaries—computer experts of varying degree—whom they can't understand either. (Partly because they talk in thick jargon and acronyms such as DOMNICS, MUMMS, TRUMP, SASSY, CIMS,

ARMACS, NAICOM, MIS, and 1^2S, the systems with which the U.S. Navy's executives have to mangle their minds.)

Most computer customers have some real need for its services, and in some cases the need is overwhelming. Employers of masses of clerks for routine processing of paper (insur-

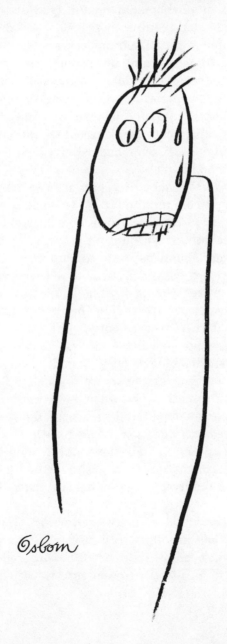

ance companies, government departments, banks, airlines, and the like) would have trouble housing, let alone hiring, the people required if, instead of the computer, they still had to rely on funny old punched card machines.

The computer can perform tricks all its own, for example, as a calculator of phenomenal capability. But the great mass of executives do not require these skills—or don't use them, which is another story. Their mistakes have mostly been in the punched card mode, and the same errors were perfectly possible with cards. One richly successful publishing firm switched its stock control and accounting system onto a computer (after a merger) and collapsed into large losses as the machine failed and customers' accounts got hopelessly jumbled up. Nobody knew who had received which books, who had paid, and who hadn't.

A similar fiasco caused Beecham's food company painful indigestion in precomputer days. A powerful new sales force was dashing around taking orders left, right, and center. When the mechanized accounting division got the account numbers wrong, shambles reigned supreme. The computer hucksters, however, were not about to tell wavering customers that all they were getting was a souped-up punched card installation. No, they were selling the future, that much more expensive and attractive commodity.

The managers, not pausing to do their sums, even imagined (or were persuaded) that they would save money in the present while waiting for the shower of golden future benefits. No wonder that something between 40 percent and 70 percent of computer users—depending on whose figures you fancy— are disappointed, or that, according to other calculations, 80 percent of computer installations don't show an economic return on investment, or that a significant deterioration of performance is reported in computerized areas by 40 percent of users.

The customers were, of course, oversold. The computer is more efficient than a bullpen full of clerks but it may well be more expensive, even if it is properly ordered and used. A computer can turn into a running sore if both the order and the application are mismanaged (which is as likely as not—the central processing units of today's computers, the most expensive parts of the system, are said to be idle for 70 percent to 80 percent of their time). There was a stocking manufacturer, now only a bitter memory in the annals of the giant that bought his firm for a sickening price, who really used his computer. He would boast that it could tell him how many stockings, of what size and color, had been sold the previous day in any part of the country.

A skeptical chain store boss asked what good the information did. The answer was none. After the merger, in fact, the rescue team did use the computer's grossly excessive capacity to improve the company's marketing efficiency, but the rescuers were thinking, and thinking hard, under the hard pressure of having to reduce costs in dire emergency.

Mesmerized executives have fallen for their own con devices. They have been persuaded that new computer models, like new cars or new soaps or new cigarettes, represent some major advance on the previous ones. So they may, but not in terms of practical use. A few of the first computers ever built are still chugging away so effectively that nobody can make a case for putting in the hotted-up, third-generation wonder. The only catch with these veterans is that their service men are gradually dying out and replacement parts have to be cannibalized. Such are the results of planned obsolescence.

Executives can with some justice protest that they are not complete suckers. They are also victims of the computer's handmaidens, their own technical staff, who have been known to desert any employer unwilling to provide the very latest toys for them to play with. So long as computer men enjoyed all the pleasures of scarcity—sharply rising salaries and total job mobility—executives caved in all along the line. Only in the 1970/71 recession, when the programmers and higher breeds of expert got lost in the unfamiliar wilderness of unemployment, was the executive able to regain the control he should never have abdicated.

But the stones that executives can cast at computer experts are no sharper than those that can be hurled back. Being logical, computers can only handle systems that are logical. The typical corporate system sprawls all over the place, working only because those in charge have got familiar with its mysteries, like travelers on the New York subway. Even though it functions, after a fashion, the established system (no matter for what purpose) is certain not to be the simplest and clearest way of organizing the flow. Therefore, the first step in computerizing is to simplify and clarify the system, and very often the main economic benefit of the computer lies in doing just that. Many customers would have been well-advised to leave it there, and not to bother about the computer. But many users didn't get the system right, and still installed a computer on top.

Never forget the late Lord Marks. That genius one day saw a sales girl filling in a form, and wondered if it was necessary. From that observation, Marks began a paper chase all over Marks and Spencer, finding, for instance, that it was costing more to check shipments from suppliers than was saved by catching their errors: that not allowing the girls to draw stock from the stockroom themselves involved quite unreasonable expense. The drive for efficiency and simplification enabled Marks to stay uncomputerized long after another British retail king had bought his first computer, as he freely admitted, because everybody else had one.

The computer will never eliminate the executive's need to think for his living; in some respects, it makes his task harder by introducing a new area of anxiety. For one day the computer may revolutionize management. Phrases such as "real time" and "on-line" will be more than sales talk. One day managements will get usable information about what is happening as and when it happens. One day computers will graduate from bookkeeping, now about half their use, to running the basic routines of the business and pitching in at the rarefied level of planning and decisions.

The parallel is with management consultants; the latter

graduated from walking around with stop watches timing production workers to (much more profitably) advising giant corporations on their future. The difference, however, is that the consultants did the advising. The computer will only act in the capacity of millions of slide rules, filing cabinets, and message centers. The information capability any big company already has will be multiplied enormously, but the function will be unaltered—to be used or misused by the human executives who now handle the slide rules, flick through the files, and accumulate memos as squirrels do nuts.

Since executives already ignore warnings of failure expressed in equations little tougher than two plus two, they will have no trouble in riding roughshod over reams of computer print-out. The computer, anyway, can only issue the warnings it has been programmed to give, and as Lockheed found with its Marietta monster, a dog that can't bark, or whose barking is deliberately ignored, is not much protection. The computer terminal in Georgia doubtless spewed out floods of information on the Galaxy C5A. All the same, so Lockheed itself says, "The impact of late specification changes was underestimated."

Worse still, although unexpectedly rapid wage-price inflation was reported starting in December 1966, only in the third quarter of 1967 were enough data available "to make possible a meaningful cost study and projection of costs." If "fully integrated management by real-time computer" can't generate enough data to signal a crisis of $2 billion dimensions for nine months, there is still a future for nonintegrated management by real-life humans.

The setup at Marietta would have coped perfectly (if expensively) with normal circumstances. But it was not set up (because its human executives were not set up) to combat the abnormal, especially abnormal circumstances that were deeply dangerous for the executives. Companies sailing toward bankruptcy have a curious vulnerability to their computers. The managing director of Upper Clyde Shipbuilders, proud builders of the Queen Elizabeth II, had an engaging explanation for the suddenness of its almost overnight collapse into illiquidity—with £32 million of liabilities against only £3.7 million of assets. The accounts, he said, had all been put on the computer and it took six weeks to get them out.

Big assumptions are by no means the only things that go wrong; so do little data. One company found that the error rate reported from the shop floor, 5 percent in the manual system, shot up to 12 percent on the computer because the men supplying the data were simply making mistakes. Even when things go right, it is unwise to give the computer all the credit and a big hand. In one car company, a computerized production control system went in so smoothly that a suspicious consultant investigated. Sure enough, the executives were continuing to operate the old manual system under their desks. Their action, though obstinate, enshrined a correct principle—the purpose of management is to operate the company to the maximum possible effectiveness, not to keep the computer happy.

Today, however, fewer executives are frightened of the computer. They have learned that it will no more take away their jobs than it will save them money. Some are actually canceling expensive computer plans after bothering to ascertain the facts—such as the bakery firm which was advised that computerizing its vehicle routing would be 50 percent more expensive than doing it by hand. For some firms, investment in computers has already reached such a size that the problem is to earn enough to pay for their nonproductive keep. As the 1970s began, on one authoritative estimate, over 10 percent of total investment in plant and machinery would be going on computer systems.

It's not enough in such circumstances to say blithely, as one typical computer user did, that it hadn't tried to justify the computer on cost savings "but was confident that its profit had come from new opportunities." Executives have no reason to fear the computer, or to jump when it or its high priests say so. Like every other machine, the computer was made by humans and needs human intelligence. It won't make executives into mindless zombies. But the executive who can't tell sales talk from real value, and who just goes on feeding the computers and their acolytes with money whenever the button is pressed, is already half a zombie.

24 *You Can't Teach Executives*

EXECUTIVES, the most intensively educated group of adults in society, are very possibly educated to the least effect. Any executive could spend three hundred working days a year—and several thousand pounds of company money—at individual seminars, without coming near to exhausting the rich table that consultants, academics, training firms, associations, publishers, and other do-gooders spread before the business world. Their altruism is spiced with lucre. The teaching of executives has been the best-paying branch of education, and by a very long way. It has also been a soft market; only a few heretical voices ever questioned whether you can really teach executives, that is, make them better at their jobs by any general course of instruction, short or long.

The Harvard Business School is the ark of the tabernacle in management education. Many schools more or less ape it, especially its "case study" method of instruction—though munching over out-of-date business anecdotes is about as helpful in actual management as waging war by tramping over old battlefields. Even those business schools that self-consciously follow a different route do so by reference to the Harvard standard. These others mostly concentrate on "quantitative" studies; in other words, as a maverick educator, Reg Revans, pointed out, they teach much the same subjects that students of economics or statistics have always fed on. The specific management element in these mind-bending studies is hard to isolate. Although executives should be numerate (and many are not), they don't require skills in higher algebra, and many great businesses have been created by men who all but count on their fingers.

A story tells of two schoolboy friends, one brilliant at math, one innumerate to the point of idiocy, who meet much later when the first is a professor and the second a multimillionnaire. Unable to control his curiosity, the professor asks the figure-blind dunderhead how he managed to amass his fortune. "It's simple," replies Midas. "I buy things at £1 and sell them for £2, and from that 1 percent difference I make a living." The business world is full of successful one-percenters who live, not by their slide rules, but by knowing the difference between a buying price and a selling price. It is also full of clever fools who work out elaborate discounted cash flow sums to justify projects and products that a one-percenter would laugh out of sight.

The clever fool syndrome would explain why one controversial study of Harvard Business School students found that, after a flying start, the alumni (presumably among the ablest young men of their day) gradually slipped back to the general level inside their chosen management hierarchies. A Harvard graduate has no reason at all to suppose that he will manage more effectively than a less instructed contemporary. The Harvard man can only claim that he is more highly educated; and high education and high achievement in practical affairs don't necessarily go together. John F. Kennedy found that assembling America's brightest brains in Washington neither got bills through Congress nor avoided the Bay of Pigs; and many companies have discovered that business school diplomas are a thin defense against incompetence.

An overwhelmingly large proportion of the highest and best American executives did study business. All this proves is that an overwhelmingly large proportion of business-minded undergraduates got the real message, which is that a diploma will be good for their careers, starting with starting salaries. It does not follow that the education was of any other direct benefit either to the executive or his firm. Nor does it follow, of course, that the schooling was wasted. As a general rule, the wise man recruits the finest intelligence he can find; and good minds are far better for good training. The question is only whether academic training in subjects that seem to have some connection with management is the best education for managing, and that is something that nobody can prove either way.

The business school is really good at teaching future business school teachers. But teaching the raw young is only the start of the money in management education. You can detach an experienced manager for hours or years and you can attempt any form of education, from familiarizing him with computers to changing his entire personality. Attempt is the critical word; for some of the objectives are very curious. They start from an odd proposition: that management is a body of abstract skills, like those of mechanical engineering, which can be applied equally successfully to any number of practical situations.

Once you've built one suspension bridge, very possibly you've built the lot—although the modern history of bridge accidents questions even that. But the abstract principles of launching a new toothpaste are too loose and vague for analogies to apply. And once you've launched one new toothpaste, it doesn't mean that you can launch the next in the same way, much less that you can use the same methods for a cake mix. The absurdity of the educational proposition is stunning when applied to personal relationships. The most successful single products in the racket are prepackaged courses for managers designed (like Midwest evangelism) to change the behavior patterns of the human beings involved.

The Blake and Moulton Managerial Grid (which sounds like an electric toaster) is a mechanism "for achieving corporate excellence." The griddled managers are supposed to plot their characteristics on numbered squares that range from 1.1 ("minimum concern for people and minimum concern for production") at the bottom left-hand corner to a 9.9 paragon at top right ("work accomplishment is from committed people: interdependence through a 'common stake' in organization purpose leads to relationships of trust and respect"). In fact, the grid really leads to a rigid, expensive, intense, and sleepless attempt to indoctrinate the executive in the philosophy and psychology of the magic 9.9.

The umbrella name of "sensitivity training" is inapt for a process that is often insensitive to the point of butchery. By confessing his shortcomings in front of others in grid sessions, T-Groups or similar gatherings, the executive becomes psychologically purified. The North Korean brainwashers and the hippies at the Esalen Institute share this same belief in inducing spiritual change by humiliation. This is achieved for executives by giving them an "unstructured" problem to discuss.

They have no points of reference, no idea what they are supposed to be doing, and no protection against attack. The more unbalanced executives have sometimes been tipped right over the brink of breakdown. Others have come away feeling better and wiser and more effective men. But all uplift wears off, and it wears off long before the uplifted one has any real chance to transform his performance through his transmogrified personality.

If the existing executives are not performing very effectively (which is probably true), it is more painful to change them than to try and change their behavior. But the only result of attempting to modify their personalities is to strengthen the conformist pressures that are already too strong inside the corporation. That is also the main, if undeclared, purpose of much so-called in-house training—when groups of executives from the same company are herded together at some away-from-it-all location such as the stately homes often maintained by British companies, or Starved Rock, Illinois, the choice of Caterpillar Tractor. "Executives don't leave Starved Rock and become better executives without working at it. How do you get to it? Feedback, results, tests, self-appraisal, counseling—you're the salami in the sandwich."

These sausage factories feature the requisite appearances of the requisite academics. But their high point is the sacramental unveiling of the boss or bosses, and it is his speech or their speeches on which the acolytes hang. The whole enterprise is surrounded by an atmosphere of forced intimacy, of flattering selection, of general devotion to the greater good of the corporation, of total immersion (like Baptist converts) in its ethos. The evangelical note is again strong—and again effective, until it wears off. These high-level in-house courses too smack more of indoctrination than of any carefully metered attempt to improve management performance in measurable, practicable ways. But they do at least let middle executives get a close-up of their supreme bosses.

In this respect, in-house courses serve the same purpose as conferences of the Soviet Communist Party. The faithful are rewarded with the opportunity to applaud the leader, who can at the same time applaud them for their faith, and seek to reinforce it. Yet in-house education actually has far greater, mostly unexploited potential. Outside courses can only get at an executive by taking him away from his job; inside courses can teach him in the best place of all—which is on that job.

Lecturers to business audiences know that the attention quotient rises sharply if the executives' superiors are in the room—the underling wants to show how alert and brisk he is, even if he has to laugh at the lecturer's jokes. That apart, any training given where the executive works and which is directly related to his work is more effective than education outside. At one-day external seminars nobody notices if the executive dozes off into langorous half-sleep, opening glazed eyes just in time to sprint for the early train. Well-attested studies show that a man absorbs only 10 percent of spoken information; he does twice as well with visual information and six times as well with sight and sound combined. So at most seminars, naturally, he gets little or no sight and sound; about 10 percent visual display, if that; and 90 percent of unadulterated, mostly unabsorbed spoken words.

Even if the seminar's subject is relevant to the man's job, even if he has absorbed a significant part of the information (both unlikely conditions), the executive still faces what is known as the reentry problem. He may have found a better way up there on the managerial moon, but will his unenlightened colleagues back on earth let him disturb the even, set tenor of their ways? Will they, hell. The more an executive is exposed to external ideas of how a modern business should be managed, the longer he spends away from the shop at Harvard or Fontainebleau or Geneva or London or Chicago, the more alien and obtuse the actual real-life conditions in his company can seem.

The company, unlike the business schools, is enmeshed in real life. The academic inevitably teaches of an ideal world in which the personalities of all chief executives (to take one illusion) are equable, open to persuasion, and eager for change, and in which (to take another dream) markets respond logically to logical plans logically arrived at. There is no other basis on which the academic can operate; but it is not the basis on which a company works.

The reentry problem is less liable to lead to burnup if external training is treated like good in-house education; that is, equip a man to do his job better, and as he moves to another mystery, equip him for that in turn. An executive in his first marketing post needs specific knowledge about certain techniques (for instance, how to fix a price or run a promotion). Most executives need better education in management accounting, which means managing by the real financial implications, not by the abstractions in the balance sheet. But no academically acquired knowledge is any use until it is applied at the crunch point, where mistakes will be made and hard real-life lessons learned. And the shorter the gap between learning and application, by far the better.

Every executive once knew enough of Latin, chemistry, history, or some similar recondite study to pass an exam of fair difficulty. Within a few years of disuse, his knowledge has decayed to the status of childhood memory. Exactly the same rusting away happens to management knowledge. So, the more general the course, the more will be wasted—simply because the executive will be limited in what he can use. On the job, anyway, he learns lessons that no course can ever teach: nobody can work out for every executive in every situation, or any executive in any situation, what will come to be the most significant, testing, and painful parts of his craft.

This presupposes that the executive has been taught how to learn, possibly the most valuable gift that education has to offer. Men who lack this general lesson are prone to take experience as a substitute for thought. All knowledge is the result of inquisitiveness—of asking why. Experience is another name for ceasing to ask because the answer has been prejudged. "We've always done it this way" is the worst reason of all, unless, that is, there genuinely is no better way; and that can only be established by inquiry. As businesses have grown more complex, this task of getting appropriate answers has also become more complicated, more difficult. And here the academic can offer analytical tools that do produce far better answers; but none of these gadgets is more than a small attachment to the great tool of skepticism.

The skeptical executive takes nothing for granted, including his own competence. He doesn't dismiss the whole effort to apply theory to business management, or to teach it. He recognizes that nobody knows, in the scientific sense of the verb "to know," how to achieve the maximum results from managing a company—let alone how to measure whether those results have been achieved. He does know that executives must be encouraged (or taught) to recognize their own ignorance. They dare not copy one chairman, since stripped of his rank, who liked to show off a chart showing how his company would coin profits once output passed breakeven and moved on toward capacity. The weakness in this inspiring analysis was that the true capacity line lay where he had drawn the break-even point.

Making executives think isn't the need that business courses publicly try to fill. But it *is* the central issue, more so than the defect the schools themselves now confess—which is that they can't teach executives how to make decisions under stress. Nor can they. But before making a decision, under stress or at ease, it helps to have been guilty of constructive thought and constructive self-criticism. Apart from any other factors, thought helps the decision to make itself—which is always the most desirable way. Saying that executives can't be taught the power of decision at school, in any case, is only another way of saying that you can't teach executives to manage: for initiating action under uncertainty and pressure is one of the activities for which executives are paid.

The interesting question is whether business education has boomed in response to the increased complexity and bureaucracy of industry or is itself part of the long march to complication. The only organizations that match business life in devotion to schooling are the military ones, which can be said historically to have started management education. Just like executives, officers can spend all their life on courses, if they are lucky. But even officers are better employed on courses that have some bearing on their needs and the army's. In peacetime, when soldiers mostly play at being soldiers, purely playful education matters less. In war the playing has to stop, and in war the amateur soldier, the civilian trained in utterly different skills and ways of thought, comes into his own. Just as the individualistic business entrepreneur outperforms the career executive, so the amateur soldier often beats out the professional, because in the battlefield, as in the marketplace, you seldom win by the book.

Great generals, like great executives, also rarely distinguish themselves academically. (Nor, for that matter, do military leaders show up well in business; in British companies they have often proved as destructive as napalm.) The qualities that win wars, like those that create fortunes for companies or individuals, are expressions of personality rather than intellect. True, Field Marshal Montgomery did make a supreme contribution to the art of business, and war. But his old El Alamein one-two is more remarkable for its simple effectiveness than its intellectuality: first, assemble overwhelmingly superior force, and second, attack where the opposition is weakest.

The games that executives play at school don't elucidate such simple truths. They are more an expression of anxiety. I am not/the company is not/my underlings are not managing as well as I/it/they should. A child who is going to fail an exam, or a golfer whose swing is slipping, is given extra coaching—and surely coaching will help the executive. So it may. Even if the business coach himself is both unqualified in real business and inept at instruction, good can always rub off. But education is no substitute for giving an executive a job he likes, letting him do it the way he wants, and demanding that he do it to the best of his ability.

In the typical situation, where the man is underemployed, overmanaged, and constantly let off the hook, a half-failed man in a half-failed organization, education of any variety won't help. And total failure must follow from the unpleasant delusion that classes can transform the adult mind and personality like some fairy wand. The less companies and educators expect to turn an incompetent into a polymath, or a bully into a Boy Scout, the more they are likely to achieve. As it is, too much of what now passes as management education isn't education: it is indoctrination, entertainment, or occupation of vacant hours. And it has very little to do with the management of business, which is the real business of management.

25 _The Consultant Game_

THERE WAS once a snappy catch answer to consultants, management professors, and other tradesmen who tell others how to mind their own businesses. "Ah yes," executives could say, "if you know so much, how come you're not rich?" There are variations to this arresting theme: "Those who can, do: those who can't, consult," or "He's never met a payroll in his life." The last gibe skirts around the fact that most executives have never met a payroll either, not in the sense of having until Friday to find the cash.

Executives rest in the safe arms of the corporation, which always (or nearly always) makes sure that the payroll gets met and the creditors paid. These days executives are more like consultants—shifting from assignment to assignment, never soiling their hands with selling or manufacture, spending their time largely on reports, meetings, and investigations.

But many consultants are more like businessmen than any executive in General Motors or ICI.

The lucrative boom in "management," as opposed to "managing," made many consultants and professors far richer than any division general manager. Very few were festooned with Rolls-Royces or Lamborghinis. But consulting paid well enough, and distributed enough of the swag in partnership devices, to retain men who could have ambled into £20,000 or $150,000 jobs managing some client company. Consultants like to say that it's not the money that retains them, but the intellectual challenge. They seldom mention an equally significant factor—consulting is much less risky than management, which for an ex-consultant can be very dangerous indeed.

The risk may only be that of losing a posthumous reputation, if, like Mark W. Cresap of Westinghouse, you die in office before the mess you made of the company lands at your door. Profits halved between 1957 and 1963, partly because of exactly the kind of snafu that consultants are supposed to clean up in their sleep. "The major problem of the company," said Cresap's successor, "in its management structure, was the fact that they had too many people reporting to the top operating man . . . A bottleneck at the top is the worst place to have one." Westinghouse, however, is not the only company (RCA was another) to discover that while most consultants are good at business, they are mainly good at their own business, which is a very specialized and lucrative form of service industry.

In that industry, consultants have performed marvels of marketing in the last two decades, elevating their status and profitability by strategic strokes that any entrepreneur would envy. The market has advanced to meet them, a usual phenomenon with hit products. Executives perplexed by the problems of operating their own clumsy corporate creations have cried for help, and they have really needed it in areas such as computers where technical advances left companies floundering in strange waters.

The consultants have been around in these quasi-technical jobs for decades, but the rewards of such humdrummery are limited by an obvious ceiling—the amount for which a company can acquire its very own full-time specialist. Some executives are not cute enough to spot this fact. But consultancy rewards in general stayed unexciting until the sharper minds in the game raised their sights to a more sublime level, the holy of holies, the boardroom itself.

Advising on marketing strategy or corporate organization has one shining virtue. The consultant breaks away from the constraint of fees related to the time of his own employees and climbs up to far more gratifying levels of remuneration based on the expected future worth of his services. Nobody does know, can know, or ever will know how to measure that worth. There may be some difference between this approach and charging what the traffic will bear, but not much.

Client boards may fight about the fee for computerizing the accounting system; they don't even try to assess the value of a new organization structure or "marketing orientation." If the company is big enough and the high-level consultant good enough, it might add £1 million a year to profits, in which case a fee of £50,000 is too ridiculous to worry about.

Since McKinsey consultants visited Shell, in fact, the latter's profits have swollen gigantically—never mind the sheer impossibility of proving that a chain of cause and effect links the consultants with the profits. The story of Shell and McKinsey started in Venezuela, where two brilliant young consultants, Hugh Parker and Lee Walton, worked so impressively for a subsidiary that they were invited to look at Shell's head office problems in London and The Hague. McKinsey at this time was still U.S.-based. But its adoption by Shell, widely supposed (and with some good reason) to lead Europe's management elite, was a gilt-edged visiting card into Europe.

If Shell, bristling with internal consultants, needed that extra something from McKinsey, then McKinsey obviously had something extra to give. Old-line British boardrooms, jammed solid with anxiety over modern problems of scale and complexity, for which they were ill equipped, rapidly took the point; so did thrusters unsure which way to thrust. One after another the blue chip names—ICI and the Bank of England, the Post Office and Unilever, Dunlop and the

BBC, and so on, and so on—found the McKinsey medicaments irresistible.

British consultants were consumed with jealousy by this American success in winning fat assignments and, adding insult to injury, publicizing it. One or two hinted darkly that the follow-up to McKinsey's work was less inspiring than its orders. Sour grapes, no doubt, but later developments, seen in this light, are still interesting. Spillers, the flour giant, went on a McKinsey course of reorganization and marketing orientation—its profits fell by one-third between 1968 and 1970. Dunlop was another good customer. In 1970, just before its marriage with Italy's Pirelli was consummated, Dunlop's pre-tax profits had been stuck for three years running.

The Post Office, set up as a new public corporation, combined big marketing fiascos with huge deficits; at least, the Bank of England didn't follow this precedent. Even Shell, after a few years, found the McKinsey scheme of boardroom organization unworkable. There are other examples, but their lesson is not that McKinsey's work was bad. On the contrary, its consultancy was probably as good as money can buy. The defects were intrinsic to consulting itself—not to consultants. The client company gets for its fee, and for a time, the services and advice of men who (if its choice has been good) have broader experience, superior intelligence, more impressive backgrounds, and sharper all-round competence than most of its executives. But the company doesn't get new management.

Most consultants tell of the assignment where the only essential, but impossible, recommendation was to heave out the chairman. One man had a tough job even getting the family chairman to resign the title of chief executive, on which a vitally needed new president insisted. The embattled chairman, after many weeks, finally blurted out that he didn't see why he should surrender, not when Henry Ford II kept his chief executive title. "Ah ha!," said the consultant, seizing his moment, "but Henry Ford runs Ford." They settled the argument by ringing Ford in Dearborn and asking if he ran the company. "Sure as hell I do," said Henry, and with that the chairman surrendered.

But consultants don't find it easy to bite the hand that hires them: they are more likely, after cozy months with the board, to unearth unsuspected virtues in the directors. The information on which the consultants work, anyway, has to come from the company itself, and consultants naturally look at the business through the directors' eyes. There is no practical point in submitting a report that incenses the customer. First, it won't be accepted, and all the consultant's labor will have gone for nothing. Second, the failed assignment will be bad for the consultant's reputation, and it is on reputation, especially in boardroom work, that a consultant's business depends. (The golden rule of consulting is once in, never out— or lose anything except the client.)

These facts play into the hands of directors who hire consultants for the most respectable bad reason—to endorse a decision that, in principle, has already been taken. Very likely, Shell knew that it was fat with surplus middle executives. But the necessary pruning was more comfortable, especially for a company that rejoiced in the avuncular nickname and traditions of "Joe Shell," when it was done, or seen to be done, on the disinterested advice of efficiency experts. This element in consultancy could be called the Pontius Pilate gambit: the hand washing comes expensive.

But suppose the Pilate gambit in no sense applies. Assume that the directors are genuinely in a quandary: they know not which way to turn, or how. At first sight, the most sensible action they can take, before going down for the third time, is to clutch at consultancy—even if it does prove to be a straw. But only at first sight. What the company needs is not consultants, but a whole new top management.

High and mighty executives draw high and handsome salaries to chart the destination of a company and decide how to get there. It may often be right, proper, and thoroughly sanitized to have competent outsiders double-check assumptions and plans. But any board that abdicates its role, and finances the abdication with stockholders' money, is worse than weak-kneed—it is incompetent to carry out the consultants' recommendations. The work will be doomed to failure, and the fees will run to waste.

Random hiring of consultants isn't justified by any exclusive expert knowledge. The textbooks on organization and strategy are all freely available; and the favored approaches of individual consulting firms can be easily recognized, like hallmarks on old silver, by the cognoscenti. If a company is told to reorganize into product divisions, install long-range corporate planning, and establish a straight man-to-man pyramid of line executives, with a single chief executive at the top—that is the authentic hallmark of McKinsey; others have similar recognizable stamps.

Whatever their brand, few consulting firms are prepared to limit their juicy range of tempting services. One American marketing consultant is happy to work on market strategy, new product development, organization of sales forces, diversification, corporate planning, and so on. The list stretches so far that very little remains for management itself to manage, and far too much remains to be provided from the consultant's own exhaustible resources: plainly, the more he specializes, the more expert, justifiable and useful his work is likely to be.

But the dynamic of consultancy dies if this line of reasoning is chased too far. The true logic of consultancy is maximization of juicy fees. Only then can the firm provide its members with the glowing reward and warm satisfaction that, rather than the grandeur of the organization, are its objectives. This is a key difference between consulting firms and the industrial corporation, to which organizational grandeur is all—which is partly why many former management consultants find adjusting to executive jobs in industry so tough.

Another part of the trauma hangs on the word "executive." The consultant, whiz though he is, merely advises; he can only put his own delectable ideas into practice by quitting the racket. In management, having ideas is wonderfully easy; turning them into reality leads to the pain of ulcers, losses, and angry stockholders. At that point, the top-level consultant is literally well out of it. His projects can only be judged, conveniently, over a period of years. If the outcome is disaster, the consultant can always argue either that the client failed to implement the advice properly, or that the glue would have been still stickier without his advice, an argument that has the great virtue of being wholly irrefutable (and wholly unprovable, for that matter).

If a company wants to employ consultants effectively, it had better not use them where effectiveness can't be measured. So don't employ those clever brains where they love to be used—in substitution pro tem for the unsure intellects on the main board. The best reason for using a consultant is because he knows something you don't know. There really are consultants pumped full with all there is to know about "physical distribution management," i.e., lugging goods about. There are consultants in how to sit, how to sell, how to plan, how to budget, how to interpret market research statistics: you name it, somebody knows it—and somebody needs it.

No management can be blamed for failure to have universal knowledge of the new business technology. But no management can be excused for failure to buy the missing knowledge. One of the feebler sights of the British 1960s, however, was to see middle-aged to aged boards of directors admitting to ignorance, all right—but assuming that their ailment was general unfamiliarity with "modern management." This produced substantial pocket money for Britain's relatively sparse population of high-ranking management academics; but whole-day seminars for the board are approximately as helpful to the company as a visit from Billy Graham.

The act of hiring and listening to an apostle of enlightened management is somehow thought to qualify the hirer as an enlightened executive. The intention substitutes nicely for the reality. Moreover, false enlightenment comes cheap. In a situation of hunger—in this case, for enlightenment—the man offering food to the starving has a great bargaining position, especially when £100 a day, or even £1,000, is a drop in the ocean of corporate waste.

But there is a real task in which the business academic, or

the professional consultant, can always help. It arises from the same causes that often negate consulting work—the fact that the consultant is outside the business and will play no long-term role in managing it. In any company, no matter how good, internal blindness becomes a besetting sin. Blinkered by obstinacy, experience, and self-regard, executives can't see their own simple mistakes. The outsider can. But his use as devil's advocate depends on having executives who will listen. Beyond this, the proper use of outside experts, in their fields of expertise, is as rifles aimed to pick off specific identified targets. To use them as shotguns, spraying in all directions, is a wasteful and uncertain method of getting bull's-eyes.

Calling in an expert to install a new management concept is like calling in the computer wizards. Unless the systems within which the new toy works are themselves effective, the toy will give no joy. In other words, it takes a high-class executive to know when he needs a consultant, to get full value, and to take the expert's advice critically and unemotionally. All consultants know that their best work is done with the best companies, a very obvious truth, even if it means that those who most need consultancy get least out of it.

The high-class executive is also less likely to run for help (or for cover) indiscriminately; it's the lower-class executive who abdicates, who lets the consultants take over. Well-found consultants can stay in a company forever, moving from one divisional trouble spot to another like Arabs wandering from oasis to oasis. Some consultants, who accept that for half of the time companies employing consultants really need new management, also feel that, for half the rest of the time consultants are misused. But they can't complain too loudly, unless, that is, they want to to lose their fees. As with all management, the possibilities are defined by the human factors.

Take the case of one supergrowth company that had plainly outstripped a rudimentary management system. One of the consultant's remedies was to kick the energetic, proconsultancy, but elderly, chairman upstairs, in favor of the highest-ranking relative. The chairman's attitude underwent radical change. While preparing to resume the reins, he was heard to mutter, "I don't think much of these consultants." That is the problem in a capsule. You can't make top-level consultancy work without breaking executives, and they purely hate to be broken.

26 *The New Product Fallacy*

ONE OBSESSION has recently united British and American executives (generally a decade apart in management fashion) : the urge to innovate. Firms love to boast that such and such a percentage of sales is, or will be, of products unborn five or ten years back. The innovatory quest has spawned new consulting firms, new gimmicks such as "venture management," and new areas of aching loss. Consumers are showered with new wonders that they don't want, which don't work, which rapidly disappear—and still executives crave more of the same punishment. Yet any wised-up executive granted one wish by the good god Mammon would beg not a new product, but one that would become very, very old. The most desirable products, self-evidently, are those that last forever—and most of the world's great businesses earn their bread from just such blessings.

This truth runs counter to a cherished concept of the new management—the product life cycle. Any academic can draw the smooth curve that shows the steep upward rise as the innovation takes off, the flattening out of profits as competition moves in—before peak sales arrive—then the slow decline through obsolescence to the morgue. From this, any student can mark the spot where new products must pick up the baton if the company isn't to drop out of the race. The picture is beautiful, beguiling, meaningless. First, theoretical life cycle charts never have an actual time scale, and it makes a mint of difference whether the palmy days will last fifty years or five. Second, the phrase "new product" needs careful analysis.

The Maverick is new compared to the Model T Ford. But the basic technology has changed little in fifty years, and this relative technical stagnation explains a commercial fantasy such as the Volkswagen beetle, unchanged forty years after its design and twenty-five years after its first sale. In food today's top brands, such as Kraft, Maxwell House, and Bird's-Eye, have been best-sellers almost since introduction. That's true, even though in food the U.S. alone spawns five thousand to six thousand new products a year (of which only eighteen hundred reach the stores and only five hundred survive twelve months).

In publishing, the *Reader's Digest* has outsold all magazines for decades. In soft drinks, no matter how Pepsi strives, nothing can touch Coca-Cola. The common-or-household light bulb of today would be familiar to Edison. The aspirin has been the world's leading analgesic since 1898. In a hot British brand market such as soap powders, Persil has kept a leading market share, even though it is technically less powerful than the new synthetics.

Nearly all these products have improved substantially since their dawn. But as technical concepts they are identical. The Maverick is more comfortable, more convenient, much faster than the Model T, and also less economical, less rugged, more costly; but the driver behind the steering wheel and internal combustion engine, on top of the four wheels, won't get from point A to point B much faster. In Detroit's heyday, the

products barely altered. Only the outer skin—the packaging—
was changed annually at an alarming cost, which was built
into the price of the vehicle.

This built-in obsolescence opened wide the doors of Detroit
to competitors who did vary the concept: minnows from
Europe and Japan beat the mightiest American management
machines in their own precious market with their own technology. The built-in obsolescence turned out to be, not of
the styling, but of the concept. The bungling of the car bosses'
did not arise from lack of new products, but from missing the
effect of changing tastes on old ones.

Brands lose market share or wither on the vine, not because
they get overtaken by the march of history, but because executives stupidly neglect them. There is no product life cycle;
there is a mismanagement cycle. A confectionery executive
once stumbled on this truth. He had an old line of cachous,
a Victorian sweet that any whizzing young brand manager
would have shot on sight. Apart from its creaking antiquity,
its sales figures were convincingly bad. Over the years they
had slid down the life-cycle slope to a quarter of their one-
time peak.

The chief executive (who, since the family owned the business, was more possessive than marketing professionals)
looked at the figures another way. Certainly, they showed that
far fewer people wanted his candy. But the miracle, for unpromoted, old-fashioned gunk, was that so many still drooled for
the stuff. It *must* have something. So he improved production
to cut costs, spent the savings on promotion—and sales
doubled. In Britain in 1971 you could still buy not only
Victorian cachous, but also products such as Beechams Pills
(b. 1847), Mackenzie's Smelling Salts (b. 1870), and Stone's
Original Green Ginger Wine, whose packaging has barely
changed since 1915. The mistake, once a company has built
a market, is to throw it away.

After World War II, the Morris company launched a car—
the Minor—which was still selling in British Leyland's hands
in 1971. But only minimal improvements were made in later
years. As the life cycle ground its way to the bitter end,

nobody admitted that continuing sales proved hard truths about both the Minor and the company's newer models. For instance, the new cars were trunkless wonders, and the Minor, which had a trunk (like competitive Fords, Hillmans, and Vauxhalls), had an advantage for anybody eccentric enough to travel with luggage.

British manufacturers, according to them, liked to run cars until they and their market dropped, to give the customer continuity. Actually, the firms couldn't afford the whopping investment in new or radically improved models. They also went on making obsolete cars on the specious financial argument that the production equipment had all been paid for with "depreciation" money. In reality, the old cars with their antique design engineering were even more expensive to produce than the new ones—and were stealing the latter's sales.

All businesses need an old product policy—how to make the best of what the company has. After the war, Beecham built its considerable fortunes on three oldies: Brylcreem, Macleans, and Lucozade. Even at the end of the 1960s, this unglamorous trio—a gooey hair cream, a crisp white toothpaste, and a sickly sweet glucose drink—were providing, with the genuinely new Beecham penicillins, about two thirds of group profits. The old brand has the cumulative weight of years of heavy advertising, of use by (more or less) satisfied customers, of high acceptability and established image. So long as astute directors improve and upgrade the product in step with the market, and modify the image with the times, the dreaded turning point in the life cycle can be put off indefinitely. Because executives get bored or complacent with old products, however, they quite unnecessarily condemn them to fast death or slow neglect. Beecham's veterans, Brylcreem and Macleans, had so much life in them that a substantial U.S. business was promoted on their backs. (A newer Beecham condiment, Silvikrin Shampoo, failed expensively, however: its name made the unacceptable suggestion to Americans that they were going gray.)

One of Beecham's American markets, contrarily, seems to prove the life cycle: toothpaste, where the old U.S. brand leaders have all been ejected by upstarts (including Macleans). The whole American industry was turned upside down by stannous fluoride. Here was a true technological advance: the first toothpaste whose advertising need tell no lies. It knocked the makers, Procter & Gamble, for a loop (P & G, of course, being a big company, didn't invent Crest—a university did). The hucksters could sing the therapeutic virtues of toothpastes that, hygienically speaking, were no better than any other. They couldn't cope with Crest, which truly was better. After painful false starts, the American Dental Association ended the agony by endorsing the product. A simple, unglamorized ad baldly stating the facts thereupon succeeded superbly, where the traditional ballyhoo had crashed.

A great new product has to differ so sharply from any joy already on sale that its qualities—so long as they are good—sell themselves. P&G's competitors made the gratuitous boob when they launched stannous fluoride toothpastes, called Ace and Cue, of making them almost indistinguishable from Crest. New products fail, and in phenomenally high proportions, because they offer no advantage worth having or, more simply, because they are bad. Even an admirable original (such as xerography or the Polaroid camera) customarily starts life badly: it is clumsy, hard to use, dear, unsatisfactory in its results. But their unique concept allowed Xerox and Polaroid to override initial error. When similar defects in use attack products that merely vary somebody else's theme, the customers will stand clear in droves.

The highest mortality—nine out of ten—is in cigarettes, where the novelty mainly lies in the marketing. Each cigarette is the same as some other cigarette, and those that fail are as good (or bad) as those that win. New product calamities, in fact, stem from confusion about newness. The pet venture may be a straight or crooked copy, or an attempt to break into somebody else's racket (IBM trying to muscle in on Xerox), or the newness may lie in replacing a similar product of your own (adding enzymes to an existing detergent mix). There may be real technological novelty in replacements. But "innovations," such as the Boeing 707, don't produce whole

261

new markets. People don't shave more because stainless blades are superior to carbon steel, and more airliners would have been sold in the 1960s if the jet engine had never been invented.

The genuine innovations, creating whole new markets, thrusting old companies into oblivion and new ones into preeminence, are so rare, and so rarely emanate from big corporations, that the giants are best off avoiding the chase. Their "new product" is usually a "me-too" (an imitation of somebody else's wow), or, far better, some variation on their own themes. The latter pays fine dividends. Stick an extra carburetor, a new paint job, and a few fancy extras on the same car, call it the GT or the GTO, and collect a bundle of extra cash from the customers without the financial and technical pain of producing a new supermodel. Far better to devise a new method of processing polyester fiber, call it Crimplene, and open up new uses, than to invent a new shoe material called Corfam and embark on the long, expensive effort to foist it on a wary world.

The second, even if it succeeds, only produces a long-haul yield. The former, with minimal fortune, pays off at once, and if it fails, costs little more than some executive's self-respect. Even that bruising will be mitigated by executives' reluctance to remember their failures. Marketing books are full of success stories, but failure has no friends and few case histories—even though collapse is far more common. On one survey's conclusions, there is an eight out of ten ratio of technical failure, while only one in every three technical successes (meaning that the product works) goes on to commercial triumph.

The lessons of failure are always the more valuable. When executives look back at the successes, like generals brooding over old campaigns, they always rationalize and mistake perfect luck for perfect performance. Triumph often catches its perpetrators completely by surprise, like the runaway hit in the U.S. of two novel light Scotch whiskies, Cutty Sark and J & B. Both were owned by respectable London wine merchants who knew far more about prephylloxera clarets than about marketing.

In quite recent hindsight, the Lesney Products tale was a marketing marvel: its two founders, with a few hundred pounds, brought new twists to the relatively old idea of the die-cast model car. Their Matchbox toys spread to every part of the world where children had pocket money—without one foot, so it seemed, being put wrong. In fact, luck led the partners to the idea (they were making a model coronation coach at the time), and luck (the arthritis of Britain's leading toy firm) left them for long almost alone in the field. Much less can be learned from their success than from their subsequent failure to anticipate a small technical improvement, which produced Mattel's Hot Wheels, and from their slow reaction to this threat, which demolished their profitability.

When Gerber and Campbell's came beefing their way into Heinz's U. K. goldmine, attacking Heinz's canned foods and ready-to-serve soups with bottled and concentrated goodies, Heinz didn't make the same mistake. It put out its own bottled baby foods and concentrated soups, just in case the U. K. housewives changed their tastes from cans to bottles and from ready-to-serve to concentrates, and it battered the opposition with massive promotion. Gerber and Campbell's were clobbered. But more often companies get locked into their technology as well as their management habits—and even more dangerously.

Maybe Xerox will come first when the inevitable happens, and its cumbersome, unreliable reprographic money spinner is replaced by a more efficient, less unwieldy process. But don't bet on it—and Xerox shouldn't bet on having the good fortune of IBM. The first Univac computer (produced by men whom IBM had sent packing) appeared, and made IBM's entire product range obsolescent, four years before IBM got a computer on the market. Univac, however, so crunched up the greatest postwar commercial discovery that IBM, despite its errors and delay, roared past Univac into staggering riches.

You can bank on the opposition being stupid some of the time, but not all the time. That is the trouble with me-too products. Assuming that the market is established, the me-too executive is gambling that his product will be better and better marketed. This ignores logic. Trying something different is always better than competing directly, for in the latter case, you may lose. The small companies that creep to riches under the skirts of large Auntie corporations do so by specializing, by doing something different. Nobody has got near Kodak's mass market in conventional cameras and films, or ever will. Polaroid got in under Auntie Kodak by offering a clear difference: instant photos.

Self-deception is rampant. No executive confesses, even to himself, that the opposition does indeed have a better product (if the opposition has been making the goodies longer, it probably does). No executive readily concedes that his time and other people's money have produced a lemon. Only the most self-aware executive takes honest account of cannibalization, or robbing Peter to pay Paul: the Mustang hits the Galaxie, the Maverick bangs the Mustang, and the Pinto crumples the Maverick—so total Ford sales don't rise by the numbers of the new winner. Similarly, Radiant eats into Omo, and freeze-dried coffee clobbers ordinary instant (in the case of General Foods and Maxim, it did so at tremendous cost, including forty-three months in test market). Without the new product, life might have been much ghastlier—but, with it, existence isn't any richer.

The hectic chase after innovation keeps executives busy and advertising agencies in funds. Executives usually argue (like the consultants who urge them into would-be innovation) that the increased speed of technological change, the dwindling time between discovery and implementation, and the shortening scale of the mythical life cycle leave progressive managements no option but to waste effort and resources on new products—even though three-quarters of the latter fail absolutely, while, of the rest, many obviously fail in relative terms. Some companies find that only 6 percent of their development money ends up in commercial successes, which is exceedingly perverse. Possibly half the products on world markets in a decade's time will be "new." But equally half of them will be antique, and within that half great fortunes and fabulous returns on capital will be made.

27 Do Tycoons Need Techniques?

ASK EXECUTIVES what they want by way of improving literature and most will call for a richer menu of management techniques. They can't have enough of barely comprehensive inventions such as Monte Carlo simulation, management by exception, statistical sampling, linear programming, Markovitz Portfolio Selection, and the other contents of the technical basket. Their approach almost suggests that management techniques are like handbooks on car maintenance: master the latter and you save garage bills by doing it yourself; master the former and the business will respond to the magic technical touch. The analogy breaks down at several points—including the fact that many techniques (among them the most valuable) can't be left to enthusiastic amateurs.

Still more discouraging is the difficulty of translating technical lore from the page to the battlefield. Imagine the higher

267

executive leafing through a spunky article on the mathematical approach to the product mix, the number and variety of products a company puts out. If the company is typical, several products could be ejected without any effect on profits. In fact, by making room for other lines (not one of which is ever made in the optimum numbers), a bout of slashing must boost earnings. But the elevating cases in the product mix article won't exactly fit any other company. And the boss's first reaction will be to call some subordinate's attention to the offending pages. If this beleaguered man is using the technique, he fires off a brisk retaliatory memo; if he isn't, his defensive mechanisms come into play—and the most valuable of these is sheer delay.

This technique, found in no textbook, works wonders. The two main defensive gambits are diametrically opposed. Method One is, Don't respond at all until forced. This way (the most common) amplifies the chances that other and weightier matters, like an overpriced bid for another company, will supervene, and the boss will forget all about it. Method Two is to respond at speed in overwhelming and enthusiastic detail. This embarrasses the boss in turn. Now he must make a decision, which he too dislikes, and his defensive mechanisms take over. With luck, he will never make the decision at all. A Method Two twist was applied within one great engineering group. Its new management ordered a full survey of production facilities to find out which could be rationalized (a euphemism of the same order and meaning as "liquidated" in Soviet Russia). The gigantic tome ended with one short arresting sentence: "Nothing can be done until future product plans have been decided."

This illustrates the difference between techniques of management and management techniques. Techniques of management are used to procure the result a manager really wants —in the above case, inaction. Management techniques are the tools that an executive may or may not use in the pursuit of those real objectives. The true aim of an executive who wants to bone up on techniques is to feel more efficient, more modern, better equipped. He isn't, like the genuine techniques expert, obsessively interested in applying a mathematical method—such as exponential smoothing or network analysis—to obtain better operational results.

This explains the conflict, often deadly, between executives and technique experts inside the corporation. Not only do executives get the big money and make the big (and small) decisions, they are also free to use, abuse, or not use the expert's expertise. To the experts, there is something deeply wounding in being forced to support their surefire cost-saving ideas with voluminous reports, while any nut in the upper echelons merely has a brainstorm in the bath, and the experts promptly have to study its inane implications—in depth too.

The inanity is often immediately apparent. Professor P.M.S. Blackett, the Briton who invented Operational Research to improve bombing efficiency and convoy deployment in World War II, wanted to restrict "systems analysis" (which is the Everest of management technology) to "calculations that can be done on the back of an envelope." Rather than use the same small tool for his simpler sums, however, the executive loads his own failure to clarify his thoughts onto the shoulders of the misnamed management scientist—misnamed because none of the sciences is in any way specific to management, and because the work is seldom scientific either. The science rests only in applying measurement and logical deduction to known fact, something that executives are supposed to do for themselves.

Take a typical case—the executive who opposes a price rise, or wants to invoke a discount, or open a second sales office in a region, or revamp the corporate image. Rude questions have to be asked: If we raise prices by half, how much will sales fall—10 percent, 20 percent, or 30 percent? At what level of sales and prices will profits drop? How much more business will we get through this discount, or new office, or company facelift alone, and what will it cost? The cost is always precisely measurable, and you can always work out simply how much in *extra* sales is needed to cover the *overall* loss of profit.

Executives fail to make this easy, speedy test, not because

they don't know the techniques of simple arithmetic, but because they are dead set on a course that they have chosen for other reasons entirely. The man wants to cut prices because he thinks vaguely that it will help the sales effort; he wants to open the new office to widen his empire; he longs to beautify the corporate image—to enhance his own. These are emotional drives. Sitting down with the back of an envelope is a cold-blooded affair that rarely satisfies anybody except the technical expert. And he is too insignificant in the hierarchy for his pleasure to matter.

The greatest operational research calculation of all time was supervised (on a blackboard, not the back of an envelope) by Henry Ford I, whose enthusiasm for management technology was only slightly warmer than his love for unions. The sum showed the economic consequences of raising Ford wages to $5 a day. The calculations proved that elevating Ford workers into potential Ford buyers would leave Henry with enormous profits. Note the sequence of events. Ford had an inspiration, which men of less peculiar genius would have missed or misunderstood. Then, like a good engineer, Ford checked his brainwave by the simplest relevant calculation. Then he put his idea into practice—again like a good engineer.

Engineering is the right analogy. Much management technology is like most production or design technology—the general manager has no business knowing the details, but must know that the technology exists. Mathematical and computational techniques are the machine tools of management—and some are as abstruse as the Moog Synthesizer. As one authority wrote, "Some of these techniques require highly specialized knowledge or equipment for their correct use. Probably only a few dozen people in the country fully understand them . . . (others) are as yet barely understood by more than a few experts." So relax. You wouldn't be able to use them if you tried.

In fitting out a factory, a good general director decides what to make, but buys an expert to tell him how. The director's judgment then tests the expert's words to confirm (say) that he isn't proposing to use a multi-spindle automatic when a hand drill will do nicely, or isn't hiring expensive computer time to try some assumption on which no profit hinges. An American chemical plant contractor was disconcerted to find that a British customer insisted on his using the sophisticated, costly technique of "network analysis." Back home, it wouldn't have been thought necessary—it wasn't either.

A second category of techniques is essential to almost any manager; it mostly boils down to applied common sense. Much of this indispensable technology is financial, meaning that the executive (although he will resist it) has to reduce the implications of his actions to money terms. There is always a simple, back-of-the-envelope truth involved, such as the basic discounted cash flow thought, which is that a pound in the hand today is worth more than a pound in the bag tomorrow. Old-line executives in their ignorance used to rely on payback—how long their money took to come home, which assumed, falsely, that money received in three years' time had the same value as today's. The supposedly sophisticated Americans still have a deep sentimental attachment to this ancient concept, and to a degree they are right.

Old-line executives were not as silly as they seemed. Payback enshrines a truth. Until you do repocket your capital, the enterprise is pointless. Say a firm invests £1 million in a plant that produces a discounted cash flow of £100,000 a year for a decade, and then has to be replaced by another plant of equivalent cost: its effort has gone for nothing. The quicker the payback too, the less an executive needs to worry about discounted cash flow or anything else.

Forrest Mars, in creating his confectionery empire, used a crude, but highly effective, measure, judging executives by their return made in real money (with no allowance for so-called depreciation) on the real money that, historically, he, Forrest Mars, had put into the business. In other words, Mars looked at his wealth as an individual proprietor naturally would, and there is more logic (and money) here than in the big bureaucracy's more complex, convoluted measures.

The tycoon grabs hold of a simple, single idea that makes

sense to him, and applies it consistently and ruthlessly. But Patterson of NCR, Watson of IBM, Lord Leverhulme of Lever Brothers, Henry Ford, the founding Agnelli of Fiat, and the other emperors had something else: they knew their businesses. Management techniques are only adjuncts to management. They don't cope with one basic fact—that the nature of the business partly determines how it is run. You don't have to be a life-long butter and egg man to sell butter and eggs. But the lifetime knowledge of those who do know one end of a cow or hen from the other is critical to the success of the business—as turnaround men, or company doctors, often find out, late and to everybody's cost.

The turnaround artist, the expert called to revive failing firms, is frequently loaded with technical lore. Often he is a renegade management consultant. To judge by recent British experiences (British Printing Corporation, J. Bibby, Harris Lebus, and the Jensen car company, which took the extreme step of importing an American consultant, Carl Duerr), there is at best a four-year rise-and-fall cycle: the technical touch first produces radical improvement, then yields diminishing returns, and is finally blunted by business troubles.

The technically adept executive manager is asked to create an effective, fast-growing, efficient, and professional company out of one that is ineffective, sluggish, sloppy, and amateurish —which is why the *wunderkind* was called in. But for all his professional equipment he lacks the one technique that the dozy oldsters all possess—feel and affection for their special market. Lasting success depends (more than professionals can see, for it reduces their personal marketability) on how fast the newcomers can absorb the facts of a strange market and on how responsive that market really is.

Uncovering and eliminating the oldsters' mistakes is the easy bit. One taken-over motorcycle veteran vehemently opposed dropping a brand name because of its popularity in the Middle East. Inquiry showed that the company's Arab sales could be counted on one maimed hand. This kind of nonsense tumbles out of the woodwork at the first application of common sense or management technique, call it what you will, as in the case of a battery company, which only struck its profit at the year-end after counting the stock in the warehouse, though its deliveries to dealers were all on sale or return. The professional will settle such follies fast. The harder problem is to discover what the old boys did right, and, still more, to avoid new disasters (which the veterans would never even have imagined) in desperate attempts to overcome inborn defects in the market.

The British Printing Corporation, passionate to fill its presses, dropped over £2 million on publishing ventures and many millions more on a joint encyclopaedia company. Lebus totally reequipped, at dreadful cost, to make a new furniture range that landed in the market with all the impact of a Laugh-In bladder. The technical skills can stop the rot, as Duerr did at a nearly bankrupt Jensen. But replacing the fungus with healthy growth requires different aptitudes. Not even a hot-gospeling American could fully solve the fundamental problem: how to make enough cars at low enough cost to finance the effort required to sell and make enough cars, and so on, and so on.

Techniques are most valuable for correcting mismanagement. Thus the most important technique, positively guaranteed to wash any business whiter, is challenge. Since every business is managed badly, in the sense that every operation is capable of improvement, savings can always be made without any loss of effectiveness—and often at little cost. Simple technical analysis will always reveal bad cases of common defects, such as the overhead obsession. One company maintained a money-losing plant just for its contribution to overhead: it was tying up £3 million for a £50,000 contribution. Another firm kept a large loser going on the same specious grounds—the loss maker, far from making a contribution, practically was the overhead.

Companies often suffer under the delusion that by juggling costs around the organization, even with no new money coming in, they can enrich its finances. The best use of technicians is not to chart corporate forays into the remote and uncertain future, but to uncover the errors of its present management. This is unlikely to be popular; it falls foul of a basic lie of management—any mistakes were made by the previous incumbents. The Tenth Truth, however, is that *the easiest way of making money is to stop losing it*. Dealing with customer complaints used to cost Heinz £4 a complaint, until some unsung genius thought of issuing a 25-pence voucher every time a tin of baked beans or tomato soup came to grief. That's real management, and it doesn't need a computer.

The task isn't to understand what is meant by, say, "a system using doubly exponentially smoothed average demand forecasts coupled with safety stocks being set with a Trigg Tracker and the modules of the Trigg Tracker used to control the parameters of the exponential smoothing." It is to know rules of thumb such as this: operational research techniques will enable most companies to cut stocks by 30 percent, saving delicious sums, but eight tenths of that saving will come from better recordkeeping. Or (and expert help will show you where) five distribution points will always provide second-day delivery to 80 percent of the entire U.S. Never disparage a good rule of thumb: that digit is as valuable as any computer. But to discover and exploit such verities, you need the ability to challenge, check, and check again.

Beyond that, the technique of management is the use of analytical methods to picture reality. Managements are always being misled, like the U.S. paper company that thought it had developed a great trade in disposable surgical dressings. It applied a much abused technique (market research) and found that doctors actually used the products as de luxe hand towels. Luck, that most valuable of all management techniques, had played its usual, indispensable part.

If you attribute your success to pure luck, you will not only be right, most of the time, but you will be better prepared for the repugnant job of criticizing your mistakes, which are plenty. An executive in one of the more efficient retail giants once remarked, "Anybody listening in on our meetings would think it was the worst-run business in the world." That is the only safe assumption. Discontent is commercially divine—the manager's best friend. But like the techniques it employs, self-criticism won't create a wonderful business: the tycoon doesn't need techniques, and can afford self-adulation, because he can think and act along the straight line between a marvelous idea and its realization. Executives, who are hired hands and tend to think in circles, need all the aid they can get —especially from themselves.

28 *The Dotted Line Syndrome*

THE MOST prevalent organizational blight is organic—the growth of the corporate organism into an end in itself. Executives may swear that they exist to make money, sell safety matches, build power stations, market lingerie, or whatever, but insensibly they slide into serving none of these ends. Instead, they serve only the corporation. The business exists to sustain the company. The company no longer exists to do business; it exists to exist.

Consequently, a mind-bending preoccupation of senior executives is with the form of the beloved organism. Like some collector of stamps or rare coins, they fiddle constantly with the object of their love, and they call in other avid enthusiasts (in this case, management consultants) to help in rearranging, pruning, and swapping. Corporate reshuffles are non-events—for everybody outside the corporation. Inside they are of lasting fascination, like a restatement of Catholic dogma. Their initiation alone accomplishes nothing measurable. A bad business can never be swung around to supergrowth by redrawing the organization chart.

Boards huff and puff about strains on the previous structure, about growth imposing new pressures for which the old machinery was inadequate, about it being time for a new look. (For the real reasons, read bad trading results, uncomfortable awareness of falling behind the fashion, a take-over bid miraculously averted). But the ultimate cause is simply that introspection, which all bureaucracies enjoy, has to come to a great orgastic climax at periodic intervals. After their game of musical chairs, the managerial bureaucrats, purged and satisfied, settle into their new seats—and carry on much as before.

The sacred scrolls of the organization's tabernacle are the manuals and, above all, the organization chart. Like the sacred documents of many religions, these charts often mean very little, even to the initiated. Some iconoclastic managements have tried to stamp them out, with as much success as Nero had against the Christians. In one American multinational, charts are officially forbidden, so the executives draw up unofficial ones. Nothing can destroy the self-preserving desire of the inhabitants of a bureaucracy to know precisely where they stand—or where they don't stand. Many executives are more eager to narrow their responsibilities (which gives them less opportunity for failure) than to widen them.

Very possibly, the unofficial charts drawn up by deprived executives are closer to reality than those blessed by the boardroom. These are abstract art, as highly regarded as Jackson Pollocks. The top management of a big company such as Honeywell is even a bit ashamed that a few years back it was chartless. But only the names and job titles are real: the lines of command reflect an idealized truth. The telltale symptom is the dotted line: the more dotted the lines on a chart, the less it reflects the way the company actually runs.

A crisp unbroken line is understood by everybody. It means that in theory Executive B reports to Executive A, who in turn supervises, controls, or pushes about Executive B. It does not mean either that B takes any notice of A, or that B manages his segment of the chart at all—A may swamp the fellow entirely. But at least everybody knows what their relationship is supposed to be. Neither A nor B may see it the same way in practice, however. In 134 cases where managers in one U.S. multi-national thought they had told subordinates what to do, the latter were only conscious of receiving 78 orders.

The dotted line, in contrast, is a thing of confused beauty and a joy forever. It fans out from boards to "advisers" or "planning units"—staff appointments, often at the highest level, whose work veers across that of the line managers. The English Electric chart, in the days before the group's disappearance, was festooned with dots of this description. Or dots connect a functional department (engineering, say) with a product division: here dots mean that the two are supposed to work together, a forlorn but pretty fantasy.

If engineers dominate the company (as they dearly love to do) the dotted line is more authoritarian than the solid one. One production manager, invited to reveal his sorrows to a new outside director, pointed out that small differences in fifty virtually identical components forced him to maintain fifty separate production lines. He thought that the technical specification could be met by no more than five varieties. The director led him by the hand over to the engineers; they readily agreed that the production manager was dead right. The corporate ethos, or the reality behind the chart, didn't allow production considerations, or production men, to intrude on the organizational dominance of the engineers— even to save money.

Other dotted daydreams cover bureaucratic miasmas such as independent overseas companies that are controlled by so-called international divisions but make the same products in the same way as domestic product divisions. Multi-national companies (the popular euphemism for American companies with overseas interests) have gone to extraordinary chart contortions to sustain the action that their foreign satrapies are independent. They have good reasons for telling stories—host

279

countries (another euphemism, meaning the occupied territory) are not fond of reminders that the control of large chunks of national assets lies somewhere in the Midwest.

This kind of problem doesn't bother the Europeans one iota. The Swiss of Nestlé and the Dutch of Philips control their overseas companies with a tight-lipped Napoleonic firmness. "I personally still hold the view," wrote one of Nestlé's chocolate generals with heavy jocularity, "that . . . we are rather decentralized. But I am often surprised when talking to our own people in the markets . . . to find that they think the contrary." As for Philips, an internal wag commented that the electrical giant is the only company in the world where, no matter what your position, there are always more people above you than below you.

The British are almost certainly more lax, or relaxed, toward managements in other lands. This has something to do with the tradition of empire (unique to the British). By the time bad news got back from India in Queen Victoria's day, it was too late to take any action, and British executives (many of whose companies, such as British Petroleum, grew up as imperially as the British raj) became used to letting far-flung executives sink or swim. So today earnest efforts at home are periodically drowned by disasters in Australia or India, the compensation being that bad domestic results are periodically salvaged by some far-flung miracle.

The American imperialists, even though bad news travels faster these days, have come to share the same experience—Chrysler in Britain, Dow in German textiles, or Celanese in France. Controlling subsidiaries with rods (or dotted lines) of iron may stop some mistakes, but it won't solve the problem, which is fundamentally one of power. The actual management of companies is determined by their power relationships, and these, because they are human and changing, cannot be depicted by anything less than a full Freudian psychoanalysis. Like all human relationships too they follow no rules. There are only well-known dangers, which you can survive, just as you could conceivably survive driving up the New York Thruway on the wrong side of the road.

First, if the man in charge does not have the power to execute that charge, he probably won't. He needn't be the man who the chart says is in charge, so long as some other executive has the power instead. But if the authority falls into an uneasy vacuum, with overlords sitting on managerial shoulders like so many old men of the sea, the results will be ineffective. Some of the bigger American success stories in Britain have come under a loose rein—or no rein at all.

Black and Decker, managed by a tough Englishman named Robert Appleby, expanded so fast that it outgrew a parent that did little more than sit benignly by. Hoover grew to dominate the British appliance market under the independent British management of Sir Charles Colston, who took Hoover into washing machines and into Europe while the home board in North Canton, Ohio, couldn't see further than the sucking end of its vacuum cleaners. After the eccentric Herbert Hoover, Jr., decided to crack his little whip, before being ousted in turn by affronted American directors, British Hoover flopped into a much more dismal decade.

This basic principle, that he who is supposed to manage should manage, has nothing to do with the letter of the chart, but everything to do with the spirit of the company. The useful purpose of reorganization is to stop that guiding spirit (whatever it is) from being bogged down in organizational routine. A brisk game of musical chairs sharpens everybody up, the catch being that, if the executives are too slow when the music starts, they will still not be speedy enough at the end.

One precise problem is the prime position—do you or don't you have one man at the apex of the pyramid? Certain companies (du Pont, ICI) have a long tradition of multiple, hydra-headed top management; others, notably in America, have been experimenting with "the president's office"—a kind of troika; while the Germans, who had enough of the *Führerprinzip* during the war, have management boards where the boss, not even a primus inter pares, is described as the "spokesman." (He may speak in a voice so loud that he drowns out everybody else. Men like Dr. Joachim Zahn of Daimler-Benz are not in the shrinking violet category.)

Where hydra-headed management has grown up over the years, and has become built into the life-style, changing it can be as difficult as altering the whole direction and philosophy of the corporation. Shell found this out after its own McKinsey-advised reshuffle. There one director ended up as something called director of coordination, oil. Catch 22 was that Shell happens to be an oil company, the bulk of whose business descended, with backbreaking force, on this one man. His position, like the reshuffle, became quite untenable. Oil companies such as Shell face in acute form the dilemma of all organizations, which is to resolve the pull between the center and the lone executive down the line manipulating the physical facts on a day-to-day basis. Because oil is the most homogenous of businesses, the spider in the middle of the web can pull everything in toward it. But what about the happiness and self-esteem of lesser insects around the rim?

The decentralize-centralize problem can never be finally resolved. The gibe goes that the management consultant called in to a decentralized company says "centralize." Show him a centralized company, and he promptly decentralizes it. The bigger the company too, the more likely the consultant is to push the top management upstairs into an ethereal chart zone known as strategy. But where does strategy begin and tactics end? British Petroleum, for example, as the 1960s ended, got caught grievously short of tanker capacity in a rising market. Is having enough tankers strategic or nonstrategic?

The larger a company is, the more often strategy gets locked in by supposedly tactical decisions taken far lower down. By the time most issues have worked their way up the chart to the board or executive committee, the titans at the top may no longer have either the freedom or the time to reverse what some remote underling has wrought. The object of a decentralizing reshuffle is to consolidate this unplanned fact into a shining system of delegated responsibility.

BP in 1970 constructed a three-ring circus—the board, a trading board one ring down, and a permanent executive committee of trading directors below that. The overlaps between the three tiers meant that the seven managing executives on the trading board were responsible for their triumphs and misdeeds to a main board that consisted mostly of themselves (making life a little easier all around). The astrological complexities of systems like BP's, with the nine trading executives as satellites of the seven managing executives, and regional and functional orbits crisscrossing all over the planet earth, practically guarantee that the delegated power, like hot air, will rise right back to where it has always resided.

But some secret force makes a company work, more or less effectively, despite the efforts of bureaucracy to turn its management totally inward. Somewhere in the organization lurk the 20 percent of executives who (according to Pareto's law) do 80 percent of the effective work. Finding the 20 percent and removing obstacles to their performance is the only proper pursuit of organization organizers. An idealist might try to uplift the 20 percent proportion, but maybe this is unrealistic. Maybe the active executives, like worker bees in a hive (only with a king bee or king bees at their head), need a large community of drones. In which case, the chartists should concentrate on keeping the drones in happy, mildly useful, and clear relationship to each other, and out of the hair of the workers.

This worker-drone breakdown could be synthesized into a new psychological theory of companies, like the popular contrast between authoritarian Theory X companies and easygoing participative Theory Y firms. The idea of hierarchical managements trying to loosen up is like Russian apparatchiks trying to give more power to factory directors. It fails because it isn't what the apparatchiks or the top executives really want. Styles of management grow out of traditions of companies and styles of people, and there is no convincing evidence that Theory Y companies, although much nicer to work for, outperform the Theory X bastards.

Even where a recognizable Theory Y company is a wow, there is a chicken-and-egg difficulty. As a company succeeds, so its executives, working cheek by jowl over the years, develop respect for each other's muscles, wariness of each other's weaknesses, and instinct for a management method that suits them all equally. Call this participation, if you will. But Theory Y can no more be credited for its success than Theory X can be applauded for ITT's swimming against the conglomerate tide under Harold Geneen, a sixteen-hour-a-day dynamo who has devised a corporate structure that revolves around him like a top. A man can make an organization, and an organization in turn makes its men. But if the company falls on evil days, it won't achieve salvation without a change in the men as well as the mechanism.

EPILOGUE
Some of My Best Friends . . .

NEXT TO BEING told how good they are individually, executives best love to hear how bad they are as a bunch. Any course of myth destruction serves this therapeutic purpose, but at a price: that of building another myth, which is that all executives, being foolish and foible-ridden, make a bad job worse. All that I know about management was learned from executives, some of whom are my friends, many of whom I admire, most of whom deserve respect—clever men who work hard according to their best lights in circumstances that are often against them. This epilogue is for them. As for the idle, selfish, stupid self-deceivers, this is how to beat them and enjoy it.

What lends the executive his peculiar charm and weakness is inability to recognize his own nakedness—his impotence, incompetence, and error. So do recognize it: the shock of recognition will improve your performance, and give you a lasting start on unshocked competitors. Make things easier for yourself by simplifying everything you can, wherever and whenever you can.

William Blackie, the chief executive of Caterpillar Tractor, never said wiser words than these: "I deride the idea that an executive's function is problem solving—it is the bad executive who is up to his neck in problems." In the standard big company bureaucracy, executives stalk new problems with the eagerness of the hunters of the snark. As if ordinary life threw up too few troubles, they invent and invite extra complexity. Any business situation can be reduced to simple terms. If it is, the solution usually appears from the reduction, and the "problem" evaporates.

The surest way to simplify is to concentrate. Don't, if you are brilliant at making record changers, reckon that you will be an expert hand at refrigerators. If the company can find one lucrative activity or market in which it functions well, sufficient unto the day be the profit thereof. Concentration also means that the single-minded company must be single-minded about its overriding objective, which is to be the best at everything from production costs (the lowest) and efficiency (the highest) in serving the consumer. If you can supply more effectively on a lower cost base than anybody else, you must win.

The more a business concentrates, the less time its executives need to waste. The single-minded company, alas, tends to become monomaniacal as well; its executives are expected to live only for power tools or whatever, and they don't like to buck the system. So every last detail of the business is regurgitated to fill long days of discussion. Even in average circumstances, discussions take up half an executive's time, and interruptions do the rest of the damage.

According to a Swedish study, fourteen minutes is the maximum for which an executive is left on his own; and nine minutes is his top time without interruption. No wonder he can't think straight. Resist this vice strenuously. The object, as in management generally, is to get the most with the least, the maximum effective management thought and follow-up with the minimum expenditure of hours. Ask of every activity, and especially of every meeting, whether it serves any purpose directly related to the company's profit. Organize the company so that a normal working day will cover normal tasks. And pack executives (including yourself) off home at decent times (that is, unless they don't want to go). Never disturb them after hours without grave cause, and with humble apologies.

A dangerously narrow line divides a company that wastes no time from a stagnant bunch of idle corporate loafers. The best way to avoid stagnation is to manage young. That is, give men high responsibility as soon as you know that they won't allow strange Italians with Swiss bank accounts to run up £4 million debts (that actually happened). Mozart was dead at thirty-five. So are many living executives. The one great idea that, if Freud was right, is all any man is given, comes early rather than late. If you wait until men are over forty, let alone fifty, to give them their most important job, you will miss their prime—and so will they. Young executives are no more all brilliant balls of energy than old ones are all sputtered-out volcanoes. But the good oldsters were better when they were younger, or would have been, if somebody had given them a chance.

And don't kid yourself that you've rejuvenated the company by lowering the average age of the executives from fifty-seven to fifty-three. That is different in degree, but not in kind, from the octogenarian British chairman who decided to retire to make way for a younger man. He meant his son, a stripling in his sixties. Somebody, preferably that son, should long before have told the old roadblock to clear himself away. But the circumstances of the people almost certainly made serious criticism impossible. Don't let it happen in your company, and don't stay where it has happened. If an executive can't be frank to his colleagues and seniors, he won't be frank to himself either; both sins are equally dangerous.

Never take frankness as far as boasting. Lord Thomson must bitterly regret (or should) the day when he described his television franchise as "a license to print money." So it was; but it didn't take long before a British government, alerted and affronted, altered the license to one to lose money. Remember, as a better example, the Swiss of Hoffman-La Roche, who have the world's most profitable drug company, but nobody, except possibly their bankers, knows how much money Roche coins. This is extreme, and not to be imitated. But "speak only when spoken to and avoid vainglory" is a sounder course than hiring a public relations army and missing no opportunity to extoll your own merits. You may not have any.

For salutary proof of your demerits, follow up a few complaints. No criticism that has reached me in my game, however rude or ignorant, has been without a valuable grain of truth, and your game is no different. In some cases, it isn't just a grain of truth, but a whole Sahara Desert. To be specific, if an auto company delivers to a customer (probably several weeks late) a model that comes to pieces in his hands, and then takes several months of acrimonious correspondence, and several returns of the machine, before its offense is put right, then that firm is rotten from top to bottom and needs total overhaul fast.

Don't skate around complaints on the grounds that detail is not your business. The argument that board level executives, or any executives, should look at the wood and forget about the trees is an incitement to, and an excuse for, unforgivable slackness. The good executive at any level can distinguish between a vital detail and rubbish, and a detail a day keeps the liquidator away. Sometimes, spotting even a beam in your own eye, let alone a few motes, is psychologically difficult. Overcoming this repression is where outside critics come in—so don't be like General Motors and try to wish your own private Ralph Naders away. Like Nader's Raiders, they will, more often than not, be right.

Every item of GM's behavior in the Nader affair was disgraceful, from its blind eye for its own faults to its harassing of Nader's private life. The great corporation deserved its great punishment for infringing a creakingly ancient moral rule. Do unto others as you would be done by; in other words, behave yourself. Few sights in world business are more unattractive than that of large companies seeking credit and praise for progressive labor policies, or for their antipollution, antiracialism, and antipoverty programs—as if they had some right, which they were generously waiving, to foul the environment, or exacerbate social tensions, or grind the workers' faces in the dust.

After Walter Reuther forced the guaranteed annual wage on GM, the company took credit for the innovation. Executives whose firms have ignored their social responsibilities for decades applaud themselves for doing so no longer. But in fact, the environment is still being polluted; and you will still find only slightly more Jews on the boards of U.S. blue chips than colored men in any executive role in any British company. If prejudice restricts a company's hiring policy, it will miss able people—and deservedly. In many mediocre giants, careers are still not open to all talents. Change that, and you will change the giants, and possibly their mediocrity.

The company's social obligations begin at home. "In many auto companies life is like a jungle," said one escapee. "Among executives, it is dog eat dog." That is no less barbaric than it sounds, and an uncivilized company is no more worth living in than a cannibal country. Even a decent company such as General Foods comes in danger of forgetting that people are not pawns. "That place is much like being in the army," an observer once said. "They rotate people terrifically."

Don't let your company be like either a jungle or the services. Executives are neither animals nor conscripts; they can be made to behave like both, but at dreadful loss in both effectiveness and ordinary humanity. Employees are not "Honeywellers" and "IBMers," as companies like to call them; they are individuals. Their loyalty to the corporation is only worthwhile if it is voluntary, nonconformist, and like undercarriages, easily retractable.

The only excuse for being displeased when a good executive retracts himself is if the move is a genuine mistake. If the manager is moving to a better job, and you can't outbid the opposition, be happy. After all, the man is supposed to be your friend; and nobody is indispensable (especially you). Huge turnover of executives is a bad sign; someone is either managing or hiring badly. But nil turnover is possibly even worse. The company can't be hiring and developing the ambitious, able, and energetic men it desperately needs; otherwise some of them would inevitably energize themselves out of the place. Moreover, if holes don't open up, you can't fill some of them with new talent, and that is fatal.

Fresh talent need not be imported; it can very often be dredged up from the company's own depths. But only these regular transfusions can save a corporation from the major surgery to which most eventually come. Unfortunately, the surgery only rearranges the same parts. The most effective shake-ups are cataclysmic, not kaleidoscopic. The best thing that ever happened to I. G. Farben, the prewar German chemical giant, was the break-up by the Allied occupiers of a lumbering, cartel-ridden mammoth into three aggressive and distinct component parts. The worst thing that happened to Krupp after the Nazi defeat was its preservation intact by a wily owner: that signed the company's death-warrant as a leading European industrial force. The first billion-dollar giant that deliberately hives off a few hundred million dollars of superfluous, profitable sales will make history and a fortune for its stockholders.

Size, apart from its other drawbacks, kills homeliness. One common factor of unusually successful firms is their hick quality. They don't have plush metropolitan offices, or, sometimes, plush offices at all. Their heart is in some undistinguished locale such as Buchanan, Michigan or Goole, Yorkshire. Their bosses know New York and London, but can't wait to get home. Homespun companies such as the boys from Buchanan, Clark Equipment (fork-lift trucks, and so forth) have built world interests in their concentrated specialities without succumbing to the tempting passion for sophistication and complication.

Simple principles sound laughably naïve: one modern tycoon built his fortune on an old-fashioned platform of paying for everything in cash, neither giving nor receiving credit, and never borrowing—but note that he made a fortune. Non-tycoons, lacking the intuitive quality of business genius, can't afford the same luxury of sticking to principles at all costs. The common-or-garden executive needs flexibility, readiness to change course, even in midstream, willingness to look acidly even at success.

The Apollo program, hailed as a triumph of "good" professional management, is a caution in itself. Because you have landed a man on the moon by 1970 for a mere $50 billion, don't assume you've managed brilliantly—maybe it should have been done for $30 billion. Worry more about the worms inside the apple. Then, maybe, astronauts won't be fried alive, and Apollo 13 won't be sent on a hazardous fool's errand to the moon, both through minor managerial sloppiness that stemmed from major procedural defects. The real lesson of Apollo is that, if the objective is attainable and there is no limit to the resources available, executives can achieve almost any task. That is not news. But don't manage (and many companies do) as if you are NASA. There are always limits to the resources of a corporation—first, that it isn't the executives' money; second, that behind the stockholders, the money belongs to the community.

Executives are highly privileged individuals. They receive sweeping power over society's economic resources—far more than that of politicians, but entirely in a private capacity—to do with what they will, under conditions of low accountability and virtual permanence. Few executives feel this burden of national responsibility. But they won't do their duty by the country's wealth until they see their work stripped of its mythological trappings and in its true, unflattering light—and thus do it better.

The ten truths of management given in these pages form a simple antimyth kit. A wise reader of the manuscript objected that hardly any of the truths apply to executives only, but are common to almost all humanity. He had holed in one. Management is precisely that, a general human activity, to which the best guides are not the management textbooks, but history, sociology, and psychology. The first myth of management—that it exists—seeks to take management away from where it belongs and to put it on a pedestal of pseudoscience. Executives placed on pedestals fall from a great height. If the ten truths keep you off the pedestal, at least the drop will be much shorter.

1. Think before you act: it's not your money.
2. All good management is the expression of one great idea.
3. No executive devotes effort to proving himself wrong.
4. Cash in must exceed Cash out.
5. Management capability is always less than the organization actually needs.
6. Either an executive can do his job or he can't.
7. If sophisticated calculations are needed to justify an action, don't do it.
8. If you are doing something wrong, you will do it badly.
9. If you are attempting the impossible, you will fail.
10. The easiest way of making money is to stop losing it.

Another truth lies behind all ten. One of the least attractive myths of management holds that nobody can get rich without at some point being a crook, a con man, or a mobster. Many crooks, con men, and mobsters have made great wealth. It does not follow that crookedness is the path to business success, nor that executives can throw private morality overboard as they plunge into corporate vice. Ponder, rather, how it is that the Quakers and similar deeply religious gentry made so much worldly lucre. It was because they treated their people honestly and decently, worked hard and honestly themselves, spent honestly and saved pennies, honestly put more back into the company than they took out, made honestly good products, gave honest value for money and, being honest, told no lies. The naked executive can never find better clothes.